Direct
Marketing

Direct Marketing

The Proven Path to Successful Sales

Kathryn Retzler

Scott, Foresman and Company
Glenview, Illinois   **London**

Original illustrations and cover illustration by Kim Muslusky.

Library of Congress Cataloging-in Publication Data

Retzler, Kathryn
Direct marketing: the proven path to successful sales / Kathryn
    Retzler.
        p.   cm.
    Includes index.
    ISBN 0-673-38088-2
    1. Direct marketing—United States.   I. Title.
HF5415.126.R47   1988
658.8 4—dc19   886892
                                                                    CIP

1   2   3   4   5   6   RRC   93   92   91   90   89   88

ISBN 0-673-38088-2

Scott, Foresman Professional Publishing Group books are available for bulk sales at
quantity discounts. For information, please contact the Marketing Manager,
Professional Books, Professional Publishing Group, Scott, Foresman and Company,
1900 East Lake Avenue, Glenview, IL 60025.

With love to Jason and Cheryl, who never complained when manuscript pages obliterated the dinner table for days on end, or when the printer ran hour after hour through the night. Your support meant a lot!

FOREWORD

This is a book that will benefit the entire business community. Written for business people, by a business person, it addresses the primary issue facing every business in America today: Profit!

For close to twenty-five years, I have been working with and consulting to businesses. My experience as an accountant has shown me that the primary problem faced by every new or small venture, and many established enterprises as well, is how to generate enough sales to cover overhead and produce a profit. Many businesses fail because they fail to understand marketing. This book could correct that.

With the increased competition in business today, every business man and woman, from entrepreneurs to seasoned managers and business owners, must become an expert in the practice of cost-efficient marketing. The technique of direct marketing clearly provides the most efficient, effective, and *accountable* means of getting a product to a profitable market. Unfortunately, many businesses don't know how to use direct marketing.

This book thoroughly covers the technique. It is the most up-to-date guide on the market today, presenting the latest technology and innovations — right down to the impact of the car telephone on direct response advertising! Radio and television advertising — frightening to many businesses because of their perceived costs — are examined in readable, understandable detail. The reader will find extensive coverage on how to define and identify a market, write a marketing plan, prospect, and close a customer. This book looks at the various approaches to direct marketing, examining each method both separately and as part of the overall marketing picture, and then assesses how each could best benefit specific types of businesses, or business plans.

The information contained in this book can save business people and their sales staff countless, frustrating hours of cold-calling, as well as thousands of dollars in consulting fees. Retzler's guide to market research and the secrets she shares about prospecting and "target marketing" make this book required reading for any businesses that want to increase their sales.

Margret Wright, C.P.A.
Wright and Geis, Inc.
San Diego, California

PREFACE

For a long time, direct marketing was synonymous with direct mail. And direct mail was a dirty word. When ordering something by direct mail, most people did it quietly, half expecting their order to be delivered by a disreputable character in a horse-drawn wagon with "Colby's Cure-All Elixir" hand-lettered on the side.

Direct mail meant sleazy. Bargain basement gadgets that didn't work. Books with pages, even whole chapters, missing. Mismatched shoes, and pants with no zipper. Advertising looked hand-made, was poorly worded, and often made outrageous claims which the advertiser could never back up. When customers had a complaint, they found the company had disappeared and left no forwarding address. No "respectable" business wanted to be associated with direct marketing.

Not any more. Today direct marketing, or direct response advertising, which is what it really is, has a new, professional image. *Accounting for over $3 billion in revenue every day, direct response advertising reaches into every corner of the market and produces returns often upward of 20 percent on a single advertising effort!*

Direct marketing works for everybody, regardless of size or type of business. It incorporates the very latest electronic techniques, taking advantage of telephone, television, database management, and credit card shopping. It is cost efficient; the "cost of reach" (or expenditure required to reach potential customers) and the "cost of sale" are far lower than conventional media advertising, and far more effective. Direct marketing is also honest. When you run a direct response piece, you know right away if it worked or it did not.

With such outstanding potential, it is amazing to note that *most business people still don't know what direct marketing is, or how to use it.* An enormous amount of potential revenue is lost because so many businesses are missing the boat!

The problem is compounded by the fact that many managers and business owners don't even know whom to question for accurate information. The books that *do* explain direct marketing are excellent, but far too technical. The average business person won't take time to wade through such a book, much less read it. Most of these books are technical guides about direct mail, and were written before the *explosion of modern technology revolutionized direct marketing*. Nowhere, for instance, is the impact of the cellular phone discussed. To add to the problem, most advertising agencies (at least until recently) are grounded in general media advertising, and have no experience with direct marketing.

Clearly, a simple, straightforward explanation is needed, something that will introduce the concept of direct marketing to the business community, explain it, tell how and where to use it, and detail how and where to find qualified professional help.

It was the perception of that need (which was spurred by the response of my students in marketing and management classes which I teach here in San Diego), that inspired this book. This is a *"show and tell"* book, one that explains, very succinctly, what direct marketing is and how you, the business owner, can use that business to increase your sales.

To my knowledge, this is the *only* book that discusses some of the latest innovations, such as cellular telephones and buyer-graphics, that impact both business and the advertising media that business uses.

For many years I have successfully used direct marketing techniques to promote my own business and those of my clients. Even with that broad experience base, however, researching this book was a treat. The people who are deeply involved in the direct marketing industry are articulate, knowledgeable, and infinitely helpful. Enlightened by them, I discovered an even broader scope of new ideas and innovations which can increase profitability.

Direct marketing opens the door to bigger and better profits for everyone. Isn't it about time you started using direct marketing too?

Kathryn Retzler, President
Greentree Consulting Group
San Diego, California

ACKNOWLEDGMENTS

The author would like to thank the following special people who provided invaluable assistance in researching this book. Each of them contributed their expertise and valuable time. Their help is greatly appreciated.
New York . . .

Lee Epstein, President of MAILMEN INC., who is without peer in the direct mail industry, and who helped immeasurably by sharing his time, expertise, and personal resources from the beginning to the end of this project.

Simon Applebaum, contributing writer for Cable Marketing magazine and Associate Producer, BTR (Business of Television Report), whose accurate, up-to-the-minute information about the various aspects of electronic media marketing were immensely helpful.

Esther Plaut, of the Direct Marketing Association, who made available the lists and resources of that organization, which appear in the Appendices of this book.

Elaine Santoro, Associate Editor, Hoke Communications, Inc., who provided much of the material used in the Appendices.
New Jersey . . .

Dr. Mark Cohen, President, Academic Guidance Services, who willingly shared advertising information and whose enthusiasm for this project carried over into using the book for licensees of his own company.
Boston . . .

Meg Asseo, *Inc.* Magazine, Advertising Sales, who shared ideas and advertisers for the section on print media.
Texas . . .

Donald Pesce, fellow "Hurricane" and Advertising Director of SMI, who contributed statistical information and examples of his company's products and advertising efforts, in a variety of media.

California . . .

Margret Wright, Managing Partner, Wright & Geiss, C.P.A., and nationally acclaimed speaker on the subject of profitable marketing, who reviewed the manuscript and enthusiastically recommended it.

Bill Hanna, General Manager, National Pen, San Diego, who shared his thorough knowledge of direct marketing in all of its aspects.

Timothy H. Von Feldt, Manager, Mail Classification, U.S. Postal Service, San Diego, who provided information about government regulations, mailings, and the unique history of the American Postal System.

Paul Muchnick, Chairman, Advisory Board, National Mail Order Association, Los Angeles, who advised from the outset, reviewed the manuscript before publication, and asked to include this book in the association's library.

Nickolas Fisher, Vice President, Executive Concierge, put the advice in the book to practical use, and offered part of a marketing campaign we did for his company as a direct mail example.

Jay Kholos, President, World Communications, Inc., Carlsbad, who shared his tremendously successful knowledge of television direct response advertising.

Jeff Anderson, KFMB TV, Channel 8, San Diego, who provided information, technical, and editorial assistance for the information in Chapter 8.

Dave Walker, Director, Creative Services, KCST-TV, who graciously reviewed the entire section on television advertising and contributed advertising examples.

Mary Sorrentino, Operations Manager, and partner, KIFM Radio, San Diego, who shared her very thorough knowledge of the local market and the industry as a whole.

Special thanks also to the following people who contributed material to be used as examples and illustrations: Bruce Strahlman, Senior Marketing Manager for The Signature Group, advertising agency for Mobil Oil Auto Club; Edward Beckman, Advertising Coordinator, UARCO, Inc.; Carla Barrows, Advertising Manager, *Inc.* Magazine; Margaret Gracey-Brena, *The Wall Street Journal*; Catherine Hartnett, Public Affairs, L.L. Bean, Inc.; Dorothy Adams, Executive Director of Mail Order, Gump's; Elaine Santoro, *Direct Marketing* Magazine; Shelley Cagner, Arbitron Rating Company, New York City; Mr. Ron Sok, Director, Advertising and Promotion, Timex Corp., Inc.; Ed Stopper, Co-Publisher, The ComputorEdge, San Diego; Gerri Kessler, KCST Channel 39, San Diego.

TABLE OF CONTENTS

Direct Marketing

A PROVEN PATH

*"Direct marketing is like six blind people trying to describe
an elephant. Whatever part they happen to touch, that's
what they think it looks like!"*

— Lee Epstein, President,
MAILMEN INC., New York City.

Direct marketing is big business. Direct mail alone accounted for $50
billion in sales in 1986 (40 to 45 percent of it in catalogue sales).[1] And,
although mail-order sales play a major role in direct marketing, selling by
mail is only one aspect of an overall marketing strategy embraced by
millions of businesses across the country from major marketers such as
Coca Cola and Ford Motor Company down to the tiniest business in your
neighborhood shopping center.

Direct marketing accounts for billions of dollars spent on advertising
every year. Yet, only a small percentage of business people actually
understand what it is, or how it works. Fewer still can define it. Attempts
to explain direct marketing vary as greatly as the replies of six blind men
trying to describe an elephant.

INTERACTIVE SYSTEMS

Direct marketing is a special way of selling which invites buyers to respond
to your advertising and enables you to *measure that response.* As an
advertising method, direct marketing is unique because, unlike any other
form of selling or advertising, it requires a direct and measurable response — an interaction between the buyer and the seller. The Direct
Marketing Association offers the following official definition:

> "Direct Marketing is an interactive system of marketing which uses
> one or more advertising media to effect measurable responses and/or
> transaction at any location."[2]

Measured response provides another special characteristic of direct
marketing: **the database.** Direct marketing relies heavily on the existence
of an identified audience of willing buyers stored in a database.

Figure 1.1

Direct marketing is like six blind men trying to describe an elephant. Whatever part they touch, that's what they think it looks like!

The theory is that if it worked before, it should work again. To elicit the desired response from prospective buyers, advertising is designed to follow guidelines created from similar ventures which proved successful in the past. So, when a product is sold, as much information as possible is recorded about that sale for future marketing efforts. The information about who bought it, why, when, for how much, and how often, along with a host of other facts, is filed away into databases to be used in future marketing efforts. (See Chapter 3 for more on market research.)

Both of these factors, measured response and market research, create a unique marketplace for the direct marketer:

We know who bought our product!
We know who is likely to buy from us again!

In general or image advertising, products and services are touted to any and all who are exposed to the ads. When a purchase is made, there is no way of knowing who made it, or why. With direct marketing, which is an interactive form of advertising, not only do we chart the response to our efforts, but also we know who bought, in most cases, right down to name, address, and phone number.

How is it done? Let's look at some common examples of direct marketing that are used every day.

Direct Mail

One of the most common examples of direct marketing arrives in most mailboxes several times a year: brand name coupons. Mailed to households categorized by one or more factors such as age, income, and geographic location, coupons offer special discounts or free merchandise when filled in and mailed back, or redeemed at local stores and businesses. When someone responds, their name is added to a database to be used in future direct mail campaigns.

Direct mail has been around for a long time. In the classic format, it includes a carefully worded letter, one or more pages long, explaining the offer and encouraging immediate response. Some direct mail pieces, such as the sweepstakes offer by Publishers Clearing House, are mailed out on a national basis, building data on responsive buyers from coast to coast. Others, such as packets of coupons put out by neighborhood movie theaters, restaurants, dry cleaners, and retailers, are mailed out to prospective buyers to provide local businesses with up-to-date information about buyers in their immediate marketing area.

Catalogues

Another popular media used by direct marketers, the catalogue provides buyers with an opportunity to purchase several items at once. Catalogues generally offer household items, clothing, office products, or some combination of merchandise or services. Orders are placed via an order blank inserted at the back of the publication or by calling a toll-free "800" number directly.

Catalogues come in all sizes and shapes, from slick-cover magazines that include exotic items such as jeweled elephants to the plain-cover business variety that pictures a multitude of office and computer products for the business owner or office manager.

Telemarketing

Soliciting sales over the telephone is another technique frequently employed in direct marketing. For example, a trained telephone salesperson may contact prospective customers with offers to replace screen doors, photograph children, or visit a vacation resort and receive a free gift in exchange for listening to an intense 90-minute sales pitch. Telemarketing offers a unique opportunity to speak directly to the prospect, gauging response and placing an order immediately without waiting for the post office to send back a coupon.

Telemarketing can be inbound, too. Many other forms of direct marketing use the telephone as a response device. The newest telephone response device is the cellular phone. Radio listeners sitting in traffic or traveling in their cars can respond immediately and repeatedly to a variety of offers heard on their car radios.

Fulfillment Offers

For those of us who like to read the back of the cereal box in the morning, this device should be very familiar. Advertising everything from wrist watches to parcels of Florida swampland, sellers often put offers for products or services on, or in, somebody else's product line. To place an order, the buyer fills in the coupon and mails it to the advertiser. In return, the buyer gets the merchandise, and the seller gets another name for the database.

Home Shopping

One of the newest kids on the block, home shopping services provide the buyer with a smorgasbord of products shown on their home television sets. The customer places an order by telephone and pays for it by punching in a credit card number. Like all other forms of EDM (electronic data marketing), the entire transaction can be handled by computer. "E.T. phone home" takes on a whole new meaning!

All of these examples of direct marketing, which, along with some other techniques, are discussed in further detail later in this book, are highly successful methods of direct marketing. They are interactive, and even more important, the seller has control over all aspects of the sale, from design of the offer to final distribution.

MEASURED RESPONSE

No other marketing method works quite so well as direct marketing, because no other selling technique grades progress so efficiently — and so quickly. With direct marketing, which elicits a measurable response, you know exactly how well your marketing program is doing. Because the results of your advertising are measured and recorded, you also have accurate statistics upon which to build future advertising campaigns.

For example, suppose you place an ad on the back of a cereal box offering a gun-toting camouflage warrior doll for the modest price of $3.95 plus a boxtop if ordered before December 31. Each "Rambo"-style doll order that you receive means that someone has read your offer and responded with an order in the required time frame. Thus, if in March, your coupons were printed on the back of 100,000 cereal boxes and if 2,000 people ordered the toys before the end of the year, the positive measure of your offer would be 2 percent in nine months. Should you choose to run the offer again, you can reasonably expect a 2 percent return again.

A campaign to solicit donations for a new church chapel might also use a number of direct marketing techniques. For example, a clerical representative might call you at home (telemarketing), solicit your donation, and follow up a day or two later with a self-mailer (direct mail), already stamped and addressed to the church. You have only to enclose your check, then lick, stick, and mail the envelope back to the church. A follow-up call a few days later (telemarketing again) assures that you have returned the mailer. The church has made effective use of two direct marketing techniques. Response to the chapel campaign is measured by the number of donations collected. Thus a church volunteer telephoning 25 people every evening for a week and receiving checks from 50 people the following week would have a 28.6 percent success rate. Better than the 2 percent for the soldier doll, but perhaps the church chapel has a more closely defined audience than the cereal company. If and when the church needs to run another campaign, it can reliably predict the outcome from the statistical database created from this one.

Sales, earnings, and income (whether for profit, as with the warrior dolls, or for nonprofit endowments, such as the chapel building fund), depend upon a successful marketing campaign. To produce income, we expect people to purchase our product or service on a *repeated or regular basis*. If they don't, we won't be in business very long. To prosper and grow (or even simply to survive) in any kind of business, we must have a positive response to our marketing efforts. Direct marketing gives us a way to improve those response odds by utilizing *proven* marketing methods and drawing upon *proven* buyers. Direct marketing provides the opportunity to use different parts of the marketing elephant, or even the whole animal at once, depending on what kind of response we need and how we plan to get it.

USERS AND PRODUCERS

Direct marketing can be loosely divided into two camps: users and producers. A **producer** of direct marketing is a firm that *supplies the actual mechanics of getting an offer to the targeted public*. A producer manages databases, maintains and rents mailing lists, designs and prints mailing pieces, produces video advertisements, or owns and operates a computer bulletin board or telemarketing service.

The producer may or may not utilize those same services. For example, MAILMEN INC.[3] in New York City, a direct mail producer, acts as a designer, mailer, or both, for clients such as American Express, Reader's Digest, and Publishers Clearing House.

User

In most cases, the **user** of direct marketing methods is not the producer. A user of *direct marketing subscribes to the providers' services to get a product to market*. American Express, for example, is a user of the services of MAILMEN INC., who mail their catalogue for them. Manufacturers sometimes offer their product through trade journal ads that provide a discount to those responding positively to the ad within a definite time frame. In that case, the manufacturer is the user, and the advertiser producing the print advertisement, as well as the journal that published it, are the providers. Books and tapes are often offered via special catalogues that require the reader to check off choices on an order blank and send it in, along with a check, to the distributor.

Users of direct marketing are not limited to the producers of "hard goods" such as a manufactured product. The service industries make extensive use of direct marketing, too. Over 70 percent of our gross national product today is made up of service producers.[4] Such diverse service businesses as interior design, education, and banking successfully use a number of direct marketing methods. Service professions including law, accountancy, and medicine, which in the past limited their direct marketing to personal sales or referrals, now use a number of more public direct marketing methods with great success. Legal services, for example, may utilize television to offer a special fee to the viewer who telephones within a set number of hours after having viewed the commercial. A dentist might offer a free cleaning and checkup to "the bearer of this ad."

Occasionally, the roles of user and producer overlap, as in the case of a company that designs, prints, and mails its own direct mail pieces. The publisher of a catalogue, for instance, that offers books and cassette tapes on self-improvement, could control the entire process (vertical market) and employ the authors of those books and tapes as well as individuals that design, print, and mail the inspirational catalogue. National Pen Corp., headquartered in San Diego, California, is an excellent example of a self-contained operation that is both user and producer. From raw material to mail-order fulfillment, the marketing of their pens and other products is controlled by the company or its subsidiaries.

Producer

For the most part, however, because the cost of self-produced direct marketing is high, smaller companies usually employ the services of one or more producers to help them with the bulk of their direct marketing campaign. As they grow, these companies may purchase a provider company along the way to gain greater control over their operations. Eventually, should they become the size of a manufacturer such as National Pen Corp., they may acquire all of the various operations needed to provide complete vertical integration of their operation as a user.

Combining the role of user and producer often happens as companies mature. Young companies frequently start out hiring all of the professional services they need as they develop a firm customer base. They may act as no more than a paper-exchange point, processing orders solicited via mail (mail order service) or telephone (telemarketing service) and filled by a fulfillment house (a company which stocks and "drop ships" the customer's order directly). Later, when growth stabilizes, the expanding enterprise may decide to produce one or more of those direct marketing services in-house.

NEW DIRECTIONS

Direct selling has been around since Eve talked Adam into biting the infamous apple. With the development and widespread use of the printing press, direct selling moved from face-to-face encounters to the printed page. Then, as the Wright brothers nudged out the Pony Express for innovative methods of moving mail (and carrying a lot more poundage per trip!), direct marketing took a leap into modern direct marketing.

But it is in the last few years that direct marketing has undergone the most startling revolution. Three innovations were primarily responsible. The postal zip system, the microchip, and that all-American favorite, the credit card.

Zip Codes

For hundreds of years, the only methods of directly marketing a product were direct selling and direct mail. At best, both methods were haphazard, because in order to close a sale, the seller had to pound a lot of pavement and send out a mountain of mail, most of it scattered over a wide area. Fortunately, shoe leather and postage were fairly cheap.

Then came the introduction of the zip system. When the U.S. Post Office announced the new system of coding mail with five digits that predirected mail to specific geographic locations, most people viewed it as an annoyance at best. To the average letter-writer, it meant keeping track of more numbers in address books and Rolodex files. To the direct marketer, it spelled disaster. For direct marketers used to filing and addressing mail-order pieces by alphabetic listing (or other groupings such as those accorded by customer preference), the new zip code heralded expensive man hours of resorting mailing lists into zip code order to meet the postal regulations which required bulk mail to be sorted and bundled by zip code.

Then direct marketers took a second look, and the zip system didn't seem such a bad idea after all. In fact, when mailing lists were coded and entered into computerized databases, it looked downright profitable. Duplicate addresses could be eliminated in no time at all. Whole neighborhoods and geographic locations could be segmented from the rest of the population and targeted as prospective buyers. (See Chapter 2.) The postal zip code turned out to be just the catalyst that direct marketers were looking for to create new solutions to bolster sagging sales.

Computerization

Then came the birth of the microchip—a cost-effective device that could store a great deal of information in a small, affordable computer. *Small* and *affordable* were the key words. Computers existed prior to that time, but

Figure 1.2

The SHOP TIL YOU DROP syndrome moves into direct marketing.

because of their size and cost, their use was restricted to all but the most wealthy, well-funded users who had sufficient space to house them.

The microchip changed all of that. Computerization came to businesses of all sizes, allowing them to store information about their customers and to sort it into pools of data with common characteristics.

Database marketing was born. On demand, computers could spit out lists of potential or prior buyers categorized by factors such as age, income, sex, or neighborhood. Computers could keep track of responses to every offer. They could even *check credit* and eliminate duplicate names. For the direct marketer, it was a dream come true.

The next step was a political one. With the advent of the Freedom of Information act even more information about prospective buyers could be gathered and stored. Commercial databases were born. Companies jumped onto the marketing bandwagon, ready to compile, rent, and sell lists of buyers, sellers, and products.

Computers can also design ads, select appropriate headlines, and create typesetting, which was formerly done by hand. Data management has become so sophisticated that it is possible to create, sort, stamp, and send out a mailing without any human intervention at all. And telecommunication makes it possible for the customer to respond and buy—electronically—with no direct interaction at all.

Direct-mail, still holding court as king of direct marketing, has taken on a whole new meaning and a sophisticated new image. Attractive, colorful advertising is designed specifically for each segment of potential buyers. And it's hitting home with a vengeance. Direct mail has never been as successful as it is now. In 1986, direct mailers sent out over 56 billion pieces of mail. By the year 2000, direct mail is expected to match the volume of first class mail processed by the Postal Service!

Careful market research selects and qualifies the most likely prospects by consumer patterns and habits. Psychographics, the study of the factors that motivate people to buy, and demographics, which point out who and where those people are, build a highly accurate buyer profile. By studying consumer buying patterns, you can determine who wants your product, and who can afford to purchase it. Extensive databases created to maintain and cross-file groups of buyers (or nonbuyers) of various products and services provide you with mailing lists. Direct market producers will even print, stuff, stamp, and mail your advertising piece for you, leaving you free to fill the order and pocket the profits. If that sounds like too much work, a fulfillment house will purchase the merchandise for you, package it, and drop ship the orders.

The blessings of computerization don't stop with the ability to qualify buyers. Computerization also provides a smorgasbord of new direct marketing methods and ideas to choose from. The same market research that revolutionized direct mail may point you in an entirely new direction, such as interactive television home-shopping services, videotext, cable TV, video tapes, audio cassettes, subliminal message tapes, or specialty advertising. Any of the new EDM (electronic data marketing) techniques can help you to take advantage of the latest state-of-the-art electronic equipment and be well-positioned for the next innovation when it comes down the stretch.

Credit Cards

Instant, plastic credit is another boon of the Age of Information. With computerization, financial institutions can give their clients instant credit far beyond their ability to pay it back. Americans have more plastic money than they know what to do with, and it has increased their buying power tremendously. No longer required to save up for big ticket items, they can buy now and pay later, the same principle that allows them to purchase a home.

Catalogue sellers were one of the first to feel the impact. The size of a typical order tripled, both in number of items ordered and in amount of sale. The buyer checks off the items he or she desires, writes in a credit card number, licks, sticks, and mails off the order. Presto! Instant gratification. Instant fulfillment.

Telemarketing was another marketing area that felt the immediate impact of the age of the credit card. No longer does the business owner wait (and hope) for the check to come in the mail. Now a telephone solicitor gets the credit card number over the phone, verifies the credit, and posts the sale immediately. Lag between closure and payment is virtually eliminated. From the customer's point of view, it seems so much easier to say, "Yes!" when it's only plastic. It doesn't even seem like spending money at all.

Credit cards and computers. A direct marketer's dream. And, there's no end in sight. Direct marketing just keeps getting better and better.

WHY DOES DIRECT MARKETING WORK?

Accountability

Another reason direct response advertising is so successful is that it is relatively cheap. Because users don't have to be producers, there is no need to purchase special equipment. No one has to buy a television station before they can advertise their product on it. Nor do they need to own a printing house before a catalogue can be assembled. In fact, an entire direct marketing campaign can be designed, produced, and completed without anything other than the profits ever passing through the user's front door.

Direct marketing is also a bargain because each penny is accounted for before it is spent, with no wasted dollars. It is the only form of selling which, because the results have been measured, tested, and perfected, can produce very specific results, and for a very specific price. Thus, you know from the start what kind of profits to expect at the end. No surprises, just pocketable profits! Designing an advertising budget for direct marketing is much easier than designing one for general media advertising, because it is possible to accurately project costs based on past performance.

Good Lists

Ultimately, the success of any direct marketing campaign depends on the viability of its mailing list. The more accurate the list, the more predictable your profit ratio will be. And each time a customer buys, your database gets a little bit better. Thus, when Sally Tillison of Great Falls, Montana, buys a pair of size 10 red sneakers from the *Good Footwear Catalogue*, that information can be coded into a database that is available (for a price) to anyone who wants to sell sneakers, red shoes, or products to big-footed people. Each time Sally buys shoes, the facts regarding her purchase go into a number of databases (red shoe buyers, big-footed women, sneaker wearers, western women, and so on). The probability of Sally's buying red shoes again can be calculated with fair accuracy. So, if you want to sell size tens, or red shoes, Sally would be an ideal customer. Sending Sally an annual ad picturing sexy red sneakers should result in a sale! Chapter 3 will provide more information about database marketing and mailing lists.

Targeted Markets

To further target your market (Chapter 2) and to control costs, you can test your marketing methods on given "segments" or sections of your customer base as defined by geographic location, or common characteristics such as hair color, favorite food, or any other statistic tucked away in a helpful database tracking buyers and their habits.

Armed with the results of market tests, profitable direct marketing campaign strategies can be devised and quickly revised when needed. A television offer might do well in one area, for example, while a direct mail piece for the same offer would pull better in another location. Testing the offer by running it in both media would point this out.

Because certain products, such as air conditioners or snowshoes, do better in specific geographical markets, successful selling often depends on successful segmenting of the market by location. Other products, like acne medicine or hair color, appeal to segments of the population defined by

Figure 1.3

Sending Sally an annual ad should result in a sale.

demographic characteristics such as sex, age, race, or even religion. Just as you wouldn't expect a big surge of snowshoe sales in Florida, it is unlikely that you would set sales records for Grecian Formula® among teenagers. Targeting your audience and selecting how to reach them go hand in hand.

Attentive Audiences

For the few moments that it takes for your buyer to open a direct mail piece, listen to a telemarketing offer, view a television spot, or respond to a videotext shopping offer, you have their full and complete attention. That prospective buyer is totally absorbed in your offer. What's more, he's got to do something about it, even if that something is a decision to pitch your offer in the trash can. For a few precious, hopefully profitable, moments, you've got him. The odds are pretty high that you'll make a sale if you've correctly targeted your market.

Timing

The requirement of a timed response is another unique advantage of direct marketing. Your prospect must clip a coupon, answer a telephone offer, or fill in the order form at the back of the catalogue. In other words, the buyer must *act on your offer within a specific time frame*. Usually the response includes payment on the spot. No wonder the results of direct response advertising are so effective. If you've targeted the wrong person or picked the wrong method, you find out right away. Nobody buys. Your offer works, or it doesn't. Either way, you know immediately if it's going to be successful, and if it isn't, you can make appropriate corrections to your sales campaign.

WHAT DOES DIRECT MARKETING DO?

Better Bottom Line

Direct marketing increases profits. Without a doubt, direct marketing will certainly improve your bottom line. First of all, closing ratios have to go up. You've got a willing buyer in your sights instead of shotgunning everybody within range. It would take an awful lot of work *not* to make a sale.

More closes mean more sales. Add in controlled costs — and that is certainly likely since you've got plenty of supportive data available to help you contain costs, and a positively booming bottom line is inevitable.

Now, add in satisfaction. Watching your business grow, and grow profitably, is the best news of all. When you feel good about yourself and can watch the reward for your efforts taking shape, business will be even better. Finally, add in the benefit of reduced frustration levels from repeated rejection. One of the biggest drawbacks to most sales efforts is the high frustration level resulting from repeated rejection. Direct sales cuts the rejection down to manageable size.

Build Customer Base

A better bottom line is only half the good news. Direct marketing also builds a strong repeat customer base. If your offer appealed once, it should do so again. If your prospect dug out the checkbook or popped the plastic the first time, she's even more likely to do it the next time (provided your offer was as good as you claimed it would be). The more you sell, the better your customer base will grow.

Then there is the psychological factor peculiar to direct marketing. It's so easy to order just one more thing when filling out the order blank. (Did you ever see an order blank with just one line on it? At the very least, the offer will ask "how many" of the item offered you would like to order.) As long as the order doesn't exceed the buyer's credit card limit (and sometimes, even when it does), your customer will continue to list item after item on a mail-in coupon until it is filled. Telemarketers do even better. Saying yes to a real person on the phone somehow obligates the buyer to fill in the check and mail it. Better yet, the buyer can just put the cost on the credit card. Think how well television donation campaigns do.

Even Cash Flow

There's even more good news. A strong customer base and measured, expected results should provide even, expected cash flow with no more of the highs and lows that sent you into your bank line of credit. With access to consumer patterns provided by market research, you will take the guesswork out of your cash flow.

A northeastern catalogue marketing firm might take advantage of their market research to offer snowshoes in their fall catalogue, Christmas ornaments and gifts for the holidays, plants and gardening tools in the spring, and barbecue and beach toys in the summer. The result will be year-round sales and year-round profits.

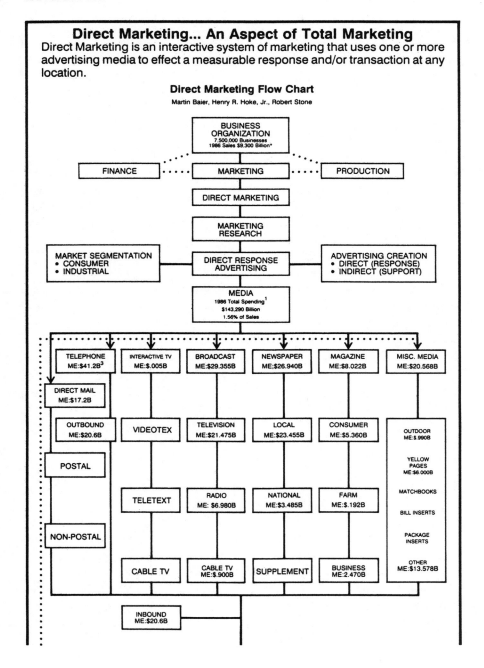

Direct Marketing... An Aspect of Total Marketing

Direct Marketing is an interactive system of marketing that uses one or more advertising media to effect a measurable response and/or transaction at any location.

Direct Marketing Flow Chart

Martin Baier, Henry R. Hoke, Jr., Robert Stone

BUSINESS ORGANIZATION
7,500,000 Businesses
1986 Sales $9,300 Billion*

FINANCE ..... MARKETING ..... PRODUCTION

DIRECT MARKETING

MARKETING RESEARCH

MARKET SEGMENTATION
• CONSUMER
• INDUSTRIAL

DIRECT RESPONSE ADVERTISING

ADVERTISING CREATION
• DIRECT (RESPONSE)
• INDIRECT (SUPPORT)

MEDIA
1986 Total Spending[1]
$143,290 Billion
1.56% of Sales

TELEPHONE ME:$41.2B[3]	INTERACTIVE TV ME:$.005B	BROADCAST ME:$29.355B	NEWSPAPER ME:$26.940B	MAGAZINE ME:$8.022B	MISC. MEDIA ME:$20.568B
DIRECT MAIL ME:$17.2B					
OUTBOUND ME:$20.6B	VIDEOTEX	TELEVISION ME:$21.475B	LOCAL ME:$23.455B	CONSUMER ME:$5.360B	OUTDOOR ME:$.990B
POSTAL					YELLOW PAGES ME:$6.000B
	TELETEXT	RADIO ME: $6.980B	NATIONAL ME:$3.485B	FARM ME:$.192B	MATCHBOOKS
					BILL INSERTS
NON-POSTAL					PACKAGE INSERTS
	CABLE TV	CABLE TV ME:$.900B	SUPPLEMENT	BUSINESS ME:2.470B	OTHER ME:$13.578B

INBOUND ME:$20.6B

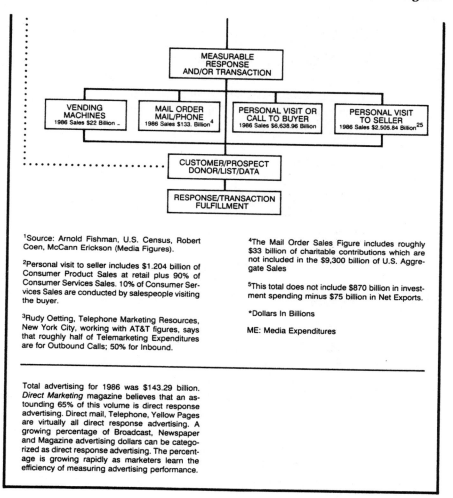

[1]Source: Arnold Fishman, U.S. Census, Robert Coen, McCann Erickson (Media Figures).

[2]Personal visit to seller includes $1.204 billion of Consumer Product Sales at retail plus 90% of Consumer Services Sales. 10% of Consumer Services Sales are conducted by salespeople visiting the buyer.

[3]Rudy Oetting, Telephone Marketing Resources, New York City, working with AT&T figures, says that roughly half of Telemarketing Expenditures are for Outbound Calls; 50% for Inbound.

[4]The Mail Order Sales Figure includes roughly $33 billion of charitable contributions which are not included in the $9,300 billion of U.S. Aggregate Sales

[5]This total does not include $870 billion in investment spending minus $75 billion in Net Exports.

*Dollars In Billions

ME: Media Expenditures

Total advertising for 1986 was $143.29 billion. *Direct Marketing* magazine believes that an astounding 65% of this volume is direct response advertising. Direct mail, Telephone, Yellow Pages are virtually all direct response advertising. A growing percentage of Broadcast, Newspaper and Magazine advertising dollars can be categorized as direct response advertising. The percentage is growing rapidly as marketers learn the efficiency of measuring advertising performance.

Figure 1.4

SUMMARY

Direct marketing is interactive. It requires an action from the seller and a corresponding reaction from the buyer. Unlike other types of advertising, the results of direct response advertising are measurable. Because each offer is aimed at a specific group of individuals (your targeted market), accurate sales predictions can be made. Testing and market segmentation allow the seller to refine marketing strategies.

Direct marketing is a selling method, not a type of business (except for those businesses that produce marketing services such as list management, telemarketing firms, and mailing). For optimum results, prospective customers are researched, targeted, and approached with offers through the utilization of one or more techniques that require a response.

ENDNOTES

1. From an article in *Advertising Age*, March 30, 1987, quoting Maxwell Sroge Publishing, Colorado Springs, Colorado. That same article notes that, according to Touche Ross & Co., San Francisco, home-shopping revenues are expected to top $5 billion by 1990.
2. The February 1986 issue of *Direct Marketing* magazine, pages 18–19, includes the following explanation of direct marketing:

> "Marketing is the total of activities of moving goods and services from seller to buyer. Direct Marketing has the same broad function except that Direct Marketing requires the existence and maintenance of a database.
>
> (a) to record names of customers, expires and products.
>
> (b) to provide a vehicle for storing, then measuring, results of advertising, usually direct response advertising.
>
> (c) to provide a vehicle for storing, then measuring, purchasing performance.
>
> (d) to provide a vehicle for continuing direct communication by mail and/or phone.
>
> Thus
>
> DIRECT MARKETING is interactive, requiring database for controlled activity: By mail, by phone, through other media selected on the basis of previous results."

(For a reprint of this article, write *Direct Marketing* Magazine, 224 Seventh St., Garden City, NY 11530. Telephone: 800/645-6132.)

3. MAILMEN INC., 342 Madison Avenue, New York, NY 10173

4. For more about service businesses, see *How to Start a Service Business and Make It Succeed*, by Kathryn Retzler, Scott, Foresman and Co., 1986.

TARGETING THE MARKET

"Target marketing is like diving 75 feet into a bucket of water. You don't want to miss. Because in target marketing, aim is everything. You have to reach the people who can buy what you have to sell."
— From an ad for the *Wall Street Journal* in *Advertising Age*, March 30, 1987.[1]

Fortunately, the aim of direct marketing is very precise. Rarely does a professional direct marketer miss the bucket. Because it is possible to analyze buyers' habits and preferences, direct marketing targets prospects much better than any other media. The theory is that if an individual has already responded to an interactive marketing method, that person is a great prospect because he or she is comfortable with that form of communication.

For example, a man who buys a book from the Book of the Month Club is likely to buy other books, tapes, or financial services. You know from research (the book-buyer database) that this person buys, that he is intelligent (he bought a literary book didn't he?), that he lives in a relatively affluent neighborhood (if he can afford literary books, likely his neighbors can too), and that he is not averse to buying by mail. Because people tend to cluster, you can overlay your bookbuyers' database with a census tract and come up with a list of people who are likely to buy books by mail.

MARKET RESEARCH

Generally, four types of identifying data are used in market research:

- *demographic* — to determine who the customers are.
- *psychographic* — to analyze their motivations.
- *geographic* — to find out where they are.
- *census-tract* — to identify them by precise geographic location.

Figure 2.1
Targeting the Market

"Target marketing is like diving 75 feet into a bucket of water. You don't want to miss!" Quotation from an ad for the *Wall Street Journal* in *Advertising Age*, March 30, 1987. Copyright Dow Jones & Company, 1987.

With this type of data, you can **segment** your market, separating it into like groups of individuals such as the young woman from Montana in Chapter 1, who regularly orders red tennis shoes from a mail order catalogue. She fits into at least four major buyer groups or clusters: (1) women, (2) westerners, (3) shoe buyers, and (4) mail order customers.

After segmenting the market, many sellers, especially those who market on a national scale, choose to **test market** their product, offering it on a limited basis to certain geographic locations or similar groups of buyers before exposing the product to the market as a whole. In that way corrections can be made early on, so that large-scale, costly mistakes can be avoided.

Finding Information

Good market research takes time; and although it can be expensive, it need not be. Because most small businesses start out on a limited budget, they frequently prefer to do their own initial research, combing library bookshelves or government offices for the statistics they need. Paid professional help from market research firms is also available, but the cost varies widely.[2] In many cases, a little ingenuity will shower you with free advice. For example, most business or real-estate brokers such as Coldwell Banker, provide demographics to assist their prospects in selecting a site to lease or purchase for their business. Business brokers usually do a complete demographic study to back up claims of potential profitability of the businesses they have listed for sale. Even though you may not be in the market to buy a business, there is no reason why you cannot take advantage of these services.

Public Sources

Local government offices (city, county, and state) are also a good resource. Most information gathered by government offices is considered public information. All it takes is time and patience to uncover a wealth of prospective buyers hidden among countless lists of new business licenses, fictitious name filings, new home buyers, business buy-outs, liquor licenses, taxpayers, and more. In many cities, this information is also available on preprinted computerized labels or paper tape for a nominal charge. The white pages of the local phone book should have complete listings of city, county, and state government offices in your area.

In the larger cities, one or more services, usually listed in the yellow pages under "Mailing Services," provide direct marketers with the latest lists preprinted on self-adhesive labels. If you can't find one of these services, ask your life insurance agent where to look. Most insurance agents use this type of service for direct mail "prospecting" for life insurance sales.

Be careful of selecting a service "carte-blanche" from the yellow pages. It is best to know something about the company you select, and to check its references carefully before you elect to use its services.

Perusing public lists offers a special advantage. It gives you a quick overview of the size of your potential market. If it appears that the group you have targeted is too small, now is the time to find out, not after you have paid to print, stuff, lick, stick, and stamp 5,000 direct mail pieces when only 1,000 of them will actually reach a potential buyer.

Private Sources

Private lists and directory listings can be helpful, too. Many companies have their own in-house lists which they may or may not be willing to rent or share. Telephone directories are a good source, as are membership lists for everything from car pools to country clubs. Some advertisers, such as newspapers, provide demographic statistics as a way of marketing their own services.

A little innovation goes a long way when it comes to gathering information. Suppose you want to determine whether there is a potential market for golfing equipment and supplies in your area. You might start with the listings under "golf" in your local phone book.

Cars and Carts
Clubs
Course Architects
Course Equipment and Supplies
Courses, Miniature
Courses, Private
Courses, Public
Equipment and Supplies
Equipment Repair
Instruction
Practice Ranges
Tournament Booking Services

Check other phone books (available at the public library or main office of the telephone company) to find out how many golf clubs and equipment suppliers there are in neighboring locations, even in the entire state. (When you look under the various headings, don't overlook facilities listed under "Tennis and Golf Clubs" or "Country Clubs." Try public courses, too.) Each of these facilities should have a membership roster of some sort, although only a few will offer to let you see it.

Call a few of the clubs on your list. If the club puts out a newsletter which is regularly sent to the members (and most do), inquire about buying space in it. As a potential advertiser, you have the right to ask for information about circulation and about demographic statistics regarding the membership. This should help you to determine if their club paper would be a profitable vehicle in which to place your advertisement. You need not actually purchase space to obtain this information, only to indicate that you are interested in doing so at some time in the future.[3] As a result, you might get a peek at the coveted membership list.

The same principle works with newspapers, magazines, and other "subscription" publications. The larger ones, such as your local newspaper or a trade journal that you regularly see at work, supply potential advertisers with a "media kit" that breaks down their readership by age, location, income, and other very helpful statistics. Papers will usually give you that information over the phone, as will most radio stations, when you inquire about their advertising rates.[4] Many publications which offer classified advertising will send you "advertisers guidelines" or quote demographics over the phone.

Mailing Lists

Don't overlook your own suppliers or direct marketing producers for help in identifying your customer base. Some of the best (and the worst) market research is available from the firms that provide database mailing lists. (See Chapter 3 for more on database marketing.) List brokers and list sellers offer a multitude of statistics, identifying and typing potential buyers by just about anything you can think of—including body type, leisure-activities, reading habits, eating preferences, lifestyles, even the typical number of bathing suits owned by a family! No matter what you want to sell or to whom you want to sell it, chances are that a professional list broker can find the right group of buyers for you.

BUILDING A BUYER PROFILE

A buyer profile usually starts by making an "educated guess" about who wants to buy your product or service. The next step is to search for supportive statistics that will prove your theory. In your search for buyers of golf equipment, for example, you found a number of establishments that sell to golfers, as well as the listings and locations of courses where they go to play, so you perused the yellow pages for clubs in your area.

Try visiting the places where golfers buy equipment—pro-shops (operated by public and private courses) and stores that sell golfing equipment, clothing, and supplies. Investigate what they sell, how much, and how often. (You are hunting for confirmation that there are a sufficient number of buyers in your area to support your marketing campaign.) A series of visits to the same establishments over a prescribed period of time—say three or four months—will give you a chance to see what sells and what doesn't. Note which items are sold as quickly as they come in, and what types of things are regularly sent to make the markdown tables. This will give you a fairly accurate picture of the *volume* of golf equipment sales—which will tell you if there is a market for your products or not.

These observations will also provide you with a picture of your buyers, or a **Buyer Profile**—who they are (demographics), where they are (census tract), and what and why they buy (psychographics). This information can be used to develop a database (see Chapter 3) or master list of names that will form the basis of your house list, your target market.

Let's try another example to see how target marketing works. Suppose that you wish to sell body building and exercise equipment. We will start out with two assumptions:

1. The market for this type of product would probably be healthy, young individuals with a fairly high income level.
2. Weight sets are a luxury, not a necessity, and are reasonably expensive.

Our buyer profile will define certain common characteristics:

1. Demographic—age and income.
2. Census tract—the specified marketing area you have selected to work.
3. Psychographic—an interest in good health, physical fitness, weight training, or other athletic activities.

4. Historical data—a prior response to one or more direct marketing methods—direct mail, catalogue, telemarketing, video marketing, etc.

When your research is complete, your buyer profile should look something like the one in Figure 2.2.

Closer inspection of both groups might suggest that the second group is slightly more favorable than the first as a primary market. Of those who are married, many have delayed starting a family until their careers were well established. Because of this factor, discretionary income is slightly higher (more time to earn, less family to spend it on), as is overall family income (working wife has less childbearing time to interrupt career advancement). The pressures of their jobs might induce them to utilize a planned physical fitness program as a stress reducer. Their higher levels of income (and perhaps lower family responsibilities) make it possible for them to devote time, energy, and dollars to a fitness program.

Figure 2.2
The Sports Buyer Profile

Buyer, type 1

Median Age:	30
Sex:	male
Location:	Suburban, N.E. section of U.S.
Median Income:	$18,000—single individual, no dependents
	$25,000—family of 2.67 with 1 wage earner
	$36,000—family of 2.67 with 2 wage earners

Buyer, type 2

Median Age:	35
Sex:	male
Location:	Suburban, N.W. and S.E. section U.S.
Median Income:	$22,000—single individual, no dependents
	$38,000—family of 2.8 with 1 wage earner
	$50,000—family of 2.3 with 2 wage earners

Figure 2.3

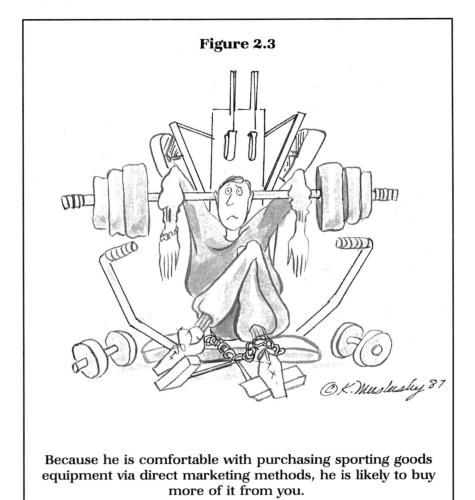

Because he is comfortable with purchasing sporting goods equipment via direct marketing methods, he is likely to buy more of it from you.

Although group one has a slight edge over group two, both groups are good markets to target. Both are the right age and have sufficient income to make your product "affordable" to them. And because both types of buyers are comfortable with purchasing sporting goods equipment via direct marketing methods, they are even more likely to buy.

DEMOGRAPHICS

Demographics, or characteristics of potential buyers, are common socio-economic factors such as age, sex, income, family structure and education, which pertain to a specific location or geographic unit such as a given zip code.

Demographics are used to identify prospects with the highest propensity to buy. Frequently, market research firms and advertisers use a survey to gather demographic information. By asking for answers to questions such as those in Figure 2.4, it is possible to verify that you are prospecting in the right market.

Surveys are done in person, over the phone, or through the mail. Sometimes they are disguised as answers to questions on order blanks or contest forms. Other times, surveys are clearly identified as a source of information for a manufacturer or advertiser. Likely, you have received several sample surveys in the mail such as those commissioned by members of the tobacco industry, or major suppliers of disposable diapers and other products for babies.

Sending a survey to every household in your marketing area (or in the U.S.) could be a costly proposition. More likely you will want to target a certain segment or section of the population. (Not everybody needs disposable diapers.) Hiring a market research firm to do it for you is the best choice. Professional researchers know where to look and probably already have a lot of helpful information on file.

If budget restraints preclude the use of a professional market research firm, try doing your own survey. Start with a visit to the local library. Ask the librarian for a directory that lists residence addresses of persons in your target market area (city, county, state, or states), with the ages of everyone living at that address. If you can't find one that meets your needs, ask for a copy of the latest U.S. census for your area. Ask, also, for other "census-type" data. Frequently this material is available through a database search done by computer (Electronic Yellow Pages, or "Dialog"). If a university or college is located in or near your town, its business library or records department should have a bundle of books, pamphlets, and government documents that will be helpful. From these various resources, compile a list showing where to find buyers who match demographic criteria of age, income, sex, educational level, or membership in athletic facilities. This, then, is your target market.

Figure 2.4
Sample Survey Questions

1. Who has traditionally bought the most exercise equipment over the last few years?

   ☐ Teenagers living at home.
   ☐ College students.
   ☐ Young professionals.
   ☐ 35 to 45 years old.
   ☐ Over 45 years.
   ☐ Dieters.
   ☐ Men.
   ☐ Women.

2. How much did they spend?

   ☐ Under $100.
   ☐ $100–$500.
   ☐ Over $500.

3. How many items did they buy at one time?

   ☐ One item.
   ☐ More than one item.

4. Where do they live?

   ☐ Cities.
   ☐ Suburbs.
   ☐ Rural areas.
   ☐ Northeast.
   ☐ Southern states.
   ☐ Sunbelt.
   ☐ Midwest.

5. Where is most exercise equipment purchased? (Rate in order of purchase preference, with (1) being the most popular.)

   ☐ Sporting goods store.
   ☐ Mail order.
   ☐ Department store.
   ☐ Health club/gym.
   ☐ Television promotion.
   ☐ Other _____ .

6. If purchased through the mail, which type of advertising was used most often? (Rate in order, with (1) being used most often.)

   ☐ Classified ad in general interest magazine.
   ☐ Classified ad in sports magazine.
   ☐ Insert in credit card statement, such as American Express.

7. How often did they buy?

   ☐ More than once a year.
   ☐ Once a year.
   ☐ Less than once a year.

Now, find out where these individuals shop and what they buy. In your search for the sports buyer you might poll local stores that sell weight-training and exercise equipment—sporting goods stores, department stores like Sears, discount retailers such as K Mart, even swap meet, or flea market, vendors. Wander through the stores, and visit with the sales people. (Try to catch them at a time when business is slow or non-existent.) Look at the equipment on the floor. Comparison shop for quality and price. Watch for trends (as you did with golfing equipment) that indicate what sells and what doesn't.

(Note: don't annoy salespeople with inane questions or take up their time when paying customers are on the floor. Conduct your research when your interviewees are not busy.)

GEOGRAPHIC AND CENSUS-TRACT DATA

When compiling data from public lists, much of what you find will be information that links buyers by location. Known as geographic, or census-tract data, this information helps to classify buyers by age, income, lifestyle, and potential buying patterns. Loosely defined, a *census tract* encompasses approximately 1,500 households and is an area defined by local governments and approved by the Census Bureau. *Geographic locations* generally define larger areas, such as states or cities, and comprise a broader mix of inhabitants. When the results of both geographic and census-tract data are overlaid with other demographics, highly accurate sales forecasting is possible.

Zip-code-ordered direct mail will help you find clusters of like buyers and will help to contain costs while pushing up closures. Encyclopedias, for example, sell best in neighborhoods where families have young children and are eager to own books. Before sending out a salesman or mailing out a flyer, it would make good business sense to find out where these people are. Concurrently, if you planned to market home-gardening products, wouldn't you want to know where the folks lived who worked in their own gardens and could afford to buy your products?

PSYCHOGRAPHICS

Buyers, profiled by age, sex, income level, and other demographic factors are only one part of the equation you must solve to be a successful direct marketer. You will also need to know if prospects are interested in buying what you have to sell.

Demographics measure who, what, where: measurable external factors that define lifestyle. Psychographics measure why people do things: internal motivators that influence buying patterns and consumer behavior.

Psychographics define motives. Why does a man demand a product today, and ignore a similar offer tomorrow? Why do some women buy jewelry or expensive, decorative household items from a catalogue, while others wouldn't be "caught dead" making a mail order purchase? Why do children besiege their parents to buy them water pistols, or robots that turn into toy cars? Why do more men than women buy flashlights? What motivates someone to buy barbecue aprons with smiling pigs printed on the front pocket? Or red rubber tennis shoes? Or paper clip holders embossed with a gold monogram?

Studying the habits and buying patterns of people who have already responded to a direct mail offer is the surest way to predict what and when they will buy again. "A buyer is a buyer is a buyer — and what he or she has already bought tells us more about what else he or she is likely to buy than all the demographic statistics available. . . . "[5]

Fulfilling a Need

Everyone buys something for a *reason*, even if that reason is the compulsion to buy something simply because the buyer saw a picture of it (impulse, or compulsive, buying is a big factor in direct marketing, especially in catalogue sales and television EDM). More often, though, people buy things which will fulfill a basic need, something they believe will improve the quality of their life, offering love, security, or status or increased knowledge.

Once they have bought, most people will buy again, forming the nucleus of any direct marketer's list, the "captive audience" of prospects comfortable with purchasing through direct response advertising. Thus, the success of your offer often depends on how well you understand and recognize these needs.

Several approaches can be used to analyze buyer motivations. Bob Stone, of Stone & Adler, suggests that people will respond to something for two reasons: the desire (1) to gain something they do not have, or (2) to avoid losing something they *do* have.[6]

The Basics

Products or services that *supply basic needs*, such as food and shelter, have a wider market and are easier to sell than unique products such as gold-embossed paper-clip holders.

The results of studies done over the last few years by professional market research firms parallel Abraham Maslow's pyramid theory of human needs[7] which places the most basic needs for survival (food and shelter) at the bottom of the pyramid, and the more esoteric ones (such as self-actualization) at the top.

Consider the direct mail coupons you receive in your mailbox. How many of them are for food or hygiene products? How many improve your home environment? Tune in to the home shopping service channel on your TV (mostly for cable subscribers), if you have it. Note the large number of products that are similar to those you could purchase in local clothing and drug stores.

Complex Needs

Direct marketing draws upon a wide range of human emotions and needs—from the bottom of Maslow's pyramid to the top of it. The interaction of those needs greatly influences a prospect's attitude and motivation to buy.

Figure 2.5
BOB STONE'S LIST OF BASIC HUMAN WANTS

The desire to gain:

To make money ✓   To have style
To save time   To gratify curiosity
To avoid effort   To satisfy an appetite
To achieve comfort   To have beautiful possessions
To have health ✓   To attract the opposite sex
To be popular   To be an individual
To enjoy pleasure   To emulate others
To be clean   To be praised
To take advantage of opportunities

The desire to avoid loss:

To avoid criticism
To keep possessions
To avoid physical pain ✓
To avoid loss of reputation
To avoid loss of money ✓
To avoid trouble

Source: Bob Stone, *Successful Direct Marketing Methods.*[6]

Couple a sales pitch for food or shelter with an offer of security or savings, for example, and you have a surefire winner. Food coupons are a good example. They offer a chance to *save money* while buying a necessity. Even those of us who routinely throw away third class mail have trouble resisting a Carol Wright® coupon envelope. The message is reinforced each time you drive by the food store. "Unlimited Double Coupons" a banner reads, reminding you to cash in the manufacturer's coupon before it expires.

Love is another complex human need. To many of us it is even more basic than food or security. While you can't sell three hugs a day by mail, you *can* sell desirability. All of us (well, most of us) want to be loved, appreciated, and wanted. Any product or service that would make us feel more attractive to others is likely to be a good seller.

Buyer motivations are not as straightforward as they might appear. In order for us to understand a prospective market, several different emotions and desires must be taken into account. Miss one, and you may well miss the market entirely! For example, the exercise equipment you researched in the demographic study of sports buyers will certainly increase desirability. The buyer will be slimmer, trimmer, and more attractive if he or she uses it. However, exercise equipment is expensive, and if used regularly, requires a heavy commitment of time and patience. If you target a market that wants to look better but won't take the time to exercise or spend money on it, then your advertising is wasted on the wrong prospects.

Selling Desirability

Consistent sellers in the "desirability" market are things that are easy to use, affordable, and *offer instant improvement*. Think of all the catalogues that offer clothing, jewelry, perfume, or cosmetics. These products are designed to improve the buyer's appearance immediately.

TRANSFORM YOURSELF FROM HOUSEWIFE TO HOSTESS, WITH OUR LOVELY SILK CAFTAN,

"SHOW HIM HOW DESIRABLE YOU ARE WITH CHANTILLE PERFUME."

Other offers improve atmosphere rather than appearance, and offer affordable luxury: custom bedspreads of tufted satin (which are washable); window treatments to flatter skin tones (through soft, filtered light);

scented, colored soaps; and coordinated bathroom accessories. All are designed to increase the buyers' sense of self-worth and to offer immediate, instant improvement to their lifestyle. After all, we look and feel better in attractive surroundings.

If all these sensual suggestions are combined, the effect is overpowering: a beautiful, Chantille-scented woman, in a bright-colored, flowing silk caftan, luxuriating on a tufted, quilted satin spread.

Psychological Appeal

Another interesting aspect of marketing desirability is that the success of your product *depends on an appeal that is often more psychological than*

Figure 2.6

The effect can be overpowering.

physical. Turn to the back of any woman's magazine and you will find offers that promise thicker, healthier hair, slimmer thighs, a bigger bust, a thinner waist. How many ads have you seen in the last month (printed, televised, or broadcast) that promised to "melt away ugly fat in minutes!"?

Improved physical appearance is not reserved only for women. Take a look at advertisements for men: same positive suggestions. From late-night television commercials to the back pages of macho male magazines, advertisements promise to replace hair or remove it, cover grey, slim waists, or build biceps. Look at a sports publication. Tiny mail order coupons in the back offer the chance for longer drives, better serves, more accurate racquetball shots, better sex.

In each case, the advertiser is selling desirability. "Use my product," he is saying, "and you, too, can be one of the beautiful people." The cost is small, the effort is negligible (and often the results are too), but the buyer *feels* better by trying it. (See Figure 2.7.)

BUYER-GRAPHICS

Buyer-graphics is a relatively new refinement to psychographics. As our population becomes more mobile and more technologically oriented, new forms have been designed to study the product-purchasing behavior of certain groups of people. One system, developed by Artitron Ratings Company, uses a system called "ScanAmerica"℠.[8] A box known as an RD 100 sits on top of the T.V. set to monitor shows being watched. Another device, this one hand-held, monitors *who* is watching the program. Viewers are prompted with on-screen signals to indicate when they are watching by punching in their own personal code. A third device, a special wand similar to those used in supermarkets and capable of reading bar codes, is "waved" across the bar codes of products purchased by members of the household whenever they return home with food, clothing, or other items bought and ticketed with the UPC (bar) code. Thus, ScanAmerica not only determines who is watching what, but also records what kinds of products the viewers buy.

The potential is enormous. Not only will they have past performance to rely on when they design an advertising campaign, *they can predict the future as well* and be on top of a rising market. (See Figure 2.8.)

Figure 2.7
FEEL-GOOD MOTIVATORS

love	happiness	comfort
pleasure	security	peace of mind
recognition	praise	self-confidence
money	beauty	entertainment
friends	acceptance	creativity
knowledge	self-improvement	sex

Regardless of their background or lifestyle, most people will buy a product that makes them feel good.

COMMON FACTORS

It is interesting to note that regardless of the product or service you intend to market or of the method you select to do it, several factors determine why people will buy something.

Appreciation

Most people are alike in more ways than you think. Look at the list of "Feel-Good Motivators" in Figure 2.7. Compare it with Bob Stone's list of "Basic Human Wants" in Figure 2.5. We all want to be appreciated. It is only in the method of appreciation we most prefer that we differ.

Group Behavior

Certain groups (designated by common characteristics such as ethnic or racial background, age, sex, or income) exhibit a buying behavior as a group, which sets them apart from the larger buying group (such as U.S. citizen or European) to which they belong. Make sure you target the right group.

Figure 2.8

Advanced technology that works

ScanAmerica is the first television ratings service to combine an advanced people meter with an in-home UPC scanner.

Both parts of the system, people meter and scanner wand, are designed with household participation in mind. The tasks are simple, and can easily fit in a family member's routine.

The household compensation plas are structured to encourage continuous and long-term cooperation.

Convenient technology combined with generous compensation ensures that households will be able to provide the information ScanAmerica needs to deliver a full range of media and marketing services.

The people meter

The ScanAmerica people meter is easy to use. It is designed to motivate viewers to indicate who's watching.

When the television set is turned on, the ScanAmerica people meter inserts a flashing question mark in the upper left hand corner of the screen.

This on-screen prompt reminds viewers to register their presence in the room. The prompt is noticeable and difficult to ignore, but it doesn't interfere with normal television viewing.

From a brochure © 1986 Arbitron Ratings Company. Adapted and reprinted by permission.

Self-Interest

Buyers are selfish. Subconsciously, the first question a potential buyer asks is, "What's in it for me?" If your product doesn't provide an immediate and obvious benefit, rethink your approach.

Time

Many families today have two wage earners to support the unit; others are supported by a single parent. In both cases *time becomes a valuable commodity*. Products or services that offer "quick" remedies are in high demand. Look at the number of families that "eat out" at McDonald's rather than "cook in" at home. Fast food is quick and convenient. How many products or services can you think of that provide an immediate solution to the demands imposed by a tight schedule?

Rewards

The vast majority of individuals (well over 80 percent) are influenced by things that affect their sense of well-being or self-esteem. They seek recognition and reward for their achievements. A product or service that causes anxiety is very difficult to sell.

Appearance

We all want to look our best, and most of us are willing to put our paychecks on the line to achieve the effect. Count the number of catalogues you receive in a year's time that advertise clothing, shoes, or beauty products. When you were a teenager, did you ever order a cream that promised to broaden your bust, dim facial freckles, or rub away unwanted body hair? Have you ever bought perfume without smelling it first, ordering it directly from a catalogue because the advertisement appealed to you? How about leather goods like briefcases and appointment books? How many credit card statements have you received in the last few months that include a filler or direct mail coupon for products that will visibly prove your affluence (thus attractiveness) such as briefcases, stereo sets, or fancy embossed keychains?

THE MARKET IN MOTION

Mobility is a big problem faced by direct marketers today. Their market is in motion, following jobs, sunshine, family ties, recreational interests, and more. Changes in economic patterns and overall lifestyles add to the burden of accurate forecasting.

Sex

Because over half of our female population works, the stay-at-home housewife is a fast-disappearing target. A large contingent of single-parent households is headed by women with low-paying jobs. Thus, many homemakers are often more concerned with family survival than personal luxury. At the same time, many young women are electing to pursue careers instead of marriage and/or children. They seek products in the "feel-good" market and buy heavily into the desirability market as well. Many who do marry choose not to have children and elect to spend money on travel or household improvements rather than salting it away for college educations for the children they will never have. Within just a few years, thousands of merchandisers have capitalized on the "working woman" or the "executive woman," whereas only a few years ago they aimed at apron-bound ladies tied to the care of husbands and households.

Age

Women aren't the only group undergoing a radical change. The median age of the population has increased. "Baby boomers" are entering middle age. Health care services and products have improved tremendously, and people are taking better care of themselves, expecting to live longer, healthier lives. Discretionary retirement income and an interest in leisure-time activity services and products have been rising steadily over the last few years. A vast new area of products and services that cater specifically to the older American have sprung up, especially in the sunbelt areas.

Economics

Perhaps the single largest factor impacted by our fast-changing society is an economic one. The change from an industrial society to one based on the processing of information means more white collar and professional jobs and less work for skilled or unskilled labor. Consequently, entire clusters of population have uprooted their families and moved from one area to another, permanently changing the demographics of both old and new locations for these people.

Education

As the work force changes, so do educational requirements. Universities for "adult students" are increasing rapidly. Conferring bachelors and masters degrees, these institutions promise to help people make the career switch from blue collar to white. It is not uncommon today for a minimum-wage secretary to have a bachelors degree in psychology, or a bank teller to boast an MBA. (They may not earn any more money, but they are certainly better educated than their counterparts of a few years ago.)

Lifestyle

With the changes in lifestyle and work patterns, terms like "Yuppie" and "Senior Citizen" and "Baby Boomer" have taken on special import to the advertisers who coined or capitalized on them. Entire campaigns have been successfully aimed at a "Pepsi Generation," for instance, who buy soft drinks en masse in order to be "hip" and "with it."

For a direct marketer to stay with it, too, he or she needs to keep a bead on the moving target.

MARKET SEGMENTATION

Whether in motion or safely ensconced in a local neighborhood, every buyer is part of a large group influenced by cultural distinctions based on the "segment" of society to which he or she belongs. Nationality, regional affiliations, community groups and other geographic factors impact them as surely as do sex, age, and economic status.

Cultural Groups

Many Americans grow up with a sense of "entitlement," which means that they expect their basic needs to be supplied by family, employer, and/or government. Americans are further characterized by relative affluence and a high standard of living. Quality of life is greatly enhanced by a number of products or services designed to minimize work time and increase leisure time. Americans are an excellent target for the direct marketer who offers to supply any *materialistic* needs.

Clusters

Within each broad market segment, subgroups or "clusters" exist. The type of material goods or services that appeal to members of a specific cluster are further defined by socioeconomic class. Socialization and traditions subtly shape much of the buyer's decisions.

Figure 2.9

**Within each broad market segment, subgroups or
"clusters" exist.**

Discount coupons for beer or jug wines, for example, would have a broader appeal to groups categorized as belonging to a middle-income class. Discount coupons for estate bottled wines would not do as well with that same group. Why? Statistically, individuals categorized as belonging to the middle-income class drink more beer and jug wine than any other group. They also respond positively (and frequently) to coupon offers. Attempts to sell large amounts of vintage wines to this group, with or without coupons, have failed. The price is too high, and the product has poor "taste appeal" as the group has had far more exposure to the lower priced products.

Segments

Consumer behavior and demographics are examined in small segments as well as larger ones. Each major group is further broken down into subcultures, groups of people who share common traits, attitudes, and interests. Often subcultural traits cross socioeconomic class lines. Frequently they break age barriers as well. Religious and racial groups, for instance, are not bound by age, social class, or income, or even by national allegiance. A catalogue offering articles and books in print for members of the Roman Catholic faith would have appeal to Catholics regardless of their geographic location or class standing.

Young people are one of the biggest segments of the buying population. And, as a consuming group, they are most likely to spend readily. Given the opportunity to do so, most of them will spend money as fast as they can get it.

The big motivator in this case is desirability. Young people want to look appealing, to be "trendy" and popular, to "fit in." Choices in music, clothing, entertainment, and environment are influenced by the attitudes of their peer group. Records, books, skin-care products, body-building tonics, hair color, magazines, video programs, and other products that would help a young person to feel more attractive and more desirable to their own social class have great mass market appeal. However, this market is also fickle! Kids change styles at the drop of a schoolbook; therefore, to stay on top of this market, the advertiser had better be truly tuned in to what teens want even before they know that they want it!

SUMMARY

Target marketing uses demographics, psychographics, and census tract data to locate a group of buyers who are *most likely* to buy your product or service. Past history is also studied, to determine *who has already bought* by direct response advertising. This group is your target market.

Direct marketing is consistently successful because it depends on the expected, measured response of a carefully chosen target market.

An important part of market research is to remember that, as far as the buyer is concerned, it is highly subjective but it must be kept highly *objective* as far as you are concerned. Never let your own personal preferences influence your research on a product's viability. Most direct marketing campaigns that fail do so because the seller ignores the basic rules of direct marketing and targets a market based on who he "thinks" will buy rather than the individual clearly defined as the most likely buyer.

Target your market as a result of thorough, scientific market research supported by a proven tract record and good solid data. Remember, direct marketing is very *precise*. If you follow the rules, it will result in phenomenal success.

ENDNOTES

1. Source: WSJ Subscriber Study, 1985. Mendelsohn Survey of Adults in Markets of Affluence, 1986. Copyright Dow Jones & Company, 1987.
2. Two such market research firms are Information Resources, a Chicago-based firm, and ASI Market Research (a division of IDC Services) in New York City. *Advertising Age* also is an excellent source of information regarding market research firms and their latest innovative ideas.
3. It is wise to have a business name and business address before you try this. Giving a home address is shaky at best. It is certainly unprofessional. Most private clubs will be reluctant to give out demographic information to an individual; however, they will be very helpful if you are a business interested in purchasing advertising space.
4. When dealing with professional publications such as newspapers, magazines, and trade journals, generally they will mail a media kit only to a business name and address. Most radio and television stations will give out demographic information over the phone if you tell them you are a business. (Telling them that you are a student working on a research project works well, too!)
5. From a quote paraphrasing Gertrude Stein in "Psychographics ... The lifestyle of the mail order buyer," a pamphlet put out by Dependable Lists, Inc.
6. Source: Bob Stone, *Successful Direct Marketing Methods*, page 263.
7. Source: Abraham Maslow, *Motivation and Personality*, 2nd ed., (Harper & Row, 1970). This text suggests that the hierarchy of human needs is like an inverted pyramid with basic survival needs on the bottom and the need for self-actualization at the top. The idea is that we go through a number of stages, from birth to maturity, and

during these stages we progress from the need for food, shelter, and sex in our earlier years to more aesthetic needs such as love, understanding, and personal achievement in our later years.

8. ScanAmerica℠ is a Registered Service Mark of Arbitron Ratings Company, Metropolitan Tower, 142 W. 57th Street, New York, NY 10019.

3

DATABASE MARKETING

"We got rich being 2 percent right. We never had to worry about being 98 percent wrong. What's needed to succeed in today's highly competitive direct marketing is an innovative way to reach 'the other 98 percent,' the folks whose direct mail goes from mailbox to trash can without a glance."

—John Stevenson, President
Experts in Direct Marketing

Being "2 percent right" is simply not acceptable any longer. To make money, you need to know where the money is, and that means keeping track of ready, steady buyers. Success in today's marketplace is based upon a solid *dependable customer base — the single most important ingredient of any direct sales campaign.*

Fortunately, building a good list that successfully taps into the 98 percent that got away is not as difficult as you might think. Thanks to the capabilities of the computer to store, sort, and retrieve information, a lot is already known about your prospective buyers. Most of them are already on file in a database[1] of some sort — a qualified list of who bought, where they are, and why they wanted it. These are the people you want, the folks that are already comfortable with direct response advertising.

From your own market research, you should already have a pretty good idea of whom you are looking for and where to find them. By overlaying your buyer profile with lists of willing customers (including your own, if you already have some), you should be able to get a fairly accurate fix on prospective buyers.

Obviously, you cannot and will not put out an offer that will attract all of the people all of the time. But with judicious use of applied psychographics, list testing, and good creative copy, you will reach most of the buyers most of the time. Dependable Lists, Inc.,[2] one of the major list brokers in the U.S., suggests the "important thing to remember is that it is better to send a poor mailing to a good mailing list than a good mailing to a poor mailing list." In other words, *no matter what you are selling, if your offer doesn't reach the eyes and ears of the right group or* **segment** *of potential buyers, you won't make a sale.*

Figure 3.1

Today's direct marketer has to find a way to get to the prospects whose mail goes from mailbox to trash can without a glance.

FINDING THE RIGHT LIST

There are two basic types of lists, the house list (or internal list) and the external list that comes from outside sources such as a list broker or another business willing to rent or lease its own house list (or a segment of it) to you.

House Lists

House lists contain *information pertinent to customers who have bought from you before, or have answered inquiries regarding your own products and services*. If your company uses a warranty or registration system, that information should be a part of your internal list along with orders, sales, and requests for information or brochures.

House lists are your best bet for prospects because they contain your own customer base, the people you know the most about, and the ones who are most familiar with the products and services you have to offer. Properly organized and maintained (kept up-to-date), **your house list is your most valuable marketing tool**. Because house lists are based on internal information, they can be (and usually are) very complete. Your list should include up-to-the-minute information about each customer's credit and buying habits as well as the person's name, address, phone number, and other personal information.

Another advantage of a house list is that, because the information contained in it is based on data that belongs to you (your sales records), it can be updated or amended at any time. Suppose, for example, that you have compiled a list of 10,000 individuals who regularly buy craft and collector's items such as colonial teaspoons and that you want to target a promotion toward a "women only" audience. If your database has been coded for sex (male or female), the list can be manipulated to produce a list of women buyers for your new promotions.

House lists can be broken down into residential and business categories or a combination of both. A **residential list** usually includes the family name, i.e. Smith, and often includes the first names and titles of family members as well, such as Mr. John, Mrs. Susan, Miss Georgina, and so on. A **business list** is used for mailings or marketing campaigns targeting other businesses. Besides providing the company name, this type of list usually (but not always) gives the name of a person to contact along with an appropriate title. With both types — residential or business — it is a good idea to keep the list fresh because people frequently move in and out of both jobs and homes.

Figure 3.2

Examples of Sources of "Free" Lists*

Professional organizations, such as the local building industry association.

Business organizations, such as a chamber of commerce.

Service club or personnel management group.

School's teacher/parent organizations or private school membership roster.

Social organizations, such as country club, baseball booster club, or square dance club.

Donors, such as orchestra, art museum, or opera supporters.

*May be restricted to members' use only.

External Lists

External lists are resources that *come from outside your own company.* They can be bought, rented, borrowed, or traded. A number of professional services are available that rent lists for a fee, but there are other alternatives, too.

Organizations.   If you belong to a neighborhood, business, or professional organization, or if your children attend private school, membership lists can usually be obtained for little or no cost. Before using one of these lists, however, check to see if there are any restrictions on its use. Some groups, such as private schools and charitable donors, do not appreciate having their house lists used for commercial purposes, unless the marketing campaign is for a "good cause" that has been preapproved by the membership.

Other private organizations require that the users of their lists also be members. Most social clubs and some service clubs fall into this category. Still other groups, such as chambers of commerce, usually place little or no restrictions on the uses of membership directories, and helpfully publish a new one every year in order to promote new business within the community.

Organizational lists are a good way for the small business to get started in direct marketing, especially for a service business such as word processing, insurance, or a marketing organization. In any community there is a nucleus of "small business" that is often interactive and mutually supportive. Frequently, the local chamber of commerce will provide either lists or the names of list brokers who can assist you in approaching this market.

Compiled.   Most external lists come from list brokers who rent or sell them to prospective users. Usually referred to as compiled lists, these lists contain names grouped together by a common denominator (such as zip code, sex, or food preference). Often a number of psychographic or demographic factors are used in compiling such a list.

Compiled lists can be divided into major groups of buyers such as these:

- Business.
- Professional.
- Membership.
- Technical.
- Agricultural.
- Consumer.

Figure 3.3

Examples of Compiled Lists

Architects, by size of firm, specialty, AIA membership, length of time in business.

New businesses, by SIC* code, number of employees, gross sales, length of time in business.

New home buyers, by purchase price, address, title company or lender, acreage, or number of persons in the household.

*Standard Industry Code: classifies businesses by the type of business they engage in.

Business groups are usually broken down by factors such as SIC (Standard Industry Classification) code, as well as size (number of employees and gross sales), and location (city, state, or regional area). Most business lists also include names and titles of the principals and/or staff persons in charge of purchasing.

Professional groups (individuals in law, medicine, education, engineering, and other professions) usually record information such as professional affiliation, area of specialization, ownership structure, and gross receipts.

Membership lists, trade show registrations, company or industry directories, and credit reporting services provide much of the information for business and professional lists, as do the actual organizations themselves.

Technical and **agricultural** lists are specialized lists generally used by a smaller group of businesses who specialize in one particular industry, such as farming. Obviously, the market for such a list, in comparison, say, to a general consumer list, is much smaller. These lists also overlap with membership and business lists, as in the lists of electrical engineers, for example, who show up on all three categories.

Consumer lists (which can be business lists, but usually are based more on home consumption of products and services) get their information from local directories (telephone) and census tract information. Polk, Donnelley, and other consumer reporting services should be able to provide you with accurate lists for reaching the household market.

Internal lists are commonly shared between two or more companies by mutual agreement. Some companies also rent out their own house lists (as an additional revenue source). The entire list, or a segment of it (based on certain psychographic or demographic characteristics) can be interchanged for various direct marketing campaigns. Each company tends to segment its list along lines best suited to its own internal use. If you plan to exchange lists, be sure to verify that the reciprocating business can provide you with a meaningful group of names. You don't want to wind up on the short end of a one-way information swap!

Rented Lists

Rented lists are usually a one-time only proposition. Names are rented, at a price per thousand ($PER/M), on contract, for a specific use. The contract usually determines what will be advertised, as well as when and how. Price is based on how selective the list may be (number of overlapping segments to be reached). A list based on zip code alone, for example, would cost less than one based on zip code, sex, age group, and recency of purchase (a total of four segments).[3]

You rent the right to use the names on the list once, and once only. If you want to use the list again, you must rent it again. If you want to change the preapproved specific use, the list owner must grant permission. Mailing (or telemarketing, or whatever it is you are doing with the list) must be done on the date specified by the contract, and for the number of names agreed upon.

To insure that the rules are followed, the list owner usually "seeds" the list with a number of names of people who report directly back to the owner. Should you attempt to use the list for something other than that specified in the contract, the "seed" names will report it, and you could be subject to a court action under breach of contract (or worse).

Reliability

Unfortunately, there is a wide range of dependability of external lists, and it is easier than not for the novice to wind up with a list that is almost useless. Generally, when utilizing the services of a list broker (or list counselors, as they are sometimes called), *less nets little and more is best.* Unfortunately, because acquisition cost is almost always the deciding factor, it is not always possible (or affordable) to have as complete a list as you would like. While a list with too little pertinent information may save money, it may also net a zero return. This is a common problem for business people who are unfamiliar with direct marketing. They try to save money by renting the cheapest possible list. Many of them even "price shop," a practice which virtually guarantees a less than satisfactory list. The trick is to strike a happy medium.

To avoid unnecessary expense (or worse yet, complete disaster) when considering an external list, check these two factors first:

1. How current is it?
2. Is it a list of buyers, or just a list of names?

Far too many commercially available lists fall into the latter category. On the average, people move every three to five years. Before deciding upon a list, you need to know how long the listees have been on it. There is no point in wasting postage on mail that will be returned marked "Not at this address" or "Moved. Left no forwarding address." Of course, you could simply address each piece to the "Occupant" or "Resident," but that may cheapen the piece, and in some cases, cause it to go straight to the trash can with the other junk mail.

The other problem encountered by novice list renters/buyers is one of validity. A multitude of public lists are available for groups such as home buyers or new business owners. But just because someone's name is on a list doesn't mean that person is comfortable with direct marketing. You are looking for the ones who are. (A buyer is a buyer is a buyer, don't forget.) So, if you want to do more than skim the 2 percent off the top of all unqualified lists, spend the time and money necessary to obtain a list of direct response buyers.

Lists with proven buyers usually come from prior direct marketing campaigns. Your own list, compiled from previous experience, is obviously dependable. Many external lists available through professional list brokers are also reliable. They cost more, but they're worth it. Your sales will increase dramatically!

Qualified lists mean higher sales — in most cases. Even qualified buyers have "quirks," however. For example, not all direct response buyers are repeat customers. Some of them may be "one shot" buyers. Mailing a list with a preponderance of those could result in heavy disappointment and scant sales. Most professional list brokers have the computer resources to locate and weed out these names from their lists.

Choosing the right list often comes down to a combination of what you can afford and how much information you can get for the time and money you are willing to spend. Finding a reliable list broker is the key. To find one, contact your local direct marketing association or club (see the Appendices for a complete list), or the Direct Marketing Association in New York City. Picking a name at random from the Yellow Pages is **not** a good way to find a dependable list broker.

WHAT'S IN A LIST?

Regardless of your sources of information — previous sales, inquiries, or shared information from other resources, when you build a house list, or rent one, it is important to include all of the information you will need for a successful marketing campaign. Because you create internal lists yourself, they tend to be far more accurate and complete. The amount of information you put into your own list is limited only by the amount of time and money you are willing to spend to put the list together. A rented list, on the other hand, should be streamlined to provide only what you need. (Why pay for information you don't plan to use?)

If you plan to cross-reference information, as all professional list brokers do, be sure to eliminate duplicate names (and/or addresses) *before* embarking on a direct marketing project. (See Merge/Purge on page 62 in this chapter.) A reliable rented list will already be purged of duplicate names (*within* that list) and can be ordered according to the minimum amount of information you need for a specific campaign.

The Basics

All lists should include the customer's name. However, because you may want to personalize your offer or to direct it to one specific individual in the household or business, it is a good idea to specify the contact person's first name, title, and appropriate salutation. For example, if you plan to send out a direct mail piece to book buyers, you might address it to Mr. James Smith at 4847 Whatswhere Street in Boulder, PA 19000, and begin your letter with, "Dear James,".

Because direct marketing now encompasses so much more than direct mail, the area code and telephone number should be included in any list you build. Already, more than half of all direct marketing orders come in by telephone. In some cases, 100 percent of the orders are placed by telephone.

Keeping track of current credit card numbers and expiration dates within your database will be helpful, too. It is already possible for customers to peruse a computer bulletin board or page through a televised catalogue in their own homes. Using a home computer system hooked to the shopping service via modem, they can key in their order and the current credit card number they want to use for their purchase. (Although this procedure is already possible, most people don't have the computer equipment needed to complete this type of transaction.)

Your list should always track the date of each customer's most recent purchase or inquiry. A "hot list" of mail order buyers, for instance, is not so hot if over half of the people on it are deceased or have moved and left no forwarding address. Unfortunately, for first-time list users on a do-it-yourself direct marketing campaign, more often than not, that's what they wind up with when they rent a list.

All lists, whether you rent them or build them yourself, should contain the following "fields" (or categories) of information.

- Name: first, middle initial, last.
- Address, including zip code.
- Title (i.e., Mr./Ms./Mrs./Miss/Dr., etc.).
- Home telephone number (with area code).
- Most recent date of purchase.
- Business address (including job title, if any).
- Business telephone number and area code.

The last two items refer, of course, to the business market. In a house list, however, there is no reason why business information cannot be stored for residential users. This practice is particularly useful if you are marketing to professionals, such as doctors or lawyers, and you wish to get past their front desk to reach them directly at home!

The More You Know

The more you know about your prospects, the easier it is to sell them. The age and sex of each individual on your list is often important. Most direct marketing campaigns are aimed at one or more broad socioeconomic segments loosely defined by sex or age category. For example, if you are selling acne preparations, your targeted market is obviously young people. But, if your advertising promotion depends upon a catalogue featuring vitamins, skin treatments, and prosthetic devices for women who have undergone surgery, a totally different type of database would be used. To make certain you are truly targeting the right market, your list should identify the following demographic factors:

- Sex: male or female.
- Age category (usually by groups, i.e., 15–20, 21–35, Over 40, Over 55, etc.).

Other information can be helpful too, regardless of the market you are targeting. Knowing the method of payment (cash, credit, or check) and the amount of the most recent or average purchase (or total purchases within a given time frame, such as a year) helps you qualify consumers. If you plan to market big-ticket items (televisions, appliances, etc.), wouldn't you prefer to mail your offer to a list of prospects who were willing and able to spend that kind of money on a direct marketing offer? In that case, mailing a list of gadget buyers whose average purchase last year was $5.95 would be a waste of your marketing dollars!

Historical data which could help identify and categorize types of buyers should include factors such as these:

- Credit card(s): number and expiration date.
- Date and amount of last purchase(s).
- Sales history, including number and amounts of past purchases with corresponding dates (or perhaps just a total number of dollars spent and number of purchases made over a specific period of time, such as two years).
- Bad credit list.
- Do not mail list.

The final two items are important. *If you are selling sexually explicit material or certain types of firearms or alcoholic beverages, you must comply with local, state, and federal regulations.* The post office maintains a list of individuals who have asked that certain types of materials not be mailed to them. Because lists are sold, rented, and interchanged frequently, it is easy to overlook a **do not mail** code and send material the recipient finds offensive. To date, the burden falls on you to avoid that mistake. *Contact your local post office to verify that your direct marketing plans are within legal limits.*

Bad credit codes can be inserted into any list, and certainly should be a part of your own house list. It's a good idea to flag customers who can't or won't pay, or fail to return merchandise as promised.

Profitable direct response marketing is a two-way street. It takes the cooperation of both parties—buyer and seller—to effect a satisfactory transaction. If your buyer doesn't play fair, stop wasting your marketing efforts. There are plenty of other people who want to buy. Aim for them instead.

BUILDING YOUR OWN LIST

Many small businesses start out by building a house list and renting additional names to use with it. Larger businesses find it essential to maintain their own house list.

Computerized Lists

The larger the company, the more complex the computer system that controls its house list. Being small, however, does not preclude having a computerized list. Because of the proliferation of small, affordable "personal" or "business computers," a number of "computerization" alternatives are possible. Because both the PC (personal computer) and its big brother the AT (much faster, and a far better alternative) are so inexpensive and easy to use, and because a number of excellent commercial database products are available that interface with ordinary word processing programs and desktop publishing packages, it is reasonably easy to create your own customer list.

Before purchasing any software or hardware, take time to investigate it thoroughly. Generally, the three things to look for are speed, storage capacity, and backup capabilities. A good rule to follow is to buy ten times what you initially need. Otherwise, you will be faced with a costly replacement before you can afford it! At the very least, you should plan on using an AT-style "personal" computer with at least a 30 megabyte hard drive system and a high-speed, heavy-duty printer. You will also need a tape backup. Your printer should be high speed — and this does not mean a $595 special at the local computer store. If you plan to *print* your own direct mail letter, for example, you must be able to process a great many letters very quickly for the promotion to be cost effective. (Most businesses subcontract the actual printing to a direct mail service.)

Although you may want to send your printing out, you will still want to create and maintain your customer list in-house. A number of commercial database packages are available for this. The one most frequently used by small business (because it interacts comfortably with most word-processing programs) is dBase III® by Ashton Tate.

Figure 3.4 shows a typical "record layout" or format for a typical customer database. Fixed fields (meaning they have defined length) are listed by name, field length, number of decimals (for numeric fields such as amount of purchase), field type (numeric, character, date), and description. If a field is a "key field," that is, one that is used for sorting, testing, etc., it is defined with a special character on the record layout, in this case, the letter X.

With the format shown in Figure 3.4, which we use in our company, the key field (a unique combination of letters and numbers which identify this particular customer) consists of the customer number plus the first 5 digits of the zip code plus the first 20 characters of the last name, [000000192101SMITH] in this example.

Figure 3.4
Customer List Layout

Field Name	Field Length	Dec.	Type A	Key field	Contents of 1st record
CUSTOMER KEY	21		C X		00000192101SMITH
CUST. NUMBER	06	0	N	X	000001
ZIPCODE	11	0	N	X	921010001
LASTNAME	20		C	X	Smith
FIRSTNAME	12		C		John
TITLE	12		C		Mr. J.C.
ADDRESS1	08		C		1234
ADDRESS2	19		C		Bluebell Ct
CITY	27		C		San Diego
STATECODE	02		C	X	CA
STATE	25		C		California
AREACODE	03	0	N	X	619
HOMEPHONE	07	0	N		555-1234
BUSCODE	01	0	N	X	1
MEDIACODE	01	0	N		1
TOTALSALES	12	2	N		5000.00
NOTIMESBOT	03	0	N		8
DATEFIRST	06		D		01/01/83
DATELAST	06		D		07/20/87
PAIDTYPE	01	0	N		2
CCT#1	01		C		V
CCN#1	25		C		4020-1111-1111-V
CCE#1	06		D		01/88
CCT#2	01		C		M
CCN#2	25		C		5020-1111-1111-MC
CCE#2	06		D		02/89
SEX	01		C		M
AGE	02		N		3

To speed mailing and fulfillment of orders, the first 3 digits of ZIPCODE 1 are also defined as PREZIP (the prezip sort for direct mail).

Because our mailing labels are 27 characters (or spaces) wide, we use a special method to "trim" the name down to that size, putting a title in front of the last name, as in "Mr. J.C. Smith." (If the "trimmed" name runs over 27 characters, the last characters are dropped and do not appear on the label.) The same system is used for the address, to insert the street name after the street number. But, because we sometimes use the *entire* name or address (in the body of a letter, for example), we keep larger fields on file in the computer.

A similar philosophy is behind the use of a state code and the name of the state itself. When we send a piece to the residents of "California," for example, that name is too long to put on a mailing label. We trim it to the state code only (a field we also use for sorting).

Because we have the capability of combining lists internally (also known as merging multiple databases), we code our master list to match (cross-reference) it with other databases. This procedure permits access to this customer from several different reference points. We can also track him through several smaller, individual databases, resulting in faster processing since we have only to look through information we specifically need. Mr. Smith, whose customer file is outlined in Figure 3.4, can be accessed by his business code or his sales history as well as his "master record" in this database.

Another reason for multiple codes is *privacy*. If we choose to rent or share our list with someone else, we may not wish to include the customer's business address. Rarely do we share specific sales history. Our database system isolates sensitive information for our own internal use only while permitting profitable rental of our lists to other businesses.

Another field we track carefully is the *Media Code*. Mr. Smith is a "1" (our code for direct mail) because that's how we originally got him as a customer. (He responded to a direct mail offer.) When the media code is combined with his sales history file, we can determine what type of media works best with him. This file lists only his total sales ($5000) and number of times purchased (8), but his sales file, which we can MERGE (join) with this one, allows us to view his sales history as well.

Mr. Smith's file also tells us that he has been with us since January of 1980 (DATEFIRST) and most recently bought on July 20 of this year. He paid with a type 2, our code for payment by personal check.

Because our customers typically pay by credit card over the telephone, and in order to speed up processing, we maintain information about their credit cards in our file. Two major cards are tracked by card number and expiration date. In this way, credit can be verified while the customer is placing the order, **before he or she gets off the phone**. If the card is bad or if credit on that card has been exhausted, we can make appropriate changes while the customer is still on the phone. This "quick credit check" and (instant approval code) saves time (and often embarrassment) for both of us, and insures us of a valid order at the time it is placed—especially important when dealing with big dollar volumes.

At the end of our list, we code John Smith (M) for male, and code (3) for age, which indicates Mr. Smith is in group three (age 35 to 45 by our age bracketing).

Your list will, of course, reflect the information that is most important to track for your firm. Any list that you rent or purchase should include all, or at least a majority, of those items that you will need to know for future market research.

Remember, direct response advertising is interactive and measurable. You must be able to calculate results based upon experience with markets chosen because they represent the best prospects (as determined by past performance and assumptions of future buying patterns). *Buying or renting a list and mailing to it is not direct response marketing unless you have a way to measure (follow-up) and record the results of that mailing.*

MAINTENANCE

Building a good list is only half the battle. The other half is maintaining it. A good list doesn't stay that way by itself. It needs regular tune-ups, just like your automobile.

Because we are a mobile society, subject to whims and wishes, your offers and marketing methods must be flexible enough to meet changing lifestyles and locations. Individuals who bought once may or may not buy again. (They usually do, though.) They may also move. (They usually do that, too, about every five years.) Marketing areas are constantly expanding or rearranging themselves to fit new geographical or economic boundaries. To "keep up with the Joneses" and stay on top of your list, you will have to perform regular service on it, regularly examining it for a number of factors, including the following:

- Duplicate names and/or addresses.
- Type of purchase.
- Recency of purchase.

- Frequency of purchase.
- Monetary response to particular offer(s).

These latter three items are also known as the RFM formula (recency, frequency, and monetary value), and are used to evaluate past buying habits and predict future sales.

Merge-Purge

The term Merge-Purge refers to the practice of overlaying or comparing one list with another, checking for duplicates, and eliminating them. More practically, the second part of the Merge-Purge formula, elimination of duplicates, should be one of your main priorities. Duplicate names mean duplicate costs. Even a 10 percent duplication between lists can get very expensive.

Set up a schedule (and stick to it) of when and how you will look for and eliminate duplicate names within your own list. In most cases (with a database of 20,000 names or more), processing will be done entirely by computer, so periodic purging is merely a procedure to be built into the overall system. When you elect to rent lists, they will generally be checked first against your own house list and then against each other.

Procedures to eliminate duplicates offer other opportunities as well. Since the process is electronic, you may choose to suppress certain names because of a psychographic or geodemographic factor (old people, poorer neighborhoods, pet-owners), or to omit those who have a low or one-time-only response rate.

Cleaning Your List

In addition to electronic purging, there are other methods you can use to maintain an up-to-date list. Use "Address Correction Requested" labels or imprints on the outer part of direct mail offers. Address correction can get expensive! Be careful not to use it indiscriminately. Instead, let the customers themselves help you keep your lists current. Do this even if you are renting the list. *All purchasers become part of your house list after they buy.* If they merely pull off a label or accept a telemarketing offer, you need *the correct address* to fulfill their orders. Address correction is the surest way to make sure that you've got it.

Figure 3.5

A good list needs regular tune-ups, just like your automobile.

Moves, Marriages, and Mix-Ups

Home address, marital status, employment, and group affiliations change constantly. So do phone numbers and credit card accounts or limits. Your buyers change preferences, discover new products, or stop buying altogether. Any change in the status of their file should be recorded.

The Time Factor

If you were to process every change that crossed your desk the minute it got there, there would be no time for creative advertising. You would, instead, become a full-time computer operator. Save changes until you have sufficient amount of them to make it worthwhile to shut down other operations and enter the changes.

TESTING

By testing a list, we can make reasonable assumptions regarding its usefulness. If a sample of the people on it respond well to the offer, then the assumption is that an equal percentage of the entire list will respond in kind.

For the most part, testing is designed to ascertain how useful the list will be in promoting a given product or service. A small segment (such as a particular given zip code or census tract, or sporting goods buyers, or women over forty) of the market is selected to receive your offer. Their responses are carefully tabulated to see how popular the offer is with that market.

Determining the size of the sample can be crucial. Factors to consider include sampling tolerance (deviation), risk, number of responses needed, price (higher-priced products usually mean a lower response), and consistency of response.

The aim is to raise response ratios to acceptable, profitable levels. Professional list brokers test their lists before they rent them, but even then, say Dependable Lists, Inc., of New York, "Response ratios may vary as much as 10 to 1." If you compare that to a ratio of 30 to 1, which Dependable says is about average for the average user working with a nonexperience list, the importance of using a pretested list is obvious.

Testing a list can be done in several ways. Each method is relative to a specific market technique. Several are discussed in greater detail in the individual chapters devoted to specific methods of direct marketing and in Chapter 12.

In determining the validity of a list, a number of factors (used singly or collectively) can be tested, including:

- Packaging.
- Formats.
- Location.
- The offer itself.
- Number of pieces sent.
- Demographic factor.

In order for a test to be effective, enough people have to respond to it. Statistical validity depends on the number of responses, not on the number of pieces mailed (or telephone calls made). Even with an adequate response, test results should be compared to a model or base-line test. One test, by itself, is usually not sufficient to give a reliable reading of a prospective market.

Several methods are used to confirm test results. In one, several identical tests are made, in equal quantities, on a number of different key codes. If all of them come in about the same, you can proceed with the list. If there is a substantial variation between responses, say 15 percent or more, the offer, the list, or both, should be reevaluated before you go any further. Another common method of checking test results is to repeat the test with a larger sample. Finally, comparing test results based on first-time buyers to persistency (reorders) is a fair indication of the reliability of a list.

The question "How many names constitute an adequate test?" is difficult to answer. Bob Stone's answer is probably as reliable as any, when he suggests that you need at least 5,000 names for an adequate test (and, that more than 10,000 names is a waste of time and money).

STATISTICAL ANALYSIS

Computerization of marketing lists is an open-ended proposition when it comes to analyzing who, why, where, or any other factor based on behavior, demographics, or census tract information. There is virtually no limit to how you can analyze your list, or how often. As a market research tool, performing statistical analysis on your own or rented lists can provide invaluable information about your present and future markets.

Statistical analysis can be as sophisticated or as simple as you want to make it. Utilizing the services of highly skilled list brokers, tests such as the following can be performed.

Multivariate methods allow the user to locate and correlate a number of variables and determine their interdependence. These common groups are then clustered by zip code and identified as key market prospects.

Regression analysis uses values established from one (or more) variable to determine the validity of another.

Correlation analysis refers to an interdependence between mathematical values (assumed to be positive) and is used to relate the validity of one factor to another.

SUMMARY

Database marketing depends on lists of prospects identified by common characteristics. A list can be as simple as a compiled zip code list of names and addresses, or as complicated as a list created by overlaying census tract data with psychographic and demographic factors tested for responsiveness to direct marketing offers. The more closely your list matches your buyer profile, the more profitable your offer will be.

As your business grows, you will develop and maintain a house list of your own customers — the most valuable tool you will have in direct marketing. To widen your market and target other prospects beyond your own customer base, lists may be bought, rented, or borrowed. Lists rented through professional list brokers (or list counselors) vary in price, with the more expensive being the most accurate, having shown positive in tests for responsive direct response buyers.

To maintain your own list or to determine the accuracy and cost-effectiveness of someone else's, you will need to eliminate both duplicate names and names of "uninterested" buyers. By testing a list, you can determine buyer response and thus predict sales in advance.

ENDNOTES

1. In his Acknowledgments to the Third Edition of *Successful Direct Marketing Methods* (Crain Books, 1987), Bob Stone says, "Inherent in all direct marketing activities is the development of a data base, *unique* lists of individuals, of companies who have inquired or bought. Such lists become prime media for stimulating repeat business, for converting inquiries to sales.

   "Media available for building data bases stagger the mind. Direct Mail. Newspapers. Magazines. Co-ops. Bingo cards. Telephone. Radio. T.V. Cable. Car cards. Catalogs. Interactive electronic media. Video discs. And any combination thereof."

   Mr. Stone's point is that a database is far more than a mailing list. It is the media and the means of increased sales and profits — your primary tool in any direct response advertising campaign!

2. Dependable Lists, Inc., puts out a number of booklets to help you effectively plan your direct mail campaign. The company maintains three full-time offices: in New York, Chicago, and Washington, D.C. For more information, contact the headquarters at 33 Irving Place, New York, NY 10003, or call (212) 677-6760.

3. A typical compiled list of names and addresses rents for $15 to $20 per M (thousand). A direct response list rents for $40–$50/M and up through a list broker. Selections for various segmentations cost extra. It is very possible to pay upwards of $100/M for highly qualified names (such as a list of home addresses and telephone numbers of chairmen of boards who are also direct response buyers of big ticket items and major donors to charitable organizations.)

DIRECT SELLING

4

"The point in sales is always to follow the Girl Scout motto, 'Be prepared.' See business when it's there. Look at everyone and think, 'Is this a customer? How do I make this person buy?'"
—Markita Andrews, top seller of Girl Scout cookies.[1]

Markita has been selling cookies since she was a Brownie Scout. She sells more of them than almost anyone else. Her formula is simple: set goals, follow through, and "go where the customers are."

Let's examine Markita's formula and see if it applies to direct marketing. Do we set goals? You bet! Except in direct marketing, we usually call it market planning. We establish whom to sell to, where to find them, and how to do it—which is how we follow through. Database marketing makes going "where the customers are" easy because it tells us exactly where to find them. And that's the big difference between just plain selling and direct selling. Although most direct marketing is more properly defined as direct response advertising, direct selling still qualifies as direct marketing because it is interactive, and because it generates a measurable response.

DIRECT MARKETING PREDEFINES YOUR SALES TRACK

Direct selling is not an accident. The whole operation, from start to finish, is preplanned. When you make a sales call, you are there because you have researched, located and qualified this prospect as positively motivated to buy.

With this much preparation, you can reasonably expect your prospecting efforts to result in a sale. No wonder the closing ratio of direct selling is so high. By carefully qualifying the prospect first, we don't waste time. We make sales.

Target marketing takes the guesswork out of sales. Your sales track has already been built by someone else. All you have to do is use it. By following in the footsteps of others who have been successful, you already

Figure 4.1

In sales, it's important to always be prepared.

know where to look for the customers and what to do when you get there. Since finding customers is the toughest job for any merchandiser or service producer, the hard part is over. Past history tells us what these people like and what kind of approach works with them — or others very much like them. We know what to do to convince them to buy again.

Suppose you are selling life insurance. "Cold-calling" (knocking on business or residence doors at random) can be exhausting and frustrating. For every hundred doors you hit, you'll be lucky to be invited inside five times, and even luckier if you make a sale. Too many things are against you. You don't know whether the person who answers wants insurance, likes it, or even knows what it is. He may not have time to talk with you, or he may hate salespeople in general. There are so many barricades to cross that making a sale is the exception rather than the rule.

If this person had been prequalified, however, if he had been selected from a list of people who already owned life insurance and had indicated they were interested in buying more, wouldn't your job be easier? You would be talking to someone who *wants* to talk to you, someone who will be receptive to you when you knock on his door.

THE PSYCHOLOGY OF SELLING

Selling is really convincing. Once you are fairly certain that someone wants or needs what you have to offer, your job is to convince the person that it's okay to take the plunge and buy it. This is where your skill as a salesperson really counts. Your job is to describe what you're selling in detail, and to make your prospects see it, feel it, taste it. You explain how it will benefit them, why it will make them feel better, happier, more important. You use the prospects' own emotional responses as a selling tool. You point out selling points, answer questions, discuss objections.

Buying is really not based on logic at all; it's based on emotion. No matter how thoroughly you prove the value of your product to prospective customers, unless you also appeal to their emotions as well, it is difficult — often downright impossible — to make a sale. You must create a positive atmosphere, one that "allows" the customers to agree to your offer. You must give them *permission to buy!*

PRESALES PREPARATION

A successful salesperson does her homework before she meets with a client or customer. She starts by learning everything she can about her product, her company, and her competition. She learns why her answer is the best, what her product can and cannot do, and why. She finds out who has used it successfully in the past, how often, and for how long. She gathers testimonials and referrals and as much information about her product and her prospects as possible, before she puts herself in front of a prospect.

The temptation here is to overprepare. Sometimes fear of actually talking directly to the prospect is so great that the salesperson spends all her time and energy on preparation. When you are ready, you will know it. While your ideas are fresh and your enthusiasm high, take the first step and start selling!

Product Knowledge

You and your salespeople should know a great deal about your product. If your product is life insurance, for example, you know that you have several kinds of policies which can provide a wide variety of benefits. Some policies have cash values which can be built up from premium payments and borrowed out when needed. Others have no cash values and a correspondingly low premium cost. Some were designed to be used in pension plans. Some help build family equity, or make mortgage payments when the homeowner dies or becomes disabled. Some policies offer family protection, and some provide liquidity in the event of the death of a business partner. The more you know about your products and what they do, the easier it is to find out what kind of need they will fill.

Prospecting

Your next job is to match the products you have to sell with the people who need them (although they may not know they need them yet.) Let's say that you manufacture Halloween costumes. Your goal is to sell those costumes to retail stores from coast to coast. Nestled within all that geography are a great many stores, most of which will not be interested in your product. You could spend years following the phone book and knocking on doors. Much better to rely on past experience (and comparative data available from your own company and other manufacturers who manufacture similar products). That way, you know that your buyer profiles look like this:

> PROFILE 1: Retail store chain. Carries full line of merchandise, including men's, women's, and children's clothing, toys, gifts, appliances, and hardware. Offers store credit and takes all major bankcards. Located in high-traffic shopping centers in major cities.

> PROFILE 2: Drugstore chain. Carries cards, cosmetics, gifts, candy, photography items, and a large line of toys, in addition to prescription medicine and standard drugstore items. Takes major credit cards. Located in community shopping centers.

With these criteria, you can develop a database or list of qualified prospects that lists stores by name, location, and contact person. When you follow up, you will be working with a group of potentially profitable customers. Even better, you can prove that your product will improve their profitability too! The profile that helped you establish your own customer base is also a source of referrals. Past history has shown that stores fitting this profile have increased sales substantially during the fall season by offering Halloween costumes. Thus, your prospecting has already provided you with your main selling points!

The top salespeople never stop prospecting. If one list is good, two will be better. Consistently high producers keep building and refining their lists of qualified prospects. When one area is exhausted, they open another. As each new profile is built, it often suggests others.

The best salespeople also use a variety of resources. Computer searches, such as Electronic Yellow Pages, are popular. Many salespeople employ market researchers, or pay someone to hunt through source books found in the library. Certain industries, such as insurance, provide "orphan" lists of their own past customers who have not been contacted for a long time by a sales representative. The best resource of all is a *qualified referral.* Successful salespeople frequently ask their buyers to personally refer them to people they know would be interested in their service or product. (Ask your customer to call the person first, though, so that your time and theirs will not be wasted.)

Direct marketing techniques are mutually supportive. Successful sellers often employ more than one technique to build a client base. (See "Market Mix" in Chapter 11.) Direct mailers often follow up by telemarketing. People in personal sales use a number of direct marketing techniques, too. With direct mailings, they mine for prospects. They use telemarketing to book appointments or sell products over the phone. Some of them buy space in the print media or cable television. Direct mail is probably the biggest friend to personal selling, however, because it, too, is a very personal media. (See Chapter 5.) With direct mail, salespeople can "pre-qualify" prospects and thus increase sales dramatically.

THE SALES PROCESS

For a sale to be consummated, there must be something to sell, and somebody to sell it to. After that, selling is merely a matter of finding out what the customer needs, and why, and then producing a solution. If you have done your job, the only possible conclusion will be a positive one. The customer will buy. A skillful salesperson leads the prospect to this conclusion by letting him do most of the talking.

Figure 4.2

So, what is it you have to sell me?

Establish Control

This is not always an easy job. Many prospects, especially those who are initially uncomfortable or untrusting, will open an interview with a remark like, "So, what is it you have to sell me?" Your reaction is crucial. This is where a new salesperson often loses control of an interview. If he does make a sale, often it is not because of his skill, but because of remorse on the part of the prospect for having acted unkindly. A skillful salesperson should take control of the sales process right at the start and then hang onto it. You might respond to that type of opening by turning it around and asking a question of your own, such as "Until we talk a little, I don't know what you need yet. I understand you are concerned about how your wife would make the house payments if something happened to you. Is that right?" You have gently placed this individual in the position of giving you valuable information. It is unlikely he will curtly reply, "I don't care about my wife or the house payments!" Instead, you have opened a dialogue, a two-way channel of communication that will let you find out what the problem is, agree with your prospect about it, and work together to find a solution.

At this point, although you should be fully in control, you must remain flexible. Bludgeoning the customer to help you "solve the problem" or even to acknowlege it is not a successful sales technique.

Learn To Listen

Listening is the factor that separates successful salespeople from unsuccessful ones. You can't solve a problem until you know what it is. And you won't know what it is unless you ask and then listen to the answer!

Consider the dialogue in Figure 4.3 between a gentleman selling a dating service and a woman interested in finding out what the service has to offer. The salesman was completely inflexible. His "track" called for him to determine "need" by asking, "How do you think our service can help you?" The prospect was expected to give some kind of an answer. Any answer at all was considered "appropriate" as it would provide an opening for the next step of the sales track. The salesman could then continue by pointing out how his dating service would benefit the prospect. In this example, when the customer failed to follow the track, which was probably one the salesman had practiced earlier in sales-training class, the salesman was lost and unable to answer any of the woman's questions. Obviously, this was not a successful interview. The salesman did not listen. He lost control. He lost the sale.

The Sales Cycle

- State the problem.
- Offer a solution.
- Prove it.
- Initiate action.
- Record progress.

State The Problem

The singles salesman provided an excellent example of what **not** to do. Now let's follow the insurance man on his sales call, where he follows the sales process correctly. When he asks the customer about house payments, the man answers, "Yes, I do worry about it. If something were to happen to me, my wife would have a tough time keeping up with the mortgage

---

Figure 4.3

Salesman:	How do you think our service can help you?
Woman:	I don't know. What exactly do you do?
Salesman:	I have to find out if you qualify for our service first — we are very choosy, you know — before we can determine if we would be able to help you. I need to ask a few questions.
Woman:	Fine, but before we waste your time or mine doing that, what does your service do?
Salesman:	This will take about an hour. Do you have a comfortable place where we could sit?
Woman:	I **really** want to know what your service does before we proceed any further. Can you please tell me what you have to offer. I really don't have an hour to spare right now, and if I did, I would want to know that my time was spent valuably. What does your service **do?**
Salesman:	This process takes cooperation. I can see that you really aren't interested in this. I don't see much point in pursuing it any further.

How NOT to make a sale!

---

payments. She would probably have to sell the house, and I don't want her to have to do that." By questioning this man further, the salesman determines how much those payments are, why the wife cannot make them, and the term of the mortgage. He also learns that this man has children, is saving for college, owns his own business, and wants to buy a vacation home in three years.

The problem, the insurance man realizes, is not mortgage payments. That's only a symptom. The real problem is lack of an organized financial plan. This customer needs to establish a plan that will cover a number of contingencies, not the least of which is house payments. When the insurance man points this out, the customer can see the true scope of the problem.

Listening and carefully restating the problem also build trust between the seller and buyer. At this point, the man is comfortable that he is talking to someone who *understands* his needs. Buying is, after all, an emotional process even more than it is a logical one. The prospect is far more likely to be receptive to the salesperson's suggestions now than he would have been had the salesman marched in and proposed a life insurance policy in response to the original overture, "So what have you got to sell me?"

Offer A Solution

When both you and your prospect are clear on the problem, you can propose a solution. Make sure, however, that both of you are working on the *same* problem before you proceed. As with the example in Figure 4.3, if the customer is not with you at this point, whatever you suggest just won't make sense. *If no need has been established, there is no basis for a sale.* You are wasting both your time and his.

When you make a proposal, remember to stay flexible. Your proposal is only a suggestion at this point, and it can certainly be amended or changed to fit the situation. You are throwing out a "best judgment" kind of answer to the problem as you both perceive it. If you are way off base, better to find out now, than to supply a lot of benefit statements and selling features to back up an unacceptable proposal. (Benefits explain what your product or service will do for the buyer. Selling points detail specific features of the product itself.) You want to make sure you are headed in the right direction.

During this stage of the sales cycle, don't get sidetracked with long-winded explanations or try to defend objections. You are merely exploring possible alternatives. Of course, the better you are at reading the prospect's problems, the more likely you will be to come up with a top-notch solution on your first try. Don't be discouraged if you don't however. At least not at first. Of course, if you *consistently* miss the mark, you had better have your ears checked. Or perhaps you should consider whether you have really mastered the art of listening!

Salespeople who tend to be pompous have the hardest time with this stage of the sale. Because they know their products so well, this is the point where they may try to bulldoze the prospect into accepting their solution. Remember, while you want to control the interview, you must also be skillful enough to do it so that the prospect does not feel he is being led. Let him participate in the selling process. Forcing a solution now can cause resentment and may later mean a cancelled order.

Prove It

Now it's your turn to talk, and the customer's turn to play questioner. Here is where you field objections, and prove how and why your solution is the right one. This takes skill, empathy, and knowledge about your product and your prospect. Again, listening is important; make sure you thoroughly understand each question before you attempt to answer it. You should welcome, even invite, objections. Each one is really a chance for you to explain another selling point or benefit. The more questions your customer has, the easier it is for you to prove that your solution is correct. If you do the job right, you will stack one proof on top of another until you have built a pile so impossibly high that the customer can reach only one conclusion: you've got the only answer to his problem.

If in establishing your "proof," you find that you really cannot solve the problem with the products you have to offer, say so! Forcing the wrong solution on an unhappy customer will follow you for the rest of your career. Better to walk away from a sale or to suggest someone or something else, than to provide a bad solution.

As you work through the customer's objections, try to have him acknowledge each point once you have reached an acceptable conclusion about it. Ask, "Does this answer the question?" or "Have we solved this situation to your satisfaction?" before you move on to the next point. In that way, the objection will not crop up again at the end of the interview. Each step of the way, each move on the sales track path, should lead inexorably toward one conclusion: a consummated sale.

Initiate Action

Generally the close is over without either one of you having realized it. As you "proved" each step of the solution, you "closed" a little piece of the sale. With life insurance, for instance, agreeing to take a physical examination (known as the "medical close") is tacit agreement that a sale has taken place. Had the singles service salesperson in Figure 4.3 been more successful, he might have gotten the woman to agree to attend a social function to meet other members of the group. The Halloween costume salesperson could have completed a "trial contract" with the customer, whereby a number of costumes could be placed in the store on "consignment" with no obligation to the store unless the costumes were purchased by a consumer.

Figure 4.4

If you do the job right, the customer can reach only one conclusion!

In most cases, the final close is anticlimactic. You have only to ask for the money, hand over the order blank, or initiate an action that confirms the sale has been made.

Gentle persuasion. Even though they have made up their minds to buy, many customers will stall at the last minute. They hesitate, waiting for you to reinforce to them that they are really doing the right thing. It's the *permission to buy* situation all over again. They want to buy, but for some reason, hesitate to do so. When Markita Andrews sells cookies to a woman on a diet, for example, she acknowledges the diet, as well as the fact that by purchasing cookies, the woman is likely to break her diet. On the other hand, as a cookie lover, this customer obviously wants to buy. By *letting her buy* the cookies, Markita has tacitly given that customer permission to do what she wanted to do anyway.

Sometimes even your best efforts will leave you empty-handed. You've done everything right. The customer obviously wants to buy. He has pen in hand, yet doesn't sign on the dotted line. Now is the time to use the "urgency close" and offer a special incentive to do the deal now. If you rent mailboxes, for example, and a customer has decided to purchase a twelve-month contract but wants to come back tomorrow, you might offer two free months if the customer signs up on the spot.

Know when to stop.   The biggest mistake made by an inexperienced salesperson happens right here at the most important part of the sale. He doesn't know when to shut up. There comes a point in any sale when the prospect smiles and looks you right in the eye. The sale is a done deal. Stop right there, hand him the pen, and keep quiet while he signs the check or fills in the order. Then smile back, say "Thank you," and leave. Don't belabor your points, rehash the sale, or take up any more of his time. You're finished. It's time to go back to the office and log in the sale.

Record Your Progress

Direct marketing is interactive and measurable. At this point, the interaction is obvious. You made a sale, didn't you? To complete the direct marketing formula, you must also record your progress.

Successful direct sellers keep some type of log. They track their progress religiously, and set competitive goals, often against themselves. Our insurance salesman, for instance, has a log book that looks like the one in Figure 4.5, where he tracks his progress for the week, quarter, and year. He also keeps a current list of "hot" prospects (Figure 4.6) that he is actively pursuing, listed by the date he acquired them and the resource he used to find them. This lets him determine which sources work best. When he fills out his sales plan for the next year, he will have plenty of historical data to use to insure that his performance will at least equal this year's, and hopefully, be even better.

Figure 4.5

Week ending: _____

$ Volume

Number of calls made: _____ _____

Number of sales opened: _____ _____

Sales in progress: _____ _____

Number of sales closed: _____ _____

Total sales this month: _____ _____

Total sales this quarter: _____ _____

Salesperson's log

SUMMARY

Personal selling is direct marketing in its purest form. Direct response techniques just make selling a little easier. Target marketing lets you pick the people you want to sell to. With general advertising, the merchant runs a couple of ads (or not), and waits for the customers to beat a path to his door.

Sometimes they do. Sometimes they don't.

The merchant's sales depend on a number of important factors — like the weather, or the amount of available parking, or maybe the new employee he hired who knows everybody in town. What he lacks is a method of *predicting* sales, a way to determine who will buy, and why, and when.

Direct marketing solves the problem. Interactive marketing based on past performance predicts the outcome before the first contact is made!

Figure 4.6

"HOT" Prospects

Date	Name	Telephone	Source
____	_____	_____	_____
____	_____	_____	_____
____	_____	_____	_____
____	_____	_____	_____
____	_____	_____	_____
____	_____	_____	_____
____	_____	_____	_____
____	_____	_____	_____
____	_____	_____	_____
____	_____	_____	_____

ENDNOTES

1. *How to Sell More Cookies, Condos, Cadillacs, Computers . . . And Everything Else*. Markita Andrews with Cheryl Merser. Vintage Books.

DIRECT MAIL

5

"MAIL ORDER—two words that both inspire and excite the mind of the business entrepreneur. More so, perhaps than any other business, mail order conjures up visions of enormous wealth, easy living, and the proverbial 'pot of gold' at the end of the rainbow."
— Paul Muchnick, Chairman, Advisory Board, National Mail Order Association

While mail order is often an entrepreneur's dream come true, it is also the hard-working advertising medium that produces almost *three billion dollars a week* in sales of products and services and accounts for more than *14 percent of all consumer purchases*. What's more, direct mail is growing at a rate of more than 15 percent per year, which is faster than conventional retailing. According to Lee Epstein, President of MAILMEN INC. in New York City, by the year 2000, the volume of direct mail pieces processed by the Postal Service will exceed that of first class mail.

Obviously, with numbers like that, direct mail[1] sales are not limited to the small business on the corner or the one operated from somebody's garage. (Although a lot of small businesses started that way.)

Mail order marketing is the foundation of hundreds of businesses whose sole marketing method depends upon mailing direct-response offers to prospective customers, and then fulfilling their orders. It is also a technique successfully used by retailers and manufacturers to supplement other sales methods such as direct selling or telemarketing. In fact, the hottest direct marketing technique today is to send out a direct mail piece and follow it up by telephone.

WHAT MAKES IT WORK?

Mail order is a form of communication between buyer and seller which involves packaging an offer in a device such as a letter, brochure, or self-mailer, and using a mail service to deliver that offer to a selected audience whose response is actively solicited.

Figure 5.1

Mail order conjures up visions of enormous wealth and the pot of gold at the end of the rainbow.

Mail order has the lowest *cost of reach* of any other form of direct marketing.[2] Unlike direct selling or telemarketing, no sales staff is required. It doesn't use expensive electronic communications whose cost per second can be very high. Unlike mass media advertising, prospects can be *selected* from extensive lists of prequalified buyers chosen to match a predetermined buyer profile, so the cost per prospect is lower. With a carefully targeted market, there is no wasted circulation. Each piece counts!

Used alone or as part of a multimedia campaign, mail order selling is highly effective because it offers an unlimited amount of formats for reaching a captive audience (i.e., qualified prospects). Because formats are so flexible, each piece can be designed to produce maximum results. Best of all, *you control the entire process*, from design through mailing, to fulfillment of the offer, thus making direct mail more "testable" than any other marketing method.

No other advertising media can make these claims. Time dictates the design of radio and television advertising. Telemarketing depends on complicated communications equipment and the sales skills of operators. Print space, type styles, page size, and editorial philosophy restrict print advertising. But with direct mail, you alone control the media, the timing, and the prospective customer list.

Direct mail is both personal and private. Each piece can be directed by name to a single individual. The only other media that can even approach that is telemarketing, which, in comparison, is still far more impersonal. With direct mail, recipients approach your offer in much the same way that they react to a personal letter from a friend. They take time to read it.

While the recipients are reading your direct mail piece, it commands their *undivided attention*. They have chosen to look at the offer it contains. Advertisements via other media, such as TV, radio, or magazine ads intrude upon the reader's or viewer's primary reason for attending to that media. Often, these intrusions are annoying. Commercials *interrupt* a television or radio program. Paid print advertisements break the reader's concentration, forcing her to skip over the offer — or stop and read it — before moving on to the balance of the article. But when a prospect reads a direct mail piece, something that was addressed specifically to her, she gives it her complete attention. She's there because she wants to be.

Put all the pieces together — carefully selected market, personalized approach, unlimited format, and the undivided attention of a direct mail prospect, and it's no wonder that direct mail continues to be the most successful direct marketing technique used today.

CHOOSING A FORMAT

There are no guidelines except those established by the post office, and even those are minimal. (See the post office regulations in Chapter 12.) Choice of a format and content relies primarily on what market research suggests will have the greatest appeal to your buyer and is limited only by your budget and your imagination.

Although choice of formats is virtually unlimited, most mailings fall into several broad categories:

1. Classic format, with outer envelop and insert(s)
2. Self-mailer, with all-in-one envelope and letter
3. Catalogues (discussed in Chapter 6)

In the classic (and most basic) format, one or more pieces are inserted into an outer envelope which can be any color, material, size, or shape, as long as it falls within postal regulations.

Inside, the advertiser can put just about anything that will fit. Usually this includes a letter explaining the offer and a response device (such as a postage-paid response card). In addition, the envelope may contain samples, contest devices (a sweepstakes offer), and one or more interactive attention-getting "involvement devices" to stick or stamp onto a response card, or special materials requiring the recipient to rub off a spot or tear out something.

Both classic styles and self-mailers may include one or more of the following pieces:

Brochure

A brochure is usually a fairly expensive, high-quality mailing piece and often contains full-color photographs as well as descriptive copy. A brochure can be used alone as a self-mailer, or as an insert with other pieces, such as an introductory letter. This format is a particularly effective way to introduce new businesses, or new products and services for existing enterprises. Because brochures are relatively expensive to produce (between $1 and $5 each), mailing them indiscriminately is not advisable. Instead, most businesses chose to send an introductory letter first, often followed by a telephone call, before they go to the expense of mailing a brochure.

Although most of them are a pricey proposition, it is possible to produce a brochure that is relatively inexpensive. Figure 5.2 shows a triple folded brochure used as a self-mailer. Printed on coated stock (shiny paper) in two colors, the cost per thousand to produce this piece was approximately $90, exclusive of design and set up charges.

Booklet or Pamphlet

Generally unbound and usually fairly small and thin, booklets containing directions, explanations, or acting as "mini-catalogues" are often inserted with the merchandise when an offer is fulfilled.

Figure 5.2

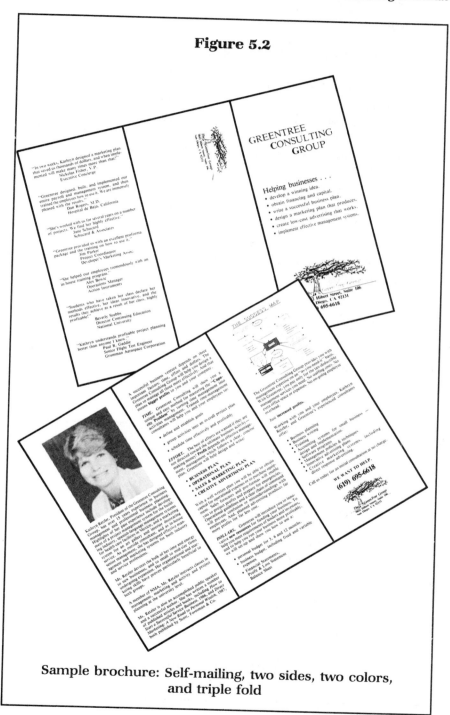

Sample brochure: Self-mailing, two sides, two colors, and triple fold

Circular

Frequently inserted in customer statements or included in packages of merchandise shipped to customers, circulars usually consist of one or two pages which contain both illustrations or photographs and copy. Because they can be produced at a relatively low cost, circulars are often used by beginning direct mailers. Larger, more expensive circulars are sometimes used in advertising products such as automobiles or cold-air inflatables. Used with an accompanying direct mail letter, circulars will usually generate a higher response to your offer than will the letter by itself.

Flyer

Often only a single page, the flyer is the cheapest direct mail piece to produce. Flyers often announce special promotions and are frequently used as inserts with other direct mail materials.

Invitation

Designed to simulate a formal invitation, such as those for a wedding or an open house, invitations (Figure 5.3) invite the reader to try a product

---

Figure 5.3

Invitation

Owen's Fine Furnishings Invites you to join them on August 20, 1988
For the Grand Opening of their new store
at 5689 Park Boulevard, downtown.

Wine and cheese will be served.
Free roses to the first 100 ladies who attend.

RSVP: 555-1234 before August 10, 1988, to Judy Simms.

Sample Invitation

---

or service and usually contain a response device such as an RSVP number or mail-back card. Invitations can be used either alone or as an insert in the classic direct mail letter package.

Simulated Telegram

Usually printed on yellow or pink paper and stuffed window envelopes of the same color, simulated telegrams often contain dated, "urgent" messages with specific time periods in which the reader may respond to the offer. (See Figure 5.4.)

Figure 5.4

T E L E W A R N I N G

DATE: AUGUST 21, 1988
TO: JOHN Q. ROADRUNNER
      1234 NATTA BLVD.
      PARKWAY, ME 23456

ONLY TEN MORE DAYS BEFORE PRICE INCREASE. MAKE YOUR SELECTIONS IMMEDIATELY TO AVOID HIGHER PRICES AND INTEREST CHARGES.

ALL ITEMS IN STORE AT HALF PRICE UNTIL MIDNIGHT AUGUST 31ST. WE PAY THE INTEREST!

NO CHARGE FOR DECORATING SERVICES IF YOU BOOK YOUR APPOINTMENT BEFORE AUGUST 31ST. CALL TODAY FOR AN APPOINTMENT: 555-2345.

                    OWEN'S FINE FURNISHINGS
                    2345 16TH STREET.
                    CORNER, PARK LANE @ 16TH.

Simulated Telegram

Sweepstakes Offer

Loaded with gimmicks, special papers, and lots of involvement devices, this format is often the most fun to create and the most fun to use. Because it can also be very expensive to produce, many advertisers use sweepstakes only with carefully preselected lists.

Figure 5.5 shows an offer produced by Signature Financial Marketing, Inc., for the Mobil Auto Club. Included in each package is a preprinted, plastic membership card and mailback response device along with full color photographs of exciting prizes. The entire package is neatly contained in a 6″ × 8″ envelope with the Mobil Auto Club visible through the window. This highly effective advertising piece pushes all the right buttons, promises great prizes, offers good value (note the chart comparing this company's auto club to other clubs), and assumes acceptance by including the auto club card as a part of the package.

The "Letter"

Usually rather formal in approach and appearance, and printed on one or more pages of good quality paper, a businesslike letter is one of the oldest forms of the classic format. It is also the most effective. (See the discussion on the letter later in this chapter on page 101.)

SPECIAL TECHNIQUES

A number of techniques are available to entice or involve the reader. Using any one, or even all of them at once, can prolong the time a prospect attends to the offer.

- Color photography.
- Special papers such as foil, plastic, or "coated stock," which is shiny and smooth to the touch.
- Special printing, such as embossing, raised letters, or messages in "invisible ink."
- Adhesive-backed papers (to stick, or lick and stick, as in stamps used to order magazines).
- Product samples, such as a packet of perfume, or rub-off samples of eye shadow or lip gloss.

Figure 5.5

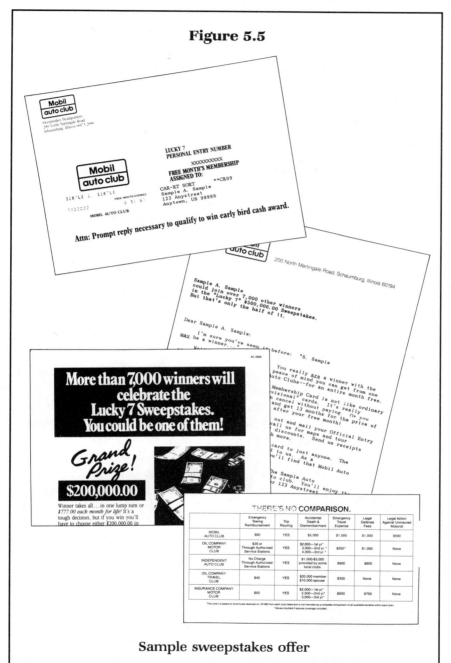

Sample sweepstakes offer

Permission to reprint materials granted by Signature Financial Marketing, Inc.

- Involvement devices such as sealed envelopes, tokens, rub-offs, tear-outs, phonograph records, or tapes (things for the reader to do).
- Attention getters that pop up or pull out.
- Customer or reader surveys.
- Second letter, usually explaining what the reader will miss if they reject the offer.

Involvement Devices

Direct mail campaigns distributing magazines via contest-type offers (sweepstakes) use almost all of these techniques. In each personalized package, the recipient can preview lavish colored photographs of houses, automobiles, and other expensive prizes to be won. A sealed envelope addressed "Open only if you aren't ordering at this time" demands immediate attention to see what's inside. Stamps of magazines, with gummed or "lick and stick" backing, are avaliable for the reader to "paste" onto the order card. Special prize stamps, which have specified "time constraints" on their use, are "hidden" in the literature and require the reader to sift through every word of the offer in order to find them. Readers must tear out, stick on, pull out, and rub off parts of their mail-order packet in order to participate in the publisher's sweepstakes and order the product.

Because this type of direct mail piece is expensive to send, many marketers carefully segment their lists. In many cases, this means mailing *only* to proven mail-order buyers. Receiving the annual sweepstakes packet such as the Readers Digest Sweepstakes was a big event in many homes. The whole family hunted for the magic winning stamps and stuck them, along with their "winning" prize numbers, in the special little slots on the enclosed order card. However, as the cost to produce such intricate sweepstakes offers increased, the number of families receiving the offer decreased. Gradually, those families that repeatedly failed to order were weeded from the list, until now, most sweepstakes offers are reserved for qualified prospects.

Other sweepstakes mailers mail to lists limited to buyers who have a proven record with the product (or service) such as the auto club offer in Figure 5.5. In that case, Mobil credit card holders are an obvious market.

Contests and sweepstakes use most all of the special devices available to the direct mailer to attract and hold the reader's attention.

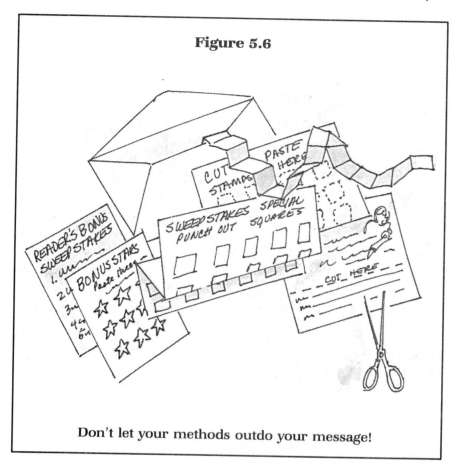

Figure 5.6

Don't let your methods outdo your message!

Other variations on this theme are frequently used that have less participatory devices for the reader to use, but are just as effective.

While inclusion of gimmicks, tricks, and special "involvement devices" is nice, it is not necessary to include one of them within a mailing piece for it to be successful. In fact, an overly "gimmicky" package can even be derogatory if the methods outdo the message!

Because such a large proportion (98 percent if the list was not prequalified) of a direct mailing often winds up in the trash can, advertisers have devised a number of clever ways to package their offer. Some of the more interesting (and more expensive) ones include these:

- Cloth bags.
- Paper sacks.
- Rolled, beribboned certificates (like diplomas).
- Cardboard tubes.
- Miniature, wrapped boxes that resemble presents.

The possibilities for response devices are limited only by your imagination and pocket book (and postal regulations, of course).

Mailers on a budget cannot always take advantage of the fancier devices, but they have found a creative, cost-effective compromise: the "personal" envelope. Computer-generated, personalized, "typed" envelopes enclosing one or more mailing pieces and designed to look hand addressed are usually more successful than those that have obviously computer generated labels stuck on the outside. Many forms companies now offer continuous form envelopes that allow the name and address to be "typed" directly onto them by the computer, thus eliminating the "computerized" look that carries such a negative connotation.

CLASSIC MAILING FOR A SMALL TO MID-RANGE BUSINESS

For the small business or new venture on a limited budget, a well-written letter addressed to the correct person still pulls best. Finding that individual may require some research *beyond* the initial list. (Usually a telephone call prior to the mailing will verify that you have targeted the right individual or company.) Figure 5.7 shows a letter sent out by a company offering concierge services to high-income multitenant residential buildings. The computer generated letter was printed on continuous form stationery imprinted with the company logo. Envelopes were pre-printed with an indicia (postage-paid imprint with sender's license number as issued by the local post office) and return address.

This letter was designed to inform prospects about services, generate interest, and elicit a response which would permit the company to initiate a direct selling effort or mail an expensive brochure to qualified prospects. (Notations in the upper right corner of the letter shown in Figure 5.7 were used to log the letter into the proper database and track results of the mailings by date.) The letter was sent out by zip code to a preselected list that met specific criteria as to building size, number of units, and rental cost per unit.

Figure 5.7

```
                                    RESPONSE LETTER
                                    FILE:L_APT.LT1
                                    DATE: XX/XX/XX
```

```
DATE

BUILDING MANAGER, TITLE
BUILDING
ADDRESS
CITY, STATE, ZIP

Dear XXXXXXXXXXX,

    One of the hottest topics today for developers and building
managers is the provision of on-site concierge services for high
quality tenants. Formerly, these services were only available through
first class hotels. Now, the same cost effective, time saving services
are available to residents of mid to high-rise, residential buildings
in affluent areas in [city, or geographic location].

    A proven concept which brings personal service and convenience
right to the front door, The Executive Concierge eliminates the
overhead costs and management time required for staffing these needs
within your own building.

    Your tenants [owners] like it. Your competition already has it.
If you would like to know more about how inclusion of The Executive
Concierge can and tip the competitive scales in your favor, call us, or
return the enclosed card today.

Sincerely yours,



The Executive Concierge
```

Sample direct mail letter

Reprinted with permission of The Executive Concierge, and The GreenTree Group, both of San Diego, California.

RESPONSE DEVICES

To truly qualify as direct marketing, a direct mail piece must include a response device. Frequently, this is a pre-posted return mail card or an order blank. A toll-free 800 number makes it even easier for the recipient to respond. A time frame should also be used, such as "Respond by September 15th to receive a free full-color Atlas of the World," or "If your answer reaches us before midnight on December 31, you will be eligible for an extra $1,000,000.!!"

Response devices vary in purpose and content, but in all cases, the primary purpose is to track the results of a particular marketing campaign.

Figure 5.8

```
                                        RESPONSE CARD #
                                        FILE:L_CARD.LT1
                                        DATE: XX/XX/XX
```

[ ] Yes. I would like more information. Please send your brochure.

[ ] Yes. I would like more information. Please call to arrange an appointment.

[ ] No. I would not like more information at this time. Please put me on your mailing list.

Sample Reply Card

Reprinted with permission of The Executive Concierge and the GreenTree Group, both of San Diego, California.

The example shown in Figure 5.8 is designed to identify four distinct possibilities:

1. Good prospect. Send a brochure.
2. Hot prospect. Send a salesperson immediately!
3. Probable prospect. Responsive to direct mail.
4. Problem. No response.

The fourth, or "no response," is interesting, because it brings up the question of "Why?" Failure to respond could have a variety of causes:

- No interest.
- Wrong address.
- Wrong approach.
- Wrong contact name.

Following up the "no response" response with a telephone call should clarify the problem and change the last three "wrongs" into "rights." In this case, the purpose of the telephone call is *not* to make a sale. (For more about telephone sales, see Chapter 8.) Instead, the person placing the call needs only to follow up on the letter, making sure the right person saw it, and verbally repeat the possible responses listed on the response card:

"May we send you a brochure?
"Shall I have one of our representatives telephone you to set up an appointment?
"May I put you on our mailing list?"

The company established a database to track its campaign every step of the way. Sending out an introductory piece first kept costs at a minimum — a major concern for any company, especially a start-up venture. Future publication costs for mailings can be estimated from past performance as new cities and territories are opened up for marketing. Scheduling of sales appointments can be controlled by how many pieces were sent out per mailing (because prior mailings predicted the number of sales calls that would be requested).

A postage-paid return-mail card is a relatively expensive response device. Printing and return postage costs add up quickly. Many advertisers, especially those conducting national campaigns, hedge their bet by including an "800 Toll-free" number in each direct mail piece. This may entail two different lines, one for in-state calls and another for national calls originating *outside* the advertiser's resident state. Rather than go to the expense of installing their own long-distance lines and training operators to use them, most companies prefer to use a professional telemarketing service.

The most common response devices include the following:

- Toll-free 800 number.
- Local telephone number.
- Postage-paid response card or order form.
- Coupon to be mailed back by prospect.
- Reader survey.
- Contest form and envelope.

Research has proven the most effective device to be a separate order form included within the offer. Regardless of your choice, however, if you *do* use a printed form, leave room for the customer's name, address, zip code, and phone number (with area code). Budget and layout permitting, include a preprinted, "peel-off" label. The customer need only peel off the address label, affix it to the order, and mail in the order. If possible, use a preposted reply card or envelope. Anything you can do to make it easier for the customer to buy will result in increased sales.

If you accept credit cards, make that fact clear in your literature and leave room on the order form for the card type and number and the expiration date. This last is very important; without it you may be denied payment by the financial insititution backing the card. If your product requires special shipping and handling, leave a space on the form where the customer can write in special instructions, such as "Leave package with neighbors across street."

If you will be using telephone response lines, the operators should be trained to ask for and record all the information needed to facilitate the customers' orders. (Professional telemarketers usually do this automatically.) Give each operator a preprinted form and a check list of questions (like those on the reply form) to ask the customer.

The key point to remember is this: *make it easy for the customer to buy*.

DESIGNING A MAILING PIECE

It takes more than a reliable list of qualified prospects to sell by mail. To be successful, direct mail advertising also relies upon a well-designed and well-written offer. Unlike direct selling where the salesperson can field objections on the spot and counter each one with a benefit statement or product feature, direct mail requires the writer to anticipate objections and answer them in advance. The written offer outlined in a direct mail piece is the sole means of communication with the prospect.

The AIDA Concept

An effective offer must accomplish four objectives. It must attract attention, generate and hold the reader's interest, create desire, and induce the reader to take positive action.

A	ATTENTION
I	INTEREST
D	DESIRE
A	ACTION

In a large agency, or within a large company having a substantial budget, the process which follows the AIDA path often involves several people, usually an art director, a direct-marketing advertising director, illustrator or photographer, and one or more copywriters. Together they plan the campaign, design an offer, and create it.

A small company may not have the budget to do all this. In that case, an advertising agency *that specializes in direct marketing* may be called in to help with the "creative process" of designing the piece. (Not all advertising agencies have experience with direct marketing. If you decide to use an agency, ask for referrals and follow up on them before signing a contract! See the Appendices for a listing of resources for direct mailers.) It is also possible to utilize various services for all or part of the direct mail process such as a list broker and a mailing service. (See the section on users and producers in Chapter 1.)

With or without outside help, because *you are still the best authority on your product or service*, you should sit in on the design stage, or "creative" phase, that provides direction and establishes a layout or outline for your direct mail piece.

Creative Process

Before the first word of copy is written or the first illustration is drawn, the whole campaign must be carefully thought out from every angle. A successful direct mail effort is not an accident.

Consider the customer's viewpoint.   Remember the common motivators of all buyers discussed in the section on psychographics in Chapter Two. The first question a buyer asks is, "What's in it for me?" Be prepared with an answer!

Review the competition.   How is your product different? How is it better? Why would someone choose your product over another? What can it do that theirs does not, and why is that of benefit to your customer?

Think carefully about pricing.   How do you stack up against your competitors? Is the price to value relationship a positive one? In other words, will the customer get what she paid for, and a little bit more?

What kind of after-sale service do you offer?   Will you take it back if it doesn't work? How much are you willing to give to make a customer happy? A full refund? Within what time period? If you are selling a service, how will you compensate a dissatisfied customer? Do you *guarantee* your product unconditionally? Many direct marketers do. The percentage of people who actually return something after keeping it for thirty days is very small, especially if the product is low-priced. In most cases, the bother to return it is not worth the cost savings. But if you are faced with a rash of returns, can your cash flow handle it?

Make a list of the features of your product.   Each of them is a selling point. How can you best demonstrate those points? Descriptively (in writing)? With an illustration? Photographs? (See the description of "call-out" features discussed in the section on copywriting in Chapter 7 for a good example on how to organize selling points.)

How do each of these points benefit the customer?   Benefits are anything that personally and positively impacts the buyer. (See buyer motivations in Chapter 2). Benefits make the buyer feel or look better, offer to give him something he wants or needs, or protect him from losing something he already has.

Don't confuse benefits with selling points. A **selling point** is something about your product or service that makes the benefit possible. Suppose you are selling encyclopedias.

Benefit statements:
Your children will enjoy using these books for years to come. With an encyclopedia, your children will achieve higher grades with less effort.

Supportive selling points:
Large, easy-to-read type and colorful illustrations.
Comprehensive set of 24 volumes with annual updates.

Benefits to the buyer ("What's in it for me?"):
High grades.
Less effort.
Enjoyment over a number of years.

Set up a budget.   How much can you afford to spend? The cost of direct mail varies widely. The more techniques you use to attract the buyer, the more expensive the piece will be. Be sure to research costs carefully before you commit to a final budget.

The Letter

The letter is both personalized and clearly directed to a specific individual, which is what makes it so effective. Regardless of format, technique, or response device, every letter will benefit by following "Bob Stone's Seven-Step Formula":[3]

1. Promise a benefit in your headline or first paragraph — your most important benefit.
2. Immediately enlarge upon your most important benefit.
3. Tell the reader specifically what he or she is going to get.
4. Back up your statements with proof and endorsements.
5. Tell the reader what he or she might lose by not acting.
6. Sum up the prominent benefits in your closing offer.
7. Incite action. Now.

Your letter says a lot about you. Its appearance should depict you as a reliable company whose products and services will provide an immediate and valuable benefit. The content of your letter should reinforce this image.

How long is too long?   A two page letter works better than one page, for example, in the standard or classic direct mail format. In the short format (such as invitations or simulated telegrams), one page works better. (If you use more than one, your message loses some of its impact.) If you choose a long letter style, don't make it too long. The reader will tire, and your message will too.

Make your offer attractive and easy to read.   Indent or separate paragraphs. Use attractive, large-size type and two colors of ink if the budget permits. If you need illustrations, photographs, or product descriptions, put them on a separate insert or flyer and inclose it with the letter. Emphasize key points with an underline or **bold** type. Your logo should be clear, simple, and easy to understand.

Reassure the reader.   No matter how good your offer is, the reader is bound to be skeptical. Whenever possible, use a testimonial or endorsement to reinforce your statement. Your readers are more likely to believe your claim if someone they know and trust publicly confirms your assertions.

Also, don't forget to include your mailing address and telephone number. (Advertisements that fail to list an address, and give only a telephone number — especially if that number is an "800" number — present an appearance of lack of substantiality. Buyers suspect companies who omit addresses on their advertising. Such a company might close up shop and disappear into the night, taking their customers' dollars with them, and leaving orders unfilled with no recourse for the unhappy customer.)

Keep the response device separate from the letter.   The purpose of the letter is to "hook" the reader's interest, to draw her into your offer. Don't break her concentration with a response card or order blank in the body of the letter. Chances are she will never finish reading your offer, but will make a decision at the point where she encounters the response device. Valuable selling points may be lost.

Copywriting

Unlike print advertising, which has strict space requirements, direct mail has no format limitations. Your offer can be as comprehensive and creative as you like. If you follow a few basic rules, you should be successful.

Be concise.   Get to the point and stick to it. Reinforce it and prove it again, but don't waste any words. Sloppy writing that wanders from point to point through a forest of words will not hold the reader's attention. Your point is lost before you make it. Don't succumb to the temptation to overwrite — the most common error in direct mail. Your purpose in writing the ad is to sell something, not to prove what a great writer you are!

Fill in your outline.   Your use of the creative process outlines the path the ad will follow. Your copywriting should fill in the details, one point following another, each one clearly explaining the benefits (backed by selling points) of your offer. When you review your copy, each statement should relate to the issue. If it doesn't, get rid of it.

Meet a motivator.   The more motivators you can meet, the better. Answer the prospect's immediate question, "What's in it for me?" Show how you will fulfill a need (see Chapter 2), improve quality of life, or give the prospect something he wants or needs. Don't make the prospect wade through two or three pages to find a motivator.

Look at the following offers. Each of them provides a distinct benefit.

PROFIT FROM SIMPLE, EASY-TO-LEARN BUSINESS AT HOME!

GAIN THE ENVY OF ALL YOUR FRIENDS WITH THE "MIRACLE-THIN DIET PLAN."

IMPROVE YOUR VOCABULARY AND INCREASE YOUR EARNING POWER WITH THE MANNING HOME-STUDY LANGUAGE COURSE.

Make a promise.   Then immediately show how you will deliver on it. If the product is a hunger-suppressant capsule that promises a "slim youthful figure" making the prospect "look younger, lovelier, and more desirable," define how many capsules, in how many days, will result in the loss of how many pounds.

Use terms the reader can easily understand.   If selling points are based on medical data, use layman's language rather than clinical terminology. If your products are computer related and if the targeted market is the business community, avoid technical terms. Make your copy readable. If the prospect needs a dictionary to understand your copy, he won't bother to read it.

Sell!   The purpose of your advertising is to sell something. Your product is wonderful. It's GREAT! It's the *best product ever invented*. Prove it. Believe it. Show some enthusiasm. Use action verbs and descriptive words. Talk in glowing terms that will make the reader want what you have to offer. Give testimonials and endorsements. Remember, this is the only chance you have to answer questions and objections, so sell, sell, sell!

Give all the details needed to purchase.   Color, size, quantity, price, discounts, delivery time: anything the customer needs to know in order to respond favorably to your offer. An amazing number of sales are lost because the advertiser did not anticipate the reader's questions. If it comes in red, blue, and green, takes six weeks for delivery, and can be exchanged for any other color if returned within thirty days, then say so! If it weighs five hundred pounds and will dent the customers' doorstep, warn them. You'll save a lot of time and effort handling complaints down the line if you give all the details right up front.

MAIL ORDER REGULATIONS

Mail order is designed to take advantage of the postal service's mail classification system (see the section on post office regulations in Chapter 12) which makes it possible to send out direct mail advertising at a lower rate than first class mail.

Before you embark on a direct mail campaign, there are several things you should know. The Federal Trade Commission, Bureau of Consumer Protection, has some very strict regulations about mail order selling:

> "The *Mail Order Rule* was issued by the Federal Trade Commission (FTC) to correct growing problems with late or undelivered mail order merchandise. Under this Rule, you have a duty to ship merchandise on time. You must also follow procedures that the Rule requires if you cannot ship ordered merchandise on time.

When there is a shipping delay, the Rule requires that you notify your customers of the delay and provide them with an option either to agree to the delay or to cancel the order and receive a prompt refund. For each additional delay, your customers must be notified that they must send you a signed consent to a further delay or a refund will be given."[4]

SUMMARY

Direct mail offers some unique opportunities. It is personal. It is private. It has almost no limitations as to format, style, or length. During the time the prospect is looking at it, *you have that individual's undivided attention!* Best of all, you control the entire process because you can design the offer, decide when to send it, and track the results in your own database.

ENDNOTES

1. Vin Jenkins, in *The Concept of Direct Marketing*, published by Australia Post, Melbourne, 1984. Mr. Jenkins states, "The term [direct mail] came into being when 'mail' was added to the generic term 'direct advertising' " (page 24).
2. Classified advertising, or print ads (see Chapter 7), is cheaper than classic direct mail advertising because one ad reaches a multitude of individuals, instead of one ad reaching one person. However, classic direct mail, because *each piece is personalized and directed to a specific individual*, has a lower "cost of reach." You know exactly who got each direct mail piece. With print advertising, you do not.
3. Bob Stone's Seven-Step Formula from *Successful Direct Marketing Methods*, pages 272–3.
4. See: Title 16—Commercial Practices, Chapter I—Federal Trade Commission, Part 435—Mail Order Merchandise.
    The FTC publishes a helpful booklet entitled *A Business Guide to the Federal Trade Commission's Mail Order Rule.* Copies may be obtained by writing to the Federal Trade Commission, Washington, D.C. 20580, or by contacting your local district office of the FTC.

6

CATALOGUE SALES

"Over the past few years giant companies and small entrepreneurs, gluttonous for high returns, have been lured into the catalogue business, while well-established mail-order merchants have been sending out more catalogues more often."

—From an article by Monci Jo Williams in *Fortune* magazine.[1]

Catalogues make a great sales tool. Many retailers routinely supplement standard media advertising with catalogue promotions. Catalogues also form the basis for successful mail order businesses such as Sunset House, Gallagher, and Spiegel. Manufacturers often market their products through catalogues, selecting one whose image best reflects their own. Distributors of products from beer barrels to building materials rely on them. Software developers and record producers find them invaluable. Originators of products such as books and tapes sometimes produce their own catalogue which contains only their own products.

The range of goods and services that can be sold by catalogue is virtually unlimited. Most publications, however, tend to concentrate on gifts, clothing, household items, and business or office supplies—all items that have a broad market. Mail order companies and retailers usually prefer to specialize in a particular type of merchandise for a specific segment of the market such as sporting goods buyers. Astute catalogue producers, such as L. L. Bean®—whose track record is long and successful, break their lists down into categories, sending specialized catalogues to hunters, for example, or fishermen, or campers.

THE CATALOGUE CONCEPT

Catalogues enjoy an unusually high rate of return. Most of them average at least 10 percent, and many boast returns of 20 percent or more! With numbers like that, it's not surprising that so many businesses—from the leanest to the largest—enter the catalogue market.

Figure 6.1

The range of goods and services which can be sold by catalogue is virtually unlimited.

Source: From the covers of the following catalogs: L.L. Bean, Hunting Specialties, 1987, © 1987 L.L. Bean, Inc. Used by permission. The American Express® Merchandise Services Catalogue, © 1987 American Express Travel Related Services Company, Inc. Used by permission. The Company Store®, October 1987. Used by permission. H & E Computronics, Inc., Catalog 26. Used by permission. Flair, Winter 1987, Alexandria, Virginia. Used by permission. UARCO, Inc., Fall Edition 1987, © 1988 Uarco Incorporated. Used by permission.

Yet, according to the article in *Fortune* magazine "The catalogue merchants still haven't reached 65 percent to 70 percent of all U.S. households that still resist shopping by mail. They have been mailing incestuously to names they rent from each other for 5 cents to 10 cents apiece, instead of generating new prospects by advertising."[2] That leaves the field wide open if you know how to build a good list.

Lists

Much of your success in this form of advertising is dependent upon your house list (or internal database — see Chapters 2 and 3). The longer you are in business, the better the list. The more repeat buyers you have, the higher your percentage of return. Supplementing your house list with rented lists that target specific groups can help to increase sales, but a dependable customer base is still the key to profitable catalogue marketing. As a rule of thumb, a catalogue list should contain at least 10,000 names, although many have succeeded with less (particularly if their smaller list is comprised of previous buyers who know and trust their merchandise).

Timing

Like most forms of direct response advertising, catalogue sales tend to be seasonal. Many retailers routinely commit a major portion of their fall and winter advertising budget to the production and distribution of a Christmas catalogue. Books such as the Neiman Marcus Christmas Catalogue are famous for their holiday gift merchandise, which can be delivered with elaborate wrappings. Many companies, such as Harry & David (whose products are edible), produce a major book during the holiday season, as well as several other supplemental, seasonal, or "theme" catalogues throughout the remainder of the year.

Spring catalogues run a close second to those designed for holiday sales. Trees, bulbs, tulips, gardening equipment, clothing, and other products aimed at spring and summer activities are popular items. Planning catalogues for more than one season, especially holiday and spring, should result in more even cash flow.

Catalogues are popular with retailers for seasonal promotions such as back-to-school clothing, winter white sales (sheets, towels, household items), new fall clothing, or "cruise wear" (lightweight summery clothing). Under this plan, the advertiser can spread receipts out evenly over the year, with peaks for spring and winter, and added revenues during slower seasons from white sales or end-of-season closeouts.

Positioning

Kenneth A. Eldred, President of IMAC, a business-to-business catalogue marketer, suggests that to be successful in the catalogue market, you must master these four "cornerstones":[3]

- Valid positioning.
- Targeted audience.
- Disciplined product line.
- Solid creative.

Although IMAC's primary marketing vehicle is a business-to-business catalogue (printed in five languages), Mr. Elred's advice applies to any catalogue marketer, regardless of location or products and services advertised.

Valid positioning.   "You must have a 'reason for being' from the customer's standpoint . . . . Pick your own position," he advises, "not someone else's."

If the market is already flooded with books such as yours, your catalogue will likely be the first to hit the trash can, with you right behind it.

Catalogue buyers tend to be *loyal.* Once they find a publication they like, one that saves time and offers good value for their money, they are less likely to spend time browsing through others that appear to carry the same merchandise for similar prices.

Time, or lack of it, is a major reason for catalogue shopping. For the busy executive or the working mother, ordering from a catalogue saves hours, even days, of hunting for just the right thing for just the right price. If your publication offers the merchandise these busy people need and if it provides an easy and convenient way to purchase those products, they will buy.

Targeted audience.   The key point is to make certain that the things you have to offer are *necessary* in the eyes of the customer. Thus, the more you know about your customers, the more likely you are to meet their needs. For example, over 80 percent of consumer catalogue customers are women. A large percentage of them have children. Over 60 percent of them work full time, and they often turn to mail order shopping because it's so convenient. Many of these women have discretionary income to spend, but little time in which to spend it.

All buyers have an established lifestyle, easily identifiable by the credit accounts they already use, current membership in sports or community clubs, or active participation in political and civic organizations. All of this information is available in a database somewhere. You have only to search it out to make use of it.

Remember, much of your success in this form of advertising is dependent upon a reliable house list. To build one of your own, you must identify your own special corner of the market, and then fill it. A lot of companies come and go in the catalogue business. To avoid becoming one that doesn't make it, take time to choose a market niche that makes your approach unique.

L.L. Bean®,[4] for example, puts out a book which targets hunters. This particular catalogue offers a wide selection of equipment and clothing that is not readily available in most sporting goods stores. To find everything the hunter wants, he or she might have to travel to several different specialty stores, probably spread out over a wide geographic area. Selecting these same items from Bean's catalogue, however, can be done from home, comfortably, even leisurely. What's more, the hunter will save not only time but money and gasoline as well.

Disciplined product line.   Catalogue marketing works so well because results are measurable. If after a reasonable amount of time, a product has a poor return (low margin contribution per average catalogue page), the advertiser can get rid of it, and replace it with something else that produces more profits per page.

Solid creative.   Before you give an item the ax, however, try to determine what caused such a poor response. Poor sales may not be entirely the fault of the product. The problem may be caused by your ad. Are photographs accurate? Attractive? Do they convey the image correctly in relation to size, shape, color, and other design elements? Sometimes the fault lies with the copywriting. Is the information confusing? Too vague? Have you given enough information about sizes, colors, shipping requirements? Make sure you have given the reader *all the information* needed to make a decision to buy. Your presentation, like the one in Figure 6.2, should clearly state what you are selling, how much it costs, and how to order it.

Occasionally, no matter how clear your presentation, a product (or service) simply does not lend itself to this form of marketing. When that happens, delete the item from your catalogue and find another way to market it.

Figure 6.2

Bean's Featherweight Rainwear

Wear for any outdoor situation where dependability is critical. High-grade neoprene-coated nylon is lightweight, windproof and guaranteed 100% waterproof. Will not leak. All seams are hand cemented and vulcanized for a permanent seal. Fabric is strong, flexible and resistant to oil, gas and sun. Garments roll up compactly for easy carrying. Cut full for freedom of movement. Made in U.S.A. Hand Wash.

Rain Jacket

Raglan sleeves for freedom of movement. Full zipper front. Vented, "cape-style" back. Drawstring at visored hood and waist. Two pockets.
Sizes: S(34-36), M(38-40), L(42-44), XL(46-48). Length about 30". Wt. 18 oz.
1305EG Men's Rain Jacket, $66.00 ppd. Two colors: Forest Green. Blaze Orange.
5849EG Camouflage Rain Jacket, $72.00 ppd. Color: Brown Camouflage.

Rain Pants

Fully cut with drawstring waist. Wt. 11 oz.
Sizes: S(28-30), M(32-34), L(36-38), XL(40-42). Inseam about 30".
1557EG Men's Rain Pants, $34.75 ppd. Two colors: Forest Green. Blaze Orange.
5850EG Men's Brown Camouflage Rain Pants, $36.00 ppd.

Rain Parka

Drawstring, visored hood. Raglan sleeves. Full zipper front. Two flapped front pockets. Length about 40". Wt. about 1 lb. 4 oz.
Sizes: XS(30-32), S(34-36), M(38-40), L(42-44), XL(46-48).
1309EG Men's Rain Parka, $69.50 ppd. Two colors: Forest Green. Blaze Orange.
5848EG Men's Brown Camouflage Rain Parka, $76.00 ppd.

Roll-Up Crusher

Takes any amount of abuse and still looks great. Crush it in your pack or roll it up in your pocket. Pull it out and put it on. Formed from a single piece of 100% wool felt, preshrunk and blocked to size. ⅜" grosgrain hatband and cotton sweatband. Made in England. Wt. about 2 oz.
1251EG Roll-Up Crusher, $16.50 ppd.
Four colors: Red. Khaki. Brown. Forest Green.
Sizes: S(6⅞-7), M(7⅛-7¼), L(7⅜-7½), XL(7⅝-7¾).

Bean's Reversible Down Vest

Blaze Orange side is 100% nylon taffeta—provides maximum visibility for big game or upland hunting. Reverses to a 65% polyester/35% cotton camouflage or tan—for waterfowl and camp use. Shows very little Blaze color when reversed. Nonblaze side has two pockets. Rib-knit collar and sides for good fit and "give." Insulated with prime goose down. Made in U.S.A. Machine Wash (tumble dry low).
2278EG Bean's Reversible Down Vest, $56.00 ppd.
Two colors: Tan. Camouflage. (Both sides reverse to Blaze Orange.)
Men's sizes: S(34-36), M(38-40), L(42-44), XL(46-48).
Length about 25".

Bean's Goose Down Guide's Jacket

The first choice of many guides, hunters and outdoorsmen. Cut to be worn over sweaters and a vest, with a snap front that ventilates instantly and fastens up against a cold wind. Filled with prime quality goose down for comfort in cold weather.
Shell fabric of Tan and Camouflage Jackets is a 65% polyester/35% cotton poplin that doesn't "rustle" when it rubs. Blaze Jacket shell is Burlington's 100% Acrilan® 10 Mile Cloth®. Highly visible and quiet. Tan and Camouflage jackets have corduroy lined collar. Blaze jacket has a nylon lined collar. Blaze Orange jacket has front handwarmer pockets are lined with polyester fleece. Rib-knit wrist cuffs seal out the cold. This is an excellent jacket for hunting big game at the higher elevations. Made in U.S.A. Machine Wash (tumble dry).
2269EG Bean's Goose Down Guide's Jacket, $89.00 ppd.
Three colors: Tan. Blaze Orange. Camouflage.
Men's sizes: S(34-36), M(38-40), L(42-44), XL(46-48). Length about 28".

15

Your presentation should clearly state what you are selling, how much it costs, and how to order it.

Source: L.L. Bean®, Hunting Specialties, 1987, page 15. Reprinted with permission of L.L. Bean, Inc.

The important thing is to make every page count, and every ad on it one that performs well on a consistent basis.

Perceptions

How your customer perceives you and your products is important. If your presentation is positive, the customer will view you as trustworthy, offering products and services that will give good value for their money and satisfy a definite need. (Review the section on psychographics in Chapter 2 for more information on selling products that fulfill a need.)

Dick Hodgson, marketing consultant and catalogue specialist, takes Mr. Elred's concept a little further. He suggests there are also four perceptions you should take into consideration when designing a catalogue:

- Availability.
- Value.
- Authority.
- Satisfaction.

L.L. Bean® offers a perfect example of this theory. Their specialized catalogues offer a wide variety of products that would be difficult to find in one location. Because their customers believe this to be true, they expect shopping by catalogue will offer a convenient alternative to the time and expense of chasing from one store to another to find the things they want.

The company has enjoyed an outstanding reputation for exceptional quality and service since before World War I. Customers easily view them as an authority in the supply of outdoor equipment, and the presentation that their catalogues make reinforces this image. On the cover, nicely rendered paintings and sharp color photographs of outdoor scenes and animals are suggestive of the merchandise offered inside. A simple title tells you if this is a specialty book or a more general one. On each page, high-quality color photographs and detailed explanations including weight and cost send a message that this is a company that knows its market well and is quite capable of supplying it.

The perception of value is implicit. For example, when the bottoms of Bean's Maine Hunting Shoes® (long a staple item in their catalogues) wear out, the company will replace them, for a nominal charge. This is obviously a company that intends to be around for a long time. (This arrangement also keeps customers coming back again and again.) To simplify ordering and to offer even greater value, Bean also pays all regular shipping and handling fees on items delivered within the U.S. The price you see on the catalogue page is what you pay. There is no need to tote up shipping charges, or add special handling fees, or compute sales tax (unless you live in their home state of Maine).

Besides services such as supplying new shoe bottoms, Bean will also take anything back. Customer satisfaction is guaranteed, and that satisfaction is the backbone of all successful catalogues.

Availability, authority, value, and satisfaction: L.L. Bean® meets the test of all four. Their catalogues are unquestionably successful. If you follow the rules of positioning and perception, your catalogue will succeed, too.

TYPES OF CATALOGUES

The original Sears Roebuck catalogue sold everything from washing machines and tractor parts to ladies' girdles and baby booties. Designed to make merchandise available to people in rural areas, the Sears catalogue, like the next few publications that followed them into the mail order market, offered an impressive array of merchandise.

Today, few, if any, catalogues try to match the, "We have it all!" slogan. Instead, many of them, such as Computronics Software Catalogue or The Company Store with its collection of down-filled products, try to specialize in a specific market niche. A few upscale catalogues, such as The Sharper Image or American Express' Christmas Gift Catalogue offer a wider range of products that include audio/visual or sports equipment, men's and ladies' furs, and other pricey products that can run into the thousands of dollars. Others, such as Lillian Vernon, a successful catalogue merchant that has been around for a long time, offer a broader spectrum of products. Frequently, these books offer household-related items or gifts in the lower price range.[5]

Retail catalogues fall into several broad categories: specialty items; general merchandise with a wide variety of products; and business-to-business supplies and services. Wholesale catalogues usually supply products or services related to a specific trade or industry.

Specialty Catalogues

Geared toward a specific market, specialty catalogues offer a range of related products, such as those in Bean's hunting catalogue. Many specialty catalogues, such as the holiday catalogue presented by Gump's of San Francisco, are intended for "upscale" audiences with larger discretionary incomes and specific tastes and lifestyles. And, like Gump's, many of them address their market directly by including a message to their customers within their publication.

Market niche.   The number of newcomers to the catalogue arena is mind-numbing. And the number of failures is uncomfortably high. To get in and stay there, you will need more than a solid creative effort or a nice-looking book. You must also understand the motivations of your customer and have a clear picture of what it is you expect to gain from choosing this media to market your merchandise.

To succeed in this highly competitive specialty market, you must:

- Know your audience.
- Fill a gap in the market.

Multiple marketing benefits.   Although the catalogue can certainly stand alone as a marketing method or can even be a business in and of itself, there are a number of other reasons why advertisers choose the catalogue as a marketing device:

- Increase store traffic.
- Broaden customer base.
- Support other marketing efforts.

Retailers often utilize catalogue marketing to increase store traffic. Advertising sale items such as school clothing or household goods, prior to the actual sale, will encourage buyers within the region to visit the store in order to preview the sale merchandise.

Overall sales—and thus profits—benefit too. Customers outside the immediate area also have an opportunity to take advantage of the sale by placing telephone orders or sending in an order coupon. Catalogue offerings also present an opportunity to reach a broad audience spread across a vast marketing area. Gump's on the west coast, for example, and L.L. Bean on the east, are able to successfully reach customers from coast to coast with the help of their catalogues.

Nonstore retailers, or pure catalogue marketers, use catalogues as the *sole* means of reaching their audience. Unlike the store retailer that selects a catalogue to *supplement* in-store sales, the catalogue seller has to rely on mail or telephone orders. Because there is no need physically to

Figure 6.3

SINCE 1861

Dear Customer,

It is with great pleasure that we bring you the 1987 edition of Gump's Holiday Gift Book. This year, we have assembled an especially outstanding collection of gifts that are as elegant and tasteful as they are rare and unique.

There are many reasons why a gift from Gump's is so special. We design and make most of our selections in our own workshops. We are renowned for, among other things, our collection of lamps, created from the jars and vases we've brought back from our travels in Europe and the Orient. And we are proud of our own striking collection of jewelry, fashioned with pearls, jade, lapis lazuli, and other fine stones and gems.

In addition to the special items we create here at Gump's, each year we travel the world in search of equally special, yet affordable, treasures that will please even the most discriminating of gift-givers and recipients. Through 126 years of changing fads and fashions, Gump's has proudly upheld a tradition of quality, value, and classic good taste.

This year, we are also pleased to tell you that our mail order service has been greatly improved. We have relocated our mail order processing facility to DeSoto, Texas (just outside Dallas). With our new, central location, larger staff and increased warehouse space, you can expect your gifts to reach their destinations faster than ever.

We hope you take as much pleasure in making your selections from our 1987 Holiday Gift Book as we have had in assembling this year's unique collection. It is for you that we work hard to make each gift as perfect a choice as possible.

Cordially,

Robert Leitstein

Robert Leitstein
President

P.S. *Please note.* When you order from this book, you will automatically receive Gump's Gift Books four times a year. If, however, you don't wish to order, you may continue to receive the books by sending $3 for a year's subscription. Just write "Gift Book Subscription" on the order form and enclose a check for $3. The full amount will be credited to your first order.

Gump's of San Francisco encloses a personal letter from their President inside each holiday catalogue.

Reprinted with permission of: Dorothy Adams, Executive Director, Mail Order Division. Gump's, San Francisco.

Source: Gump's. Since 1861. President's letter from "Gifts from Gump's, Holiday, 1987.

display the merchandise in a location where customers can see, touch, or taste it, direct mailers have a lot more leeway than a retailer does in their selection of products and services to market.

Limit choices. This heady opportunity to sell anything and everything can be overwhelming—both to the seller and to the buyer. When selecting merchandise for inclusion in your own publication, stick to the highest quality for the price, and don't offer too many similar items. Many customers find it difficult to make a choice. If too many competing items vie for their attention, they will likely not choose anything at all. The obvious solution is to limit the number of choices. Again, the old rule "Make it easy to buy!" applies.

Theme promotions. Specialty catalogues often use a theme, such as winter sports or spring cruises, to promote their merchandise. Models in ski clothes might be posed against the backdrop of a ski lodge or snowy mountain. Apres-ski clothing could be photographed in romantic, firelit settings. Spring cruise wear, on the other hand, may be worn by people relaxing on the deck of an ocean liner, or by a man and a woman standing next to their luggage in an airline terminal. If you decide to follow a theme, make it look realistic. Props and backdrops that look artificial will make your merchandise look artificial, too. Some of the most effective fashion catalogues are photographed on location, in exciting towns, or picturesque countrysides, taking advantage of local scenery and architecture. Models are posed in front of interesting-looking buildings or against expensive cars. The temptation here is to put so much artistic effort into the background that your merchandise suffers in comparison. Theme merchandising should be subtle, supportive of the products, enhancing rather than competing with them.

Sometimes theme is really the philosophy or specialty of the merchandiser. Gump's, for example, is known for high-quality jewelry, gifts, clothing, and items for the home with an exotic, oriental flavor. Most of their catalogues artfully carry this theme from page to page and item to item.

Business-to-Business

Business catalogues are really another form of specialty catalogue. As with other specialty publications, avoiding the "me, too!" syndrome is important. Because the needs of most offices are similar, your publication will likely overlap with others. But, to get into the market and stay there, follow the advice of IMAC's president, Ken Eldred, and verify that you have a bona-fide, valid position in the market before you enter it.

Pricing structure is often a key element to the business-to-business book. Because competition is so high, even with your own corner of the market, you will have to be highly competitive. The other key ingredient is service. Tell your customers what you will do for them if they are dissatisfied. Provide clear instructions and define requirements for return-ing or exchanging merchandise. If there is a particular situation in which merchandise *cannot* be returned, say so.

Essentially, you are competing with local office-supply stores, which can deliver faster, and give quicker, one-on-one attention to their cus-tomers. To overcome this disadvantage, you should offer a wider range of products and services than they do. Custom-printed forms, for example, or specialized computer support equipment, are excellent choices. To meet the criteria of good service, have trained sales and service personnel on hand *who can answer questions knowledgeably* about your products and services. UARCO®, widely known as a supplier of quality computer supplies and continuous forms, offers their customers all the personal assistance they need. (See Figure 6.4.) They provide the customer with a comfortable and convenient variety of ordering styles—direct, by toll-free telephone; via a written order blank within the catalogue; or through the personalized assistance of one of their sales representatives.

General Merchandise

Consumer catalogues offer a great many items and gadgets. The common denominator is often price and quality. Presentation varies from illustra-tions and drawings for the low-end products to high-quality, glossy, full-color photographs for high-end merchandise. Because this type of publication covers such a broad audience, it is difficult to target a market correctly. To resolve the problem, many catalogue merchants produce several books instead of one, each of them aimed at a specialized market.

Wholesale

Wholesale catalogues are another form of business-to-business catalogues. A supplier of products for beer distributors, for example, may send out an annual, or semiannual catalogue to his distributor customers. Manufacturers

Figure 6.4

UARCO *Sales Representatives... experts in development of efficient Computer Form Systems*

UARCO sales professionals take pride in being able to help you make better, more effective use of your information management systems. They can bring a fresh outlook to your organization...and provide you with time- and cost-saving innovations for more efficient processing.

Their dedication to professional forms design and excellent service has set the standard in the forms industry. That's why UARCO is widely acknowledged as the leader in innovative data processing forms and systems.

UARCO Sales Representatives work closely with their customers to find solutions for improving legibility, reducing printing costs, and developing more efficient forms. In some cases, combining several applications into fewer documents is the cost-saving answer. In others, a Sales Representative will manage a customer's forms inventory levels. Better forms utilization increases productivity and decreases printing time to keep your printers running smoothly and efficiently. That reduces your costs and saves you money.

UARCO's library of thousands of forms currently in use by businesses of all types is an excellent resource for you. Your Sales Representative can show you what others in your industry are doing to maximize the efficiency of their information management systems.

Every UARCO Sales Representative is thoroughly trained in computer forms systems design. Let us share this knowledge with you today and show you what we do best!

State-of-the-Art Manufacturing
Highly efficient manufacturing facilities across the United States serve you promptly and cost-effectively. UARCO technicians often design and build new printing equipment specially for new computer applications. In keeping up with the constantly changing demands of today's data processing requirements, we're committed to providing you with quality forms and excellent service.

▲ Plants
• Sales Offices
★ Distribution Centers

Innovations in Information Management
UARCO is known as the industry innovator in developing new computer form systems. We pioneered developments such as E-Z READ* stock computer paper, TRIM EDGE™ continuous stationery, Convelope* continuous envelopes, and the Data Mailer* form. Our 2 newest systems are also designed to increase productivity and decrease your cost:

1) Bar-coded labels and forms that enable your computer to streamline inventory control and automate pricing.

2) A new line of color-coordinated continuous statements, invoices and checks that can be imprinted to give you a custom look at low stock form prices.

Your knowledgeable UARCO Sales Representative is available now to discuss your forms and systems requirements. Give us a call TODAY...and let us put our extensive experience and know-how to work for you.

Efficient, Eye-Catching Forms
Professional forms design increases your efficiency...enhances your company image with prospects, customers, and suppliers. UARCO's fully staffed corporate Forms Design Department is always ready to work with your Sales Representative to streamline your forms and give them a fresh, professional look. Our skillful designers can even develop a unique logo for you, producing a coordinated look for all your forms. Discuss your specific forms needs with your UARCO Sales Representative.

40

Need Personal Sales Assistance?

Your UARCO sales representative can provide you with a complete product line of business forms, as well as data and information processing supplies. This knowledgeable professional can supply valuable systems analysis, too. Ask about UARCO's Data-Mailer* forms, TRIM EDGE™ stationery, stock computer forms, labels or any forms system needs you may have. Your representative will be glad to help.

Yes! ☐ Please have a UARCO sales representative contact me about my business forms/computer supplies needs.

Name _____

Title _____

Company _____

Address _____

City/State _____ Zip _____

Telephone Number (___) _____ Date _____

Mail to: **Uarco Incorporated**
Attention: Marketing Department
West County Line Road
Barrington, Illinois 60010

UARCO offers their customers a variety of comfortable, convenient ways to order.

Reprinted with permission of UARCO, Incorporated.

Source: UARCO® Quality Computer supplies and continuous forms, Fall Edition, page 40.

and distributors of hardware, building supplies, automobile parts, beauty supplies, or technical equipment often use this form of communication to keep their customers informed of the latest prices and products available.

Even food suppliers now use a catalogue system. Grocers select merchandise from a preprinted price list. Their orders are then mailed or telephoned to the distributor, who fills and delivers them.

HOW TO ADVERTISE IN A CATALOGUE

It is *not* necessary to produce your own catalogue in order to advertise in one. Many manufacturers, especially new ones, often test their product in someone else's catalogue. If you plan to try this, review as many nonstore retail catalogues as you can. (Most store catalogues offer only their own merchandise. To be included in one, your product must first be available in the store itself.)

Finding the Right Catalogue

Search for catalogues which carry merchandise that is compatible with your own. If you have invented a portable camera holder, advertising it in a catalogue specializing in camera supplies and photographic equipment would offer a greater chance for success than offering it in a general merchandise catalogue. Avoid choosing a catalogue that offers too many products that are similar to your own. Remember, customers are easily overwhelmed. If too many choices are available, most customers will avoid making a choice altogether.

Asking the Right Questions

After you have selected several appropriate catalogues, contact the publishers of each one and ask about their advertising requirements. You will find that most catalogue producers will ask to see a sample of your product first, and expect you to supply camera-ready art (either a photograph or a drawing depending upon their format), along with a complete description, pricing structure, and shipping information.

Experience has shown that the more direct your approach, the better your chances of a quick response. A telephone call will get action much faster than a letter. (You should certainly follow up your call with a confirming letter; always get *everything* in writing.) Telephoning also gives you a chance to ask important questions such as these:

Figure 6.5

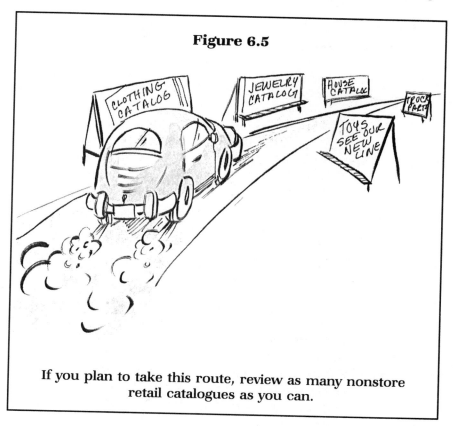

If you plan to take this route, review as many nonstore retail catalogues as you can.

- To whom should I address my request?
- Where do I send a sample?
- Who is responsible for shipping the order?
- Do you drop ship?
- How does your pricing work?
- How do I get paid?
- How are credit card sales handled?
- How long does it take to get paid after the order is placed and filled?
- Do you send each order to me (to be filled) as soon as you get it? Or do you hold it until you have a batch of orders and then send all of them at once?
- Do I have to have a certain minimum number of pieces in stock before you will carry my item in your catalogue?
- Who warehouses my merchandise? You, or me?

- Do I need to have a credit line with my bank before my item can be carried in your catalogue?

A surprising number of manufacturers and vendors never consider these questions, and are amazed to find out that the time between filling and order and getting paid can run up to ninety days or more. In some cases, because the catalogue company requires their advertisers to produce and stock minimum inventories (to insure that orders can be filled once they are placed), special credit arrangements must be made to cover the added costs.

Copyrights

A new problem that has surfaced in recent years is the problem of copyrighting. Many designers and manufacturers of software programs sell them through mail-order catalogues. If these programs are to be classified as "public domain" products, that is, belonging to the general public who are free to make as many copies of the program as they wish, there is no problem. The programmer writes the program and sells it to the catalogue company, which in turn markets it to the end user. Payment for the program concludes the author's association with it. If the program developer retains the copyright, however, the problem arises as to who is ultimately responsible when unauthorized or unlicensed copies are made. Legal entanglements can, and often do, result. To avoid being caught in this trap, check with a patent attorney (or one specializing in copyright law), before selling any original, reproducible work, and be sure to get the catalogue merchant's guidelines and policies covering copyrights *in writing*.

Be careful about selling unauthorized copies of name brand merchandise such as jewelry, perfume, tapes, records, and "designer" clothes. In such cases, special licensing is required and you will need—at the very least—written permission from the holder of the trademark or patent you are duplicating.

DESIGNING YOUR OWN CATALOGUE

Instead of offering your products in someone else's catalogue, you may decide to put together a book of your own. This can be extremely profitable if you know how to do it and have plenty of previous experience in catalogue design and marketing.

Professional Help

Catalogue production is not for the novice. For your first few attempts, it would be wise to seek the advice and assistance of professionals. To find them, look through the Advertiser's Index at the back of *Catalogue Age*, a monthly publication which encompasses all aspects of catalogue marketing. As an additional resource, contact the Direct Marketing Association in New York, (telephone 212/689-4977) and ask for their brochure on catalogue marketing. A few books on the subject should be available through your local library. And of course the information in the Appendices at the end of this book should provide you with a complete list of associations, publications, and companies that offer help in a wide variety of services you will need.

There may also be a local advertising agency with experience in this field. Advertising agencies specialize, just as you do. Some of them are familiar with direct marketing techniques — and some of them are not. Very, very few of them have experience in catalogue sales. If you decide to seek help from one, make sure the agency understands direct response advertising in general, and catalogue marketing in particular, before you hire the agency!

Creative

Even with professional help, you should be involved in the creative stages of your project. Because the market is already saturated with catalogues competing for the upscale and business markets, outstanding creative (conceptualizing and design) is imperative for a successful catalogue. Being unique is simply not enough anymore. Offering difficult-to-find or one-of-a-kind items certainly helps, but to stay in the ring, your catalogue must also look good. It must motivate, entice, and make a clear, concise, *believable* presentation.

This is a tall order! And, it can't be filled unless you are involved in it right from the start. Among the elements you will have to consider:

- Type of catalogue.
- Point-of-view.
- Price range of merchandise.
- Budget.
- Image you want to project.
- Use of photographs or drawings.
- Graphic layout and overall design.

Start with the type of catalogue you want to produce — general or specific, retail or wholesale, seasonal or year round. Then decide how you want to present the catalogue — considering factors such as overall appearance, market motivation, sales strategies, and, of course, the market you want to target. Within the advertising industry, this step is known as "conceptualizing."

The next decision is price, and it's a double-edged sword: the price range of the products you want to include, and the price you are willing to pay to put the catalogue together. The cost of products within your catalogue can range from under a dollar to over ten thousand dollars apiece; the price to produce the book varies even more. No matter what budget you initially consider, it is likely that your final product may cost much more.

Quality controls cost. If you plan a first-class image — full-size pages with full-color photography printed on coated stock (shiny paper), the cost will be considerably higher than a smaller book with drawings and illustrations printed on a standard rag bond.

The quality of the merchandise you wish to sell should be commensurate with the quality or image your catalogue projects. If your products are expensive, the book should look expensive, too. And don't drop the ball halfway through the project. If the cover conveys the image of quality products and services, continue the image from first page to last. There is nothing worse than a book that looks like the advertiser ran out of money after designing the cover. The inference is that when the customer receives an order, the packaging will be great, but the contents of questionable quality!

Conversely, if your specialty is $1.98 gadgets for the kitchen, decorative rubber rings for shower curtains, and handy little gifts for Uncle Harry and Aunt Rose, your customer will be frightened away by a "too-slick" presentation. In that case, you should bring the book down to the level of the merchandise, trying to create a "folksy," homey image that will make your customer feel comfortable. Presented with an expensive-looking catalogue, Rose and Harry see their hard-earned savings zipped away by the glitzy catalogue company. Unwilling to take a chance that they might find something they want but cannot afford, Rose and Harry shake their heads and toss your catalogue into the trash.

Internal Design

Whenever the budget permits (or unless they will be inconsistent with your image), photographs should be used rather than drawings. Each page

Figure 6.6

Create a homey, "folksy" image that makes them feel comfortable, if your book offers handy little gadgets for Uncle Harry and Aunt Rose.

should be pleasing to the eye, with a pleasant variety of items selected for pictorial compatibility and graphic design. Whenever possible, let your layout flow from the left side of the left page, across the center of the book, to the far right-hand edge — like an opened book. Many designers carry photographs and copy right across the center dividing point. Try to vary the size of photographs or illustrations, and to avoid the look of a home-made photograph album. Keep copy clean, simple, to the point, and very, very thorough. Place the captions next to the photographs. Use a letter or number system to identify which description belongs to which picture.

Another trick is to divide the book into sections, giving a catchy title to each section. Look at the following titles used by American Express in their Christmas 1987 book. Although they sound more like titles for popular soap operas than pages in a catalogue, each title follows the rules of psychographic target marketing: they hit almost every one of the "feel-good motivators" listed in Chapter 2.

Hi-tech Style
Life's Rich Rewards
Dazzle and Drama
The Connoisseur
Lap of Luxury
Private Lives
Sight and Sound
All the Comforts
An Easy Mood
Corporate Level
Treat Your Senses
Just For Fun
Prized Possessions

Within each of these cleverly titled sections, beautifully reproduced photographs printed on high-quality paper entice the reader to buy. The designers also remembered the other basic rule of catlogue marketing: Make It Easy to Buy. Each page bears this neat little message: "CALL ANYTIME. 24 HOURS A DAY . . . 7 DAYS A WEEK. WE PAY FOR THE CALL."[6]

The Cover

Whatever type of catalogue you finally decide to build, the cover is what determines if it will succeed or not. You've got three seconds to sell the customer. If he likes what he sees, he'll open the book. If he doesn't, into the trash it goes. Generally, the cover should suggest the theme or season. Saks[7] uses a bright red one with their distinctive gold seal in the center. Many catalogues display at least one key piece of merchandise. Gump's pictures one exquisite piece of jewelry. The Company Store's Fall 1987 catalogue, for example, shows a tempting down bed ensemble in soft blue with white accessories. If photographs are being used, select one that is crisp, clean, and enticing. Notice the different cover designs in Figure 6.1. Each advertiser makes it clear what the catalogue is selling. The theme, style, and taste of the catalogue is apparent from the cover.

Sales Stimulators

To add extra spice (and insure a high return), try using a few tricks to stimulate sales. Bob Stone suggests six ways to draw the reader into a sale:[8]

1. Overwrap, extra sheets which offer incentives and are wrapped around the catalogue prior to mailing.
2. Early order stimulators, which offer free gifts in return for ordering before a specific deadline.
3. Toll-free phone orders, which make it easy, convenient, and cost-efficient for the customer to place an order.
4. Charge privileges using cards such as Visa or MasterCard, which make ordering even easier and quicker.
5. Free trial periods. Watch this one. Most people will not return something if they keep it for more than thirty days. Others, however, will buy a product, use it up, wear it out, and return it for a full refund. OK if you are a big marketer and can afford to absorb the potential losses. Not so good if you are new in the business and on a tight budget.
6. Free gifts, which get larger as the order does. The more she buys, the more goodies the customer gets for free! This one works really well at holiday time when most customers — harried and hurried to finish their shopping — appreciate the extra gifts and little stocking stuffers that the catalogue merchants supply free with their order.

Response Device

The easier you make it to buy, the better. Convenience really counts here. Offer more than one option: an order blank for the orderly person who enjoys browsing through the book and filling in the order coupon with various selections, noting color, size, quantity, and so on; a toll-free telephone number for the customer who likes to think fast and act faster; personal help, if it is appropriate, as UARCO provides to speed the order and insure that the correct order is placed. (When custom forms or monogrammed items are part of the order, personal contact, or at the very least, verification of the personalized aspect of the order is imperative if you are to create and maintain satisfied customers.)

MEASURING RESPONSE

Ultimately, a catalogue is only as good as the sales it induces. No matter how nice your book looks, or how attractive the merchandise pictured within it, if the customers don't buy, you're out of business. Surprisingly, many catalogue marketers forget to measure the success of the products they have to offer.

The professional approach is to set up a database which tracks each item in the catalogue by item number. Track cost versus selling price. Sometimes a slight change in the latter is all that it takes to make a page productive. If an item is not moving well, re-think the presentation. Look at the amount of page space taken up by the item. Would a larger illustration help? Finally, how does each item stack up against the others on the page? If you've got an item that consistently draws poorly, try changing price, or positioning, or replacing it with a similar item which has a better track record.

To see how this works, refer to back issues of a catalogue from a merchant who has been selling for a number of years. Notice how some items appear year after year, while others disappear after just one offering. With time, you will be able to assess what your market will buy and what they won't.

The process of weeding out poor producers takes time. Hasty judgments give unreliable data. Give your products time to produce a track record. On the other hand, it is important to keep catalogues fresh and interesting. Take a chance. From time to time, offer a product or service that may have a questionable rate of return but that is exciting enough to have reader appeal anyway.

MAIL ORDER REGULATIONS

Catalogue shopping, like any other form of direct mail, allows you to take advantage of the more favorable rates available to direct marketing advertisers. However, there are a number of strict rules regarding its use. Among them are the regulations regarding certain types of mail (notably pornographic material and firearms), and the Mail Order Rule of the Federal Trade Commission (FTC) (see page 104). This latter requires that you inform customers when there will be a shipping delay, and offer them "the option to either agree to the delay or cancel the order and receive a prompt refund. For each additional delay, your customers must be notified that they must send you a signed consent to a further delay or a refund will be given."[8]

SUMMARY

Catalogue marketing is specialized. It provides an opportunity to offer the reader a wonderful variety of products and services all at one time, with one convenient way to buy. However, because of the heavy competition in the catalogue market, fallout is high. To insure that your catalogue will be a winner, make sure that you know your market and your position in it, and that you can justify your own reasons for choosing this medium.

Finally, unless you are a direct marketing pro, this is not a good place to learn the business. Nobody knows yet what the full impact of the new tax laws on catalogue sales will be. But you can bet that if you are targeting a middle income market which relies heavily on credit for purchases, your overall sales will be affected. Before you jump on the bandwagon, make sure you know where the wagon is headed!

ENDNOTES

1. "Glut and Gluttony in the Mail-order Business," *Fortune* Magazine, July 9, 1984, page 134.
2. *Ibid.*
3. *Direct Marketing*, Feb. 1986, page 70. Quotes from Kenneth A. Eldred, President, IMAC, on Business-to-business catalogues.

4. L.L. Bean® is a registered trademark of L.L. Bean, Inc., Casco Street, Freeport, ME 04033. L.L. Bean Specialty Catalogs include:
   Hunting
   Fly Fishing
   Home & Camp
   Spring Sporting
   Women's Outdoor
   Winter Sporting

5. Software Catalogue, H&E Computronics Inc., 50 N. Pascack Rd., Spring Valley, NY 10977
   The Company Store®, 500 Company Road, La Crosse, WI 54601.
   The Sharper Image, 650 Davis Street, San Francisco, CA 94111.
   American Express®, published by Travel Related Services Company, Inc., American Express Tower, World Finance Center, New York, NY 10285.

6. The American Express® Merchandise Services Christmas Catalogue. © 1987 American Express Travel Related Services Company, Inc.

7. Saks Fifth Avenue, Folio Collections, Inc., 557 Tuckahoe Road, Yonkers, NY 10710.

8. *Successful Direct Marketing*, by Bob Stone, page 321.

9. From *A Business Guide to the Federal Trade Commission's Mail Order Rule*, published by the Federal Trade Commission, Washington, D.C. 20580.
   See: Title 16 — Commercial Practices
        Chapter I — Federal Trade Commission
        Part 435 — Mail Order Merchandise

PRINT ADVERTISING

7

"The print media are where people go to read about what's happening now."
— Irving Burstiner, Ph.D.
Associate Professor of Marketing
Baruch College, City University, N.Y.

Direct mail marketing reaches a specific market by mailing an offer directly to individuals who have been selected to receive it.

Print advertising takes another approach. Instead of mailing one offer to each individual prospect, the advertiser buys space in a publication such as a women's magazine or a trade journal and attempts to reach all potential prospects at once. This method allows the advertiser to reach a large group of prospects simultaneously. The drawback is that prospects are targeted to fit the publisher's buyer profile rather than the advertiser's. While they may be similar in many respects, demographics of the publisher often differ from those of the advertiser. Thus, the potential for sales may decrease dramatically from that of a selected direct mailing to individual prospects.

Print advertising does offer some distinct advantages over personalized direct mail. Right at the top of the list is the cost factor. *Most newspapers and some magazines will design and produce your ad for free.* That's right! To insure that your ad will have as much success as possible in their publication, most of them offer the services of their creative art department to help you design your ad, even providing typesetting, graphics, and canned illustrations (usually known as "clip art") at no additional cost. They will *not* supply original art or photographs, however; these are your responsibility. Low-cost or no-cost services of print advertising make it a frequent favorite of new business owners or smaller firms with a tight budget.

Of course, the help of a professional advertising firm, especially one that specializes in direct response advertising, is usually a good idea, if you can afford it. (To find such a firm, contact your local direct marketing

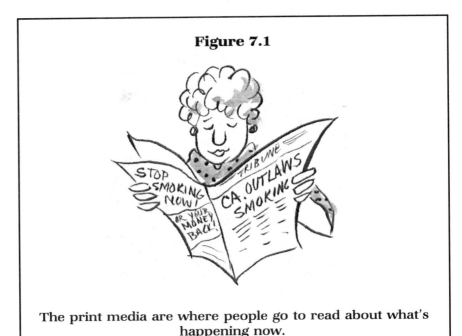

Figure 7.1

The print media are where people go to read about what's happening now.

association for a list of firms in your area that specialize in direct response advertising. See the Appendices for a list of these organizations.)

Buying space is also economical because of the sheer numbers one ad can reach. Producing one paid print ad read by hundreds (or thousands) of readers normally costs far less than producing a direct mail piece for each prospective customer on your list. Furthermore, every response or order from a print advertisement can add to (or initiate) your house list, another cost savings. For a new business, buying space may offer a quick and inexpensive way to get started.

Print advertising is also a good way to test your market. Seasoned sellers often use it in conjunction with other media to test new products or markets, or to verify the interest in established ones. Catalogue marketers find paid print advertising particularly helpful. Before adding an item to their own catalogue, they will test its salability by advertising in other publications whose demographic and psychographic profiles parallel their own.

Direct mail print advertisements should not be confused with general or "image" advertising through mass media. A *direct mail print advertisement is interactive: it includes a response device. It is also measurable:*

the success of the ad can be measured by responses received and sales made. With general media advertising, you really have no way of knowing if it was responsible for a sale or not; there is no way to measure the effectiveness of an ad because there is no specific response device.

Space usually dictates the type of response device used in direct response advertising. Often there is room for only a toll-free number, or a tiny coupon to be torn out, filled in, and returned by the reader. In many cases, the advertiser hedges the bet by providing more than one way for the reader to respond to the ad.

CHOOSING A MEDIA

Most print advertising appears in magazines or newspapers. Before deciding which would work best for you, spend some time looking at the choices your competitors have made. As a test of the publication and your competitor's luck in it, check *duration and frequency*. If an advertiser's offer appears (in one form or another — to be effective advertising must adapt to the market) for a number of months or even years, that particular media must produce profitable results.

Scanning the contents of a publication is also helpful. A quick review of a magazine's table of contents, cover headlines, and lead articles tells you a lot about its readership. From one or two issues, you can tell if this publication would be suitable for your product or service. Previewing the classified section (usually at the back) will tell you how many other direct mailers use the publication. If you would be the only advertiser, find out why. (You could be starting a new trend, or you could be following in the footsteps of a parade of losers.)

Newspapers usually have a distinct editorial content, just as magazines do. One newspaper might appeal to an upbeat, sophisticated national audience. Another might target a mid-size metropolitan area or a small rural community. As with the magazines, take time to peruse several issues, reading articles and editorials, and reviewing advertising to see what kind of readers (and advertisers) it attracts.

Research

The local public (or university) library is always a good reference source. Most libraries keep copies of magazines and newspapers on file for several years. If actual copies are not available, many libraries offer microfiche copies of major papers such as the *New York Times, Los Angeles Times,* and

Figure 7.2

Newspapers and magazines usually have a distinct editorial content and appeal to a specific type of reader.

Wall Street Journal. Magazines, with the recent copies usually unbound, and the older ones bound and stored in the stacks, should also be available. Many city or university library systems also permit borrowing between affiliated branches. In San Diego, for example, most universities carry a computerized or printed list that indicates where various periodicals can be located. Filling out an interlibrary request form is all that is necessary to have something forwarded to a branch near you.

Library reference section.   To find out about magazines, visit the reference section of the library and peruse a recent copy of *Writer's Market*,[1] or the *Directory of Magazines with Classified Ads*.[2] These reference books are excellent resources for information about magazines. The *Writer's Digest* lists publications by type (women's, business management, entertainment, sports, travel, etc.) and often gives brief demographics as well. If your product is trade-related, pay special attention to the listings under the business section. If the library does not retain copies of magazines you wish to investigate, write to each magazine at their address listed in the *Writer's Market* or *Directory of Magazines with Classified Ads* and request a copy. Most publishers will send a free copy if you send a SASE (self-addressed, stamped envelope).

To find out what newspapers are published and where, review the publications of Standard Rate and Data Service of Skokie, Illinois. One of their publications, *Community Publications Rates and Data*, lists newspapers by three categories: (1) Metro Area Urban/Suburban Weekly Newspapers, (2) Nonmetro Area Weekly Newspapers, and (3) Shopping Guides. If you write for a copy of their paper and send appropriate postage, most publishers will provide you with a free copy.

Circulation.   Newspapers and magazines are classified primarily by circulation, which includes both subscribers and newsstand buyers. If you request it, most publications can give you both the subscriber circulation and the total readership of their publication. They will generally provide a demographic profile of their readers as well. Because magazines may be given as gifts or ordered as part of a school or sweepstakes promotion, the *newsstand readership* is important. Those readers have elected to buy the magazine because they have a genuine interest in it. With newspapers, pay attention to the number of *subscribers*. Some newspapers inflate circulation figures. Just because a paper was printed doesn't necessarily mean it was read.

Competition.   While you are researching newspaper and magazine advertising placed by competitive advertisers that sell products similar to your own, pay attention to what attracts you to their ads. When you see a good headline, write it down. Look at the copy, layout, illustration, spacing, and timing of offers. Ask yourself what works, and why. When you are ready to design your own advertisement, you may want to emulate some of the competition's best points. You do *not* want to copy them, however. At the very least, you will be violating the copyright laws.

Reviewing the competition's advertising also has another interesting consequence. You learn what not to do. One of the most common mistakes made by novice advertisers is to sell for the competiton. That's right! Many novice advertisers produce ads so bland and generic that it's hard to tell what they are selling, let alone for whom. If, for example, you are selling aloe-based hair products, be sure to point out the *specific* features that your product offers, which sets it apart from all other similar products, rather than talking about how wonderful aloe is in general (a selling benefit attributable to any one of dozens of products).

Try to find an advertisement that appears in both a newspaper and a magazine. Contrast its appearance from one medium to the other. Obvious differences exist in the quality of paper, use of color, photographs, type-size, and general layout and placement on the page. Determine which would work best for your own product or service. The choice of media has significant impact on product presentation. It's possible to overwhelm or underwhelm your audience, and lose them, because you chose the wrong media.

Newspapers

Newspaper advertising has several advantages. It has the widest circulation of any mass media. Over 30 percent of the population reads the paper. On Sundays, that number jumps to almost 50 percent. Newspaper advertising is generally inexpensive. Ads can be placed in local "shoppers" for as little as $15. And, most offer complete design help through their creative services department *at no extra charge.* That translates to zero cost for ad preparation!

Also, rates for "local" advertisers are especially favorable. If you take advantage of co-op advertising (splitting the cost with the manufacturer), newspaper advertising is almost cost-free.

Newspaper advertising is also quick. From deadline to fulfillment, many advertisers can turn their cash in less than thirty days. Most replies are received within one week of publication. For that reason, newspapers also offer an excellent test medium. Ads that pull poorly can be quickly changed, reinserted, and tested again—all within a few days.

Because ads can be placed in specific sections such as food, business, or sports, cost can be offset by placing advertising where it will have the highest readership. The larger papers, such as the *New York Times*, carry a special mail order section. Almost all papers allow "preferred positioning" (sometimes for an extra charge), which allows you to request specific placement of your ad. The upper, right-hand corner of the right-hand page pulls better, for instance, than an ad placed on an inside corner (next to the fold) of a left-hand page.

There is also a psychological advantage to direct mail newspaper advertisements. By virtue of the media that printed them, each ad is inferred to be news. "Advertising in the final analysis should be news. If it is not news it is worthless." said former newspaper publisher Adolph Simon Ochs.[3]

Where to advertise.   Newspapers come in all shapes and sizes. National papers with distinct editorial content and readerships, such as the *Wall Street Journal* or *U.S.A. Today*, reach millions of readers every day. So do the papers of large metropolitan areas like New York and Los Angeles. Circulation (the number of readers a newspaper has) in big cities like Detroit, Miami, and Washington, D.C., is in the hundreds of thousands. Smaller cities boasting circulations of 50,000 or more also publish daily. Most of the metropolitan papers also offer Sunday supplements which have an even higher readership.

Getting the most for your money.   Generally higher than for smaller papers, rates for nationally read publications may run into the thousands for one ad, but because the circulation is so high, the *cost of reach* is comparatively small. If your product (or service) is one that can be sold and *delivered* to such a large audience, national papers provide an excellent media. For sellers in major metropolitan areas (which often encompass an entire county), papers such as the *Miami Herald, San Diego Union*, or *Detroit Free Press* may cost thousands of dollars, but the large readership should justify the cost.

Community newspapers, smaller papers that publish once or twice a week (or even daily), offer a less expensive, local forum, often reaching into nearby towns and rural areas with stories and advertisements of local interest. Many communities also publish "shoppers" or "penny-savers." Used as inserts, or distrubuted directly to residents and businesses, these little papers offer a quick, inexpensive way to attract local readers, especially with "dated" offers such as:

BUY NOW AND SAVE $10!

LAST CHANCE! BUY 1, GET 1 FREE!

NEW MODELS ARRIVE NEXT THURSDAY.

NO FINANCING CHARGE TO FIRST 20 PEOPLE TO BUY A NEW MODEL CAR.

Special papers.   Newspapers that target special-interest groups such as Chicanos, Catholics, or college students offer an opportunity to reach demographic markets that closely parallel your own buyer profile. Sometimes their *secondary* readership can be as important as their primary readership. In Figure 7.3, the demographic profile of this weekly publication for microcomputer users affirms that this is a good publication to select if your product is computer-related. Look at it again, however, and you will realize that this targeted buyer is also a good prospect for office supplies and equipment, automobiles, travel or vacation services, and a number of other products or services that take advantage of the discretionary income and business interests most of these readers have.

A few special papers are more like magazines than newspapers. Magazine supplements such as *Parade* Magazine are inserted in Sunday papers across the nation and read by more than 25 million readers each week. "Supermarket" papers that line checkstands are read by millions of readers who pick them up as last minute or "impulse" purchases while standing in food-store lines. Although both are popular with direct mail advertisers, publications such as *Parade* are often too expensive for the small mailer. Rates in the supermarket shoppers such as *National Enquirer*, however, are very reasonable. These papers produce excellent results for direct mailers. *A large portion of their readers are already direct mail buyers.*

Rates.   Rates and rules vary from paper to paper. Advertising cost usually drops in proportion to circulation. The bigger papers cost more by virtue of their larger audience. But most larger papers also offer special rates to direct mail advertisers. Those newspapers that do not offer a special rate for direct mail advertising, bill it as display (billed by the column inch) or as classified (billed by the line). Either way, the net cost works out to be about the same. Before planning your campaign, contact each paper you intend to use, find out how they determine their rates for mail order advertising, and ask for a rate card. (See Figure 7.4.)

The bad news.   While it is true that newspapers offer a quick, often inexpensive, easy way of direct mail advertising, there are also a few drawbacks. Most obvious is wasted circulation. Your ad may never be noticed, much less read. Look around your own home. How many papers litter your kitchen table or family room floor at any one time? Did you read every single page of those papers?

What's more, not all newspaper readers are direct mail buyers. Of the thousands of copies of your ad distributed to newspaper readers, a large percentage is wasted. Unlike direct mail, where prospects are carefully

Figure 7.3

The ComputorEdge Demographics Profile

Readership studies by the ComputorEdge have indentified our typical reader as male, college educated, a computer user at work with an annual income of $35,000–40,000. Most significantly, our readers are advocates of computer technology with extensive plans for equipment purchases in the near future. Their projected purchases for the next year put the Computor-Edge reader at the top of your customer list.

PROFILE: Influential and upscale

Male	80%	
Age	25–44	65.%
College grad		60%
Income	$20,000–50,000+ year	
Married	65%	Single 33.8%
Own home	50.5%	Rent 28.6%
Female	20%	
Age	25–44	67%
College grad		36.1%
Income	$12,000–50,000 +	
Married	56.8%	Single 40.9%
Own home	48.4%	Rent 30.3%

COMPUTOREDGE READER'S PURCHASE PLANS FOR 1987

Desktop computer	32,623
Portable computer	12,941
Multi-user system	6,065
Computer network	7,819
Printer	51,091
Modem	49,877
Software	84,657
Hard drive	35,184
Floppy drive	23,186
Expansion boards	35,184
Computer furniture	23,186
Computer supplies	71,446
Computer training	11,458
Maintenance/repair	17,255

Don't miss the opportunity to reach this exciting, poised-to-purchase market. Call your account representative or the marketing director for more information about the ComputorEdge magazine at 573-0315.

The ComputorEdge Profile

Figure 7.4

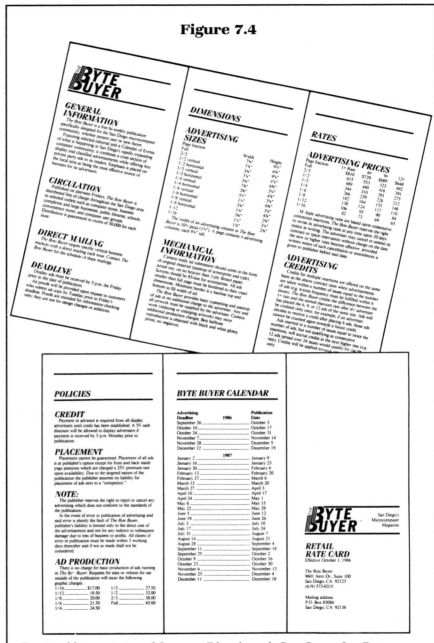

Reprinted by permission of ComputorEdge, formerly Byte Buyer, San Diego, California.

selected to receive your offer, newspaper advertising is like a crap shoot. Some people read your ad. More people don't.

Worse yet, many subscribers never even look at their paper. It lies, unopened, on the doorstep or front porch. Next day, or next week, it is replaced by another, also unread. Your ad doesn't stand a chance. If the paper does get in the house chances are that each person pulls out a favorite section, glances through it, and seldom takes time to look at the rest of the paper. The balance of the news—and your advertising along with it—goes unnoticed.

The toughest part of newspaper advertising is finding a way to measure accountability. You can never really be sure what went wrong if your ad was unsuccessful. Was it surrounded or overpowered by other, larger ads? Was it poorly laid out? Was the offer unappealing? Or was the problem that no one saw it at all!

Advertising requirements.   Before you can run an ad in their paper, almost all publications have a few basic requirements. They want to know that you are a legitimate business. Even if you use a PO box in your ad, most advertisers want to see an official street address. They usually want to *see* your product before they will advertise it. Most of them also require a reference from the Better Business Bureau or another publication. Only a few years ago, mail order had a bad reputation for offering "sleazy" products sold through "fly-by-night" operations that disappeared when customers asked for a refund or an accounting when a product was defective. It's not surprising that before they will take your ad, most publications want to know you are reliable, findable, and accountable.

Magazines

Magazines tend to have a more closely defined audience than newspapers do. And, like cats, magazines seem to have more than one life. In addition to being read by the subscriber, many of them are resurrected and perused by family members, friends, or mere qcquaintances. Often they are read by people in waiting rooms, hotels, corporate lobbies, and airplanes. The readership of a magazine usually extends far beyond the original purchasers.

Unlike a newspaper, which is frequently tossed or used for the bottom of the parakeet cage, magazines stay around a long time. Although most ads are answered within a month of publication, some are answered months, even years later. (This is a good reason for putting a date restriction on your offer.)

The loyal and long-lasting audience tends to be reflected in the cost of magazine advertising which is directly proportional to the quality of the publication as well as the quality of its audience.

Many publications have strict guidelines about submissions. To find out what they are, contact each magazine for a "media kit" to explain them.[4]

Advertising costs.   Display advertising cost is based upon a one-time insertion rate or a "contract" rate for multiple insertions (such as 12 times for a monthly publication, or 52 times for a weekly). The higher the number of insertions, the lower the cost. You cannot save money, however, by purchasing space at the cheaper contract rate, and then cancelling out of the balance of the contract. If you do, the magazine will back charge you for the advertising already printed with a "short-rate" charge to collect the difference between what you paid at the contract rate, and what you should have paid for the actual number of insertions at the appropriate rate (usually a one-time-only rate).[5]

Classified rates are usually listed at the beginning of each classified section (or inside the front page with the publisher's information). Costs for special treatments and typefaces are often given as well (or may be obtained by asking for a media kit).

Overlapping readership.   Most magazines are published weekly or monthly, so people often buy or read more than one magazine at a time, especially ones that relate to specific issues or interests. Contrast this to newspaper readers who usually have time to read only one — or two papers at the most — before the next issue comes out. Although the overlapping readership makes it difficult to determine exactly how many subscribers actually saw your ad, because so many of them read more than one publication, your offer stands a higher chance of being read if you publish it in a number of different magazines.

Within each major magazine classification — general interest, special interest (or class), and trade or professional publications — a number of subgroups exist. (See Figure 7.5 for a partial listing.) Although they cover a broad audience, magazines fall into one or more of these special categories. Because of this, magazines tend to more clearly reflect the personality of their readers than newspapers do. Stories and articles within each issue are a clue to the likes and tastes of the audience. You will find this can be very helpful in pre-determining a positive response to your marketing efforts. (Endnotes 1 and 2 suggest sources for finding magazines by category. Also see the Appendices.)

Figure 7.5
Sample Listing Of Magazines By Classification

COMPANY PUBLICATIONS (company newsletter, magazine, or bulletin)

ADVANCES FOR MEDICINE	Hewlett-Packard Medical Products Group
BAROID NEWS BULLETIN	Petroleum industry
CATERPILLAR WORLD	Caterpillar Tractor Co.
CORRESPONDENT	Aid Association for Lutherans
CORVETTE NEWS	GM Photographic
THE LEADING EDGE	Society of Exploration Geophysicists
RURALITE	For small towns and rural families

CONSUMER PUBLICATIONS (by subclassification)

ANIMALS

CALIFORNIA HORSE REVIEW
CAT FANCY
PET HOSPITAL NEWS
THE GREYHOUND REVIEW

AUTOMOTIVE AND MOTORCYCLE

BMX PLUS MAGAZINE
CAR AND DRIVER
CYCLE WORLD
THE EJAG MAGAZINE
ROAD AND TRACK

GAMES AND PUZZLES
DETECTIVE AND CRIME
ETHNIC/MINORITY
GAMES AND PUZZLES
GENERAL INTEREST
HISTORY
HOBBY AND CRAFT
HOME COMPUTING
IN-FLIGHT
JUVENILE
WOMEN'S

ASSOCIATION, CLUB, & FRATERNAL

CALIFORNIA HIGHWAY PATROLMAN
THE ELKS MAGAZINE
NATIONAL 4-H NEWS
THE TOASTMASTER

BUSINESS AND FINANCE

NATIONAL—
    BARRONS
    THE EXECUTIVE FEMALE
    WASHINGTON REPORT
REGIONAL
    COLORADO BUSINESS MAGAZINE
    HOUSTON BUSINESS JOURNAL
    WESTERN INVESTOR

LIFESTYLES
LITERARY
MILITARY
PHOTOGRAPHY
POETRY
POLITICS AND WORLD AFFAIRS
RELIGIOUS
SPORTS

TRADE, TECHNICAL, AND PROFESSIONAL JOURNALS

ACCOUNTING	JEWELRY	PLUMBING
EDUCATION	LIBRARY	TOYS
HOSPITALS	MANAGEMENT	VETERINARY

Source: Writer's Market

The prestige factor.   One of the biggest advantages of magazine advertising is prestige and appearance — good quality paper, clear photographs, crisp reproductions. Also, to many readers, advertising in a quality magazine is viewed as having "arrived in the big league" (as compared to newsprint).

"Big time" can mean big cost, though; even more important, it can mean lost or delayed revenues. Producing a top quality publication takes time. Several months, even years, go into the design and makeup of a first class magazine. Ads are planned far in advance, and the lead time for insertion of advertising is often three months or more. Generally, the cost is directly proportional to the quality. Print ads in the big, national magazines are so costly — often running into tens of thousands of dollars per page — that only a few big advertisers can afford them. The beginning business or new advertiser should consider a number of alternatives before deciding on print space in glossy or "slick" magazines, most of which require that the appearance of the ad be in concert with editorial content. That, too, can be costly, requiring countless dollars in agency help, photographers, and copywriters. If magazine advertising is part of your campaign, start small, and test carefully (see the section on calculating the cost of newspaper advertising on page 155).

Co-ops and Stuffers

Another possibility for the direct mailer is to combine advertising with other advertisers. *Direct Marketing* magazine, as well as other mail order publications, companies,[6] and associations[7] can provide you with a list of companies that will include your ad with their own (see the Appendices). Prior approval is required.

One common method is to insert your flyer or "stuffer" with someone else's mailing. You have probably received offers like this inside a cable TV bill, or within a statement from a department store or bank card company.

Another type of co-op mailing groups the marketing efforts of several advertisers together and mails them out in one package. Frequently, neighborhood businesses, anchored by a movie theater, bank, or restaurant, will use this technique.

Many of the major manufacturers, such as the producers of automobile tires, will cover part, or even all, of your advertising costs for their brands. By inserting the ads as a local advertiser, which qualifies the ad for local rates, the advertiser gains a wide network of coverage at a considerable cost savings. (Regular and national rate advertising is much higher, even after deducting the agency fee, than are local rate promotions.)

For the start-up company, co-ops can be very cost effective. They offer a fast, efficient way to place well-designed advertising in a media with a wide readership.

TIMING

Seasonal. Mail order shopping is largely seasonal. Statistically, the five best months to advertise are September through November, January and February. In the fall, people plan ahead for cold weather and the holidays. Pouring over advertisements, filling them out, and placing orders can be fun. December ads usually don't pull too well. Distributed too late for most holiday shoppers to place and receive an order in time for Christmas or Hanukkah, few publications contain much direct mail advertising during that month. January and February pick up again, especially with orders for outdoor and vacation gear, cruise wear, spring planting materials, and exercise equipment.

Lag between preparation and publication. With any print media, the time between creating the ad and fulfilling the orders can easily be thirty days or more. With most magazines, it is usually three or four months. Many of them go to press at least a month in advance of the issue date and close the date for receiving advertising one or two months before that. Thus, the June 1st issue of *Fabulous Homes Magazine* might appear in mailboxes and newsstands in early May. If deadline for advertising was a month prior to pub date, your ad (in final, camera-ready form) would have to be on the publisher's desk before April 1st to be included in the June issue. Obviously, magazine advertising requires careful budgeting and planning.

Newspapers have a shorter turnaround time, and they generally require final copy of advertising to be in their office one or two weeks prior to publication. Unless you have a credit contract with them, payment is usually required prior to publication.

Magazine advertising can cause serious cash flow problems if the advertiser is not aware of the lag between the time the ad is paid for and the time orders will be received. Using a mix of several magazines and periodicals will help. Spreading the risk helps too. A good rule of thumb for print advertisers is to proportionally space out advertising over good and bad months to even out cash flow.

CREATING AN ADVERTISEMENT

Copywriting is the backbone of a successful ad. However, because space is limited (by column inch, agate line, or number of words), and format dictated by the publication, print advertising relies heavily on instant impact, on catchy headlines and hard-selling copy—all packed into one finite space. The key to both is to *know who you are selling to and why*. (See Chapter 2, Targeting the Market.) You must design an ad that, better than anyone else's, will *motivate someone to read it and buy your product.*

The same motivator may not direct both actions (reading the copy and making a purchase). If the buyer already wants what you've got, then he will look at your ad to see if your product meets his selection criteria for that specific item. If he doesn't know anything at all about the product but is attracted to it by a personal motivation such as the need for self-improvement, then he is attracted by an *idea* rather than the specific product. Here is where a thorough buyer profile and comprehensive psychographic studies really pay off.

Before beginning the actual design work, write out a complete buyer profile of your prospects. List their motivations, from the most obvious to the most obscure. Then list selling points and specific benefits of your product or service which match your buyers' motivations. Pick out the key points. One of these will be your headline. The other points will support it.

With print media, time and attention are severely limited. Your ad may rate no more than the flick of an eyelash. Most people only glance at a headline. *Few actually take time to read copy (less than one in three), unless it offers something they really want.* As John Caples, Direct Marketing Hall of Famer, puts it, "The success of an entire advertising campaign may stand or fall on what is said in the headlines of the individual advertisements." His ad, with the following headline, is considered a classic in direct response marketing because it generates curiosity and forces the reader to look at the copy that follows it.

> **THEY LAUGHED WHEN I SAT DOWN AT THE PIANO**
> **BUT WHEN I STARTED TO PLAY!—**

Headline and Hook

A headline has one purpose: make the reader look at the copy. The best ones are both simple and direct, and appeal to the reader's self-interest.

For a few prospects, this will be easy. They already want what you have. Let them know you have it, and they will buy.

To sell the rest of them, you will have to work a little harder. Even then, the more hot buttons you push in one headline, the better the chances you have of making a sale. Offer them a quick solution or an effortless answer. Arouse curiosity. Use words like *how, now, this, what,* (**hooks** that entice the reader to find out the answer), or use words like *wanted* that make them want to prove that they already know it. Personalize the headline with the magic words **YOU** or **YOUR**. Use *action* or *newsworthy* words. Notice how the following headlines take advantage of these techniques.

1. ## DOUBLE YOUR INCOME INSTANTLY WITHOUT ANY EFFORT!

2. **Announcing a New Technique to Double Your Income in 90 Days!**

3. *HOW TO DOUBLE YOUR INCOME IN 90 DAYS.*

4. **WANTED: PEOPLE WHO WANT TO DOUBLE THEIR INCOME IN 90 DAYS!**

If the product or service is one that is yet to be proven, or something that is relatively unknown, such as musical toilet seats or electric toenail clippers for dogs, immediately explain the benefits that the product offers. "Impress Your Friends with Extravagantly Comfortable, Musical Toilet Seats in Your Own Bathroom!" "Save Time and Money by Clipping Your Dog's Toenails at Home." If most of your audience is familiar with the *type* of thing you are selling, then point out its advantages.

Take care not to go overboard with enthusiasm. Try to be realistic. If your headline promises a quick, easy solution to something, make sure it is believable. Try substituting the number 100 for the number 3 in the headline below. It stretches credibility, and turns the reader off. Advertising must be truthful; otherwise, the publication won't print it. And, even if it did get by their advertising editor, it won't get by the reader!

NOW, YOU CAN HAVE A COMPUTER TWICE AS SMALL AND
3 Times Faster Than Anyone Else's...

— Complete correspondence in 1/3 the time.
— No more need for a second shift to finish the workload!
— Fast, economical, and efficient.
— Takes up less space on your desk.

Be careful also, to use positive rather than negative connotations. The following **split run** ad (see the section on split-run advertising on page 231 of Chapter 11) for Milk Bone Dog Biscuits is frequently cited as an excellent example of the two approaches. The first headline was far less effective than the second because of the connotation it implied: a dead pet. In the second, instead of murdering the poor beast, you saved it. Much better image. Much better ad.

"DON'T POISON YOUR DOG!"

"KEEP YOUR DOG *SAFE* THIS SUMMER!"

If the success of an ad depends on the headline, it is even more dependent upon the first few words (or a few special key words). To appeal to the reader's self-interest, try using words or phrases like these:

How To	Wanted	"Your" or "You"
Advice	Make	Save
Get Ahead	Enjoy	End
Reduce	More	Better
Free	Easy	Quick
Fast	Learn	Have

For a presentation that uses an announcement approach (particularly useful when introducing a new product or upgrade of an existing one), try starting off with one of these words:

ANNOUNCING	NEW	INTRODUCING
NOW	AT LAST!	PRESENTING

Copy That Sells

Most print ads are small, only a few "column inches" and only one or two columns wide. There is precious little space in which to promote your product, so it's important to get your message across efficiently. The biggest mistake most novice copywriters make is writing too much. Save creative writing for the classroom or for magazine fiction. Direct mail copywriting is tight and to the point. The more you know about your prospect, the easier it will be to write something that hits home.

Provide a solution.   Your product or service provides a solution, presumably the *best* solution, to your prospect's problem. In a classic approach to copywriting, the writer uses headlines, subheads, copy, and even illustrations to establish the problem, promise to solve it, and show how the product or service will do it. The ad concludes with a call to action. "Call now, and SAVE!" "Don't wait. This may be your last chance to . . . ."

Sometimes the problem is implied. The ad for a business opportunity in Figure 7.6 *assumes* the reader is dissatisfied with present income levels and offers a quick, easy solution (that is **believable**) for an extremely reasonable cost. In fact, this ad did so well, that in the ten year span from December 1975 to December 1986, AGS jumped from number 214 to number 179 on *Inc.* Magazine's list of the fastest growing privately owned companies in the nation. Responding enthusiastically to the offer, one of their licensees will earn over $300,000 this year! And that's working only part time.

AGS places this ad in a number of magazines aimed at the closet entrepreneur. By utilizing the database of these publications as if the mailing list was its own, AGS can accurately target a prospective market for its own unique product. The ad hits all the right buttons: catchy headline, motivators, and use of the word "YOUR." It is believable, short, and to the point, and gives succinct instructions on how to respond. No wonder it does so well.

Figure 7.6

START YOUR OWN COMPANY FOR $495

Make up to 300% Profit Providing Students with Today's Most Desperately Needed Service

Computerized Scholarship/Matching Service

As an AGS Licensee, you become President of your own prestigious business. Parents and students seek you out. You take charge, but we do all the servicing for you. NO experience necessary...because we guide you step-by-step.

SEND FOR OUR FREE BROCHURE

ACADEMIC GUIDANCE SERVICES

The AGS Building, 300 So. Route 73, Dept. IM

Marlton, NJ 08053 • 609 - 983 - 3737

or

CALL TOLL FREE 1-800-USA-1221

Features and benefits.   Whether your points are overt or implied, support your headlines and subheads by smoothly continuing on from one point to the next, stressing benefits to the buyer, or product advantages when the type of product is well known. An ad for Timex Watches,[8] for example, makes the following statements about their Timex Ironman® Triathlon Watch:

- the official timepiece of the Ironman® Triathlon
- delivers precision accuracy to 1/100 of a second for peak performance
- 16 hour chronograph with 8 lap Memory Recall to record individual lap performance
- 3 mode, 10 hour countdown timer for cross training and pacing runs
- water resistant to 100 meters
- tough, yet lightweight at 1.1 ounces
- large, easy-access, top-mounted controls
- lighted display for night workouts
- alarm, calendar.

No words are wasted here. Each word of the copy counts. All of these *feature call-outs* specifically detail a product advantage of the Timex Ironman® Triathlon Watch, and four of them add a benefit statement to clarify an individual selling point.

Testimonial.   The ad also takes advantage of another technique: the testimonial. Using pictures and names of famous people or events helps to sell the product simply by association. The inference is that by using this watch, the wearer, too, will have star quality. Quotes and comments from satisfied users can also be your best and most original source of copywriting. "I took off so many pounds with your saunabelt that my mom didn't even recognize me at the family reunion!" says it all.

Uniqueness.   In many cases, stressing the uniqueness of a product or service is helpful, especially if you are selling an intangible such as life insurance.

> "Our product not only protects you at term rates, it also provides you with a readily accessible cash account which you can draw on at any time. No other term life insurance product offers this benefit!"

The "Essay" Ad.   In some instances, there is so much to say, and the topic is so vast, a complex approach has to be used. Here the copy reads more like a series of little essays or stories, each one a "mini" classic ad with its own problem, solution, and invitation to take action. Suppose your product is a course designed to teach someone how to build an investment portfolio. Each "lesson" is self-contained, and each one addresses a specific subject such as mutual funds or the bond market. A presentation of this product might describe the various "lessons" covered in your course and invite the reader to "try the first two lessons for free with no obligation," before signing up for the complete program.

Regardless of how you structure the copy, be sure to keep the following ten key points in mind:

1. Keep it simple. Use short, strong words.
2. Don't waste words. Make every one of them count.
3. State your case clearly. Don't get lost in rhetoric.
4. Stick to the subject: benefits and/or selling points.
5. Follow the lead. Copy should support and expand the headline.
6. Make it personal. Use the word "You" whenever possible.
7. Don't overwrite and don't underwrite. Say what you have to, then stop.
8. Avoid the "hard-sell." It will offend the reader.
9. Don't write an ad for the competition. Benefits and selling points should be specific, not generic.
10. Urge the reader to act.

Layout And Design

The visual appeal of your ad is important. For a long time, mail order ads looked like somebody cooked them up at the kitchen table and had the kids draw them out by hand. They were sloppy, with too many words and extravagant promises that made the reader wary.

In today's educated society that won't work. Mail order advertising must affirm that:

1. **Your company is honest.**
2. **Your products are reliable.**
3. **Your offer is believable.**
4. **You are licensed to do business.**

(Most publications won't print your ad if you do not have a business license.)

The appearance of your ad also says a lot about you. Make the message a positive one. Using illustrations or photographs is helpful, but will raise the cost as they must first be prepared as "halftones" or made "camera ready" before the publication can print them. Sometimes the mere layout of the ad can provide a pleasing visual appearance without your having to contract for art or photographs.

Look at the ads for SMI in Figure 7.7. (Both ads have proven very successful.) They utilize a special technique — neither of them explains exactly what it is that SMI is selling. You *must* respond to find out. In Figure 7.7b the advertising director artfully weaves in plenty of white space with a variety of type styles and type sizes, to make the ad pleasing to the eye. Two different response methods are offered — a coupon and a toll free number.

Figure 7.7a uses a different format and less white space. As in Figure 7.7b, two different response methods are offered. But, in the first example, a personal testimonial is also introduced.

Both ads draw your eye from one point to the next, as the message follows a path from headline to call for action.

If you use pictures or graphics, try to space them out with the copy. Sketch a rough of the ad first (or have the creative department of an agency or the publisher help you do this). Work for balance and rhythm, without losing continuity. Pictures should emphasize a point, or substitute for a word. Sometimes they can even be used to illustrate an abstract point, as in the photograph of two fingers used by Avis to call attention to their status as the number two car renter behind Hertz.

When the rough is completed, you may want to turn the job over to a professional (an agency, or your publisher's creative department) to prepare the mechanical. This involves typesetting and photostating, then "pasting-up" the pieces on a board for a final photostat or "camera ready" copy.[9]

*Be sure to **OK the proof** before your ad goes to press.* Check carefully the phone number, name, address, and other relevant details. Many new advertisers skip this step, and a lot of strange ads get printed every week. Take time to approve it before you print it!

Action Now!

The purpose of the headline is to entice readers to look at the copy. The copy should make them want to act, to do something to solve the problem outlined by the ad, and to undertake the solution it presented. Don't leave it to chance. Give specific instructions. Look again at Figure 7.7a. The

Figure 7.7a

SEND FOR IT . . . FREE

THINK & GROW RICH

AN ALL TIME CLASSIC CASSETTE AND VALUABLE ADDITION TO YOUR CASSETTE LIBRARY

SMI INTERNATIONAL, INC., the world's largest and leading producer of motivation, training, and management programs is looking for people who want to own and manage their own profitable business.

Along with your free cassette, we will send you information about the SMI business opportunity.

To get your cassette, just call toll free, or mail the coupon. Our advertising department will send it to you immediately.

SMI now has over 26 years of successful experience in the industry. Let us explain how you can become a part of our growing organization.

CALL TOLL FREE
1-800-433-1003

Please send me without cost or obligation a copy of THINK AND GROW RICH on cassette tape, and information about your business opportunity.

⊘SMI®

SMI INTERNATIONAL, INC.
P.O. Box 2506, Dept. IC 10-7
Waco, Texas 76702-2506

Name _____

Address _____

City _____

State _____ Zip Code _____

Home Phone _____ AC _____

Business Phone _____ AC _____

Offer good in
the Continental
U.S.A. only.

Reprinted with permission of SMI International and Advertising Marketing Associates, Waco, Texas.

Source: Inc. Magazine.

advertiser gives you the opportunity to "CALL TOLL FREE" or to fill out a coupon, requesting a free copy of the cassette tape and information about the opportunity SMI is selling.

When your offer requires the reader to send in money to place an order, explain what to do and when to do it. *Make it easy to buy.* Space permitting, include alternative response devices as SMI does, such as a toll-free number *and* a clip-out coupon. (Experience has shown that toll-free numbers do better *as long as there is someone to answer them.*) Remember, magazines have a unique life of their own. Your company's image and credibility will suffer if you run ads for short-term telephone service or lines, and then cancel the service as soon as the bulk of the orders come in.

Code your response devices so that you can track the customer's response, especially if you are testing different ads or techniques at one

Figure 7.7b

Reprinted with permission of SMI International and Advertising Marketing Associates, Waco, Texas.

Source: Inc. Magazine.

time. One method commonly employed by advertisers is to use a department number (see the address in Figure 7.6) or room number which is really a fictional number that identifies the advertising source. Mail addressed to you in that manner alerts you to the origin of the advertisement. With telephone responses, have the operator ask the respondent a simple question such as, "Where did you hear about us?"

Review Your Priorities

When the ad is finished, look it over. Ask yourself if it will command attention. Does it point out benefits and specific features? Does it answer the question, "What's in it for me?"

Is your ad exciting? Enticing? Will the reader feel compelled to sample your product, or will the ad turn her off? Is the ad honest, objective, *believable*?

Before the ad goes to the typesetter or appears in a publication, make sure it gives the right message. Ask friends or employees to read it and make suggestions. Keep in mind, however, that you are still the best judge of your own material. You know your product and your prospect better than does anyone else. Advice is helpful, but in the end, it is your pocketbook that pays for the advertising. Listen and learn all you can, but keep the final say for yourself.[9]

CALCULATING THE COST OF NEWSPAPER ADVERTISING

It is possible to run ads that pull and still lose money. Often the problem is the choice of publication. Should you decide to use newspaper advertising, try the following test before making an initial selection.

Milline Rate

To find out how much your ad will cost per reader, calculate the milline rate by multiplying the line rate (amount charged for each line of copy) by one million, then divide the result by the circulation. Contrast the milline rate of one paper with that of another to find the best rate.

$$\frac{\text{Line rate X } 1,000,000}{\text{Total circulation}} = \text{Milline rate}$$

	1	2	3
Circulation:	250,000	400,000	750,000
Line rate:	$0.95	$1.20	$1.90
Milline rate:	$3.80	$3.00	$2.53

If you are considering a paper that charges by the *word* rather than by the line, use the same formula, substituting word rate for line rate to calculate the milword rate. Be careful not to compare milword rates with milline rates. The results won't make any sense.

Use either of these formulas as a *rough comparison* only. You will also need to consider the *quality* of the publication as well as the type of reader it attracts. A cheaper reader cost may not be your best choice.

Most advertisers test their ads by running them in several different magazines or periodicals and then comparing the results. The decision to continue a print ad depends on the relationship of these ratios. After running your ads in one or more publications, calculate how effective they are by computing the following costs.

Response Cost

Although you may have an exciting number of replies, are they worth the cost? To find out, divide the total cost of the ad by the number of replies sent in.

Be careful where you put the zeros! In the following example, both ads cost $75. The first resulted in 820 replies, at a cost of 9 1/2 cents apiece, an acceptable ratio. In the second example, however, each reply cost the advertiser almost a dollar. This ad is far too expensive and not worth continuing unless an unusually high number of responses are also sales. Since the normal ratio for sales to responses is between 3 and 5 percent, the second example does not appear to be cost effective.

	Example 1	Example 2
$\dfrac{\text{Cost of ad}}{\text{replies}}$	$\dfrac{\$75.00}{820} = \$0.091$	$\dfrac{\$75.00}{82} = \$0.91$

Percent of Return

Replies mean your ad generated interest, but the big question is, *"Did it sell?"* To find out what percentage of your responses resulted in a sale, add two zeros to the number of sales and divide by the number of replies you received. If the sales in Example 1 were 205, that would mean a 25 percent return, which is unusually high. In Example 2, the percent of return was just under 5 percent, or about average.

	Example 1	Example 2
$\dfrac{\text{sales }(+00)}{\text{replies}}$	$\dfrac{20500}{820} = 25\%$	$\dfrac{400}{82} = 4.88\%$

Cost Per Sale

Now we can compute the cost of each sale by dividing the total cost of the ad by the number of sales.

	Example 1	Example 2
$\dfrac{\text{Cost of ad}}{\text{sales}}$	$\dfrac{\$75.00}{205} = \$0.37$	$\dfrac{\$75.00}{4} = \$18.75$

Analyzing this information, we find that the ad in Example 1 was well within an acceptable cost range in terms of the number of replies, but had unusually high sales (25 percent), resulting in a low cost per sale.

Example 2, on the other hand, was expensive to produce when viewed by the number of responses. The number of sales per reply was only average, resulting in a cost per sale of $18.75. Assuming that ad number two is identical with ad number one, the publication used for Example 2 should be dropped. The one used in Example 1 should be continued.

Direct marketing is a numbers game. To win at it, you must track each effort carefully, weed out the ones that are weak, and put your time and money into the ones that have a proven track record.

ENDNOTES

1. *Writer's Market*, published annually by Writer's Digest Books and distributed by Prentice Hall, is also available at most major bookstores for about $18.95. It lists all publications by category and gives a brief description of content and editorial requirements, thus giving you insight into the publication. Many listings also give demographic information about readers, which will further help you to identify if the publication's readership fits your buyer profile. *Literary Marketplace*, also published annually, is a comprehensive guide which includes information about book publishers as well as magazine publishers. Most major booksellers also carry it; however, as it costs over $50 per issue, the best resource is the public library.

2. If the *Directory of Magazines with Classified Ads* is not available through your local library, it can be ordered from SpeciaList, 134 Manchestor Road, Ballwin, MO 63001. The directory lists the name, address, circulation figures, and line or word rates for each publication.

3. *The New York Times Magazine*, March 9, 1958.

4. Media kits almost always include a demographic profile of the publication's readership, along with the rates for display advertising, and classified advertising, if they have it. Most kits also include a chart or diagram showing the actual size of various display ads (1/2 page, 1/3 page, 1/4 page, etc.), and explain extra charges for special type sizes, halftones, layout, and any other services the magazine provides.

5. Contract rates are based on multiple insertions—usually 12 times for a monthly publication, 52 times for a weekly, and so on. If a contract advertiser cancels prior to the end of the contract, the publication will usually "short rate" him, billing for the difference between the more economical contract rate and the single insertion rate. Be careful, though, because agency or national contract rates could be higher than one-time or local rates. Always check rates very carefully before agreeing to a contract.

6. Contact Dependable Lists, Inc., 257 Park Ave., New York, NY 10010, for their brochure about co-op mailings and specialized inserts.

7. A list of local direct marketing organizations appears in Appendix B of this book. For additional information about co-op mailings, contact the Direct Marketing Association, 6 East 43rd St., New York, NY 10017, telephone (212) 689-4977.

8. The ad appeared in the May 26, 1987, issue of *Sports Illustrated*. Reprint permission granted by Timex Corporation. Ironman® Triathlon is a registered trademark of the Hawaiian Triathlon Corporation.

9. To save money, many advertisers design the rough themselves; take it to a typesetter for typesetting, paying the typesetter for a layout; and then send it to the publication. Of course, in newspaper advertising, the creative department of the paper will likely do this for you. For magazine advertising, however, you will probably be asked to submit "camera ready" copy, which means a final photostat, ready for printing.

TELEMARKETING

8

"Every day telephone salespeople place more than 7 million calls and sell more than $30 million worth of products, ranging from swimming pools to life insurance."
— G. Scott Osborne, author of
Electronic Data Marketing[1]

In every direct marketing technique, it is what's up front that counts. After that first glance, or in this case, first few words, the fate of your presentation is set. When a prospect chooses to ignore printed advertising, he throws it away. When she doesn't want to watch your televised commercial or hear you on the radio, she turns you off. Rarely, however, does she hang up on you when you call.

Unlike most other forms of direct marketing, telemarketing gives you a second chance. It's not a big one—most professional telemarketers say you only have about 15 seconds to get a prospect's attention and confidence. But, if she stays on the line long enough to hear your initial opening, you still have an opportunity to open communication.

The best tool you have (in fact, the *only* tool you have) is your voice. A pleasing telephone voice, one filled with tones of interest, concern, and desire to communicate with the customer will go a long way toward closing a sale. Conversely, no matter how good your product or how reliable your company, if your phone manners are surly, or your voice tired, frustrated, and dejected, making a sale will be an uphill job.

A SMILE GOES A LONG WAY!

Many sales trainers teach their pupils to practice telephoning in front of a mirror *before* they pick up the instrument. Try this test. Sit in front of a blank wall, pick up the phone, and repeat the following sales track.

> "Mr. Brown? This is Tracy from the Ajax Cleaners. Would you like an opportunity to have your entire office cleaned this week at a 50 percent savings?"

Imagine you are seated at the telephone with a list of 200 names in front of you, and imagine repeating this message to all of the names on that list. How many times could you do it without sounding bored? The trick, of course, is to make each call sound like the first one.

Now, sit in front of a mirror, smile at yourself, and picture the person you are calling smiling back at you. Try the exercise again. When you pick up the telephone this time, the smile in your voice will come through. You will sound so much better to your caller than if you were speaking in a bored, uninterested voice.

Of course, there is a lot more to telemarketing than smiling at a mirror. Like all other forms of direct marketing, this is a professional sales technique. If you plan to incorporate telemarketing into your overall marketing plan (or use it exclusively), it is important that your operators be trained in the fine art of telephone sales. The closing ratio you will enjoy can be very high—higher even than direct mail or print advertising, primarily because of the personal contact between seller and buyer. A high ratio, however, depends on skill and technique. Not luck.

A common mistake many businesses make is to take untrained people or their own secretarial staff, and put them on the phones. Invariably the results are disappointing, and the manager who made the decision to use untrained people decides, "Telemarketing is not for us. It just doesn't produce."

Figure 8.1

Smile. It makes it easier to sell!

PREPLANNING

Part of your success certainly comes from your calling list. However, costly professional lists don't always spell success. In fact, some companies who have a closing ratio that exceeds 20 percent work strictly from the phone book! Obviously there is a lot more to telemarketing than working a list of hot prospects.

The real secret to successful telemarketing is preplanning your sales efforts from start to finish. A well-planned telemarketing campaign works best when the people conducting it are comfortable and pleasant on the phone; skillful at handling objections and questions; and very knowledgeable about the company, its products, services, history, and basic philosophy. Everyone, even long-term employees, will benefit from a training program before you begin a telephone sales campaign. Several companies, most notably the major telephone companies, offer extensive workshops which can help train your employees.[2] In addition, several books have been published on the subject.[3] However, before you embark upon a training program, there are several decisions you must make regarding the objectives of a telemarketing campaign.

Company Philosophy

Time is money. How much of both are you willing to expend to gain a sale? One telemarketing philosophy places its primary importance on time. Not a second of it should be wasted. Unless an operator is in the bathroom or taking a very short lunch break, every phone should be in operation and every operator in hot pursuit of a sale. Prospects are never called back a second time.

In the traditional telemarketing philosophy, however, emphasis is on making the sale, no matter how long it takes to do so. Objections are answered carefully. Second, even third and fourth calls are sometimes made to the same prospect. Direct mail is often used as a backup to the telemarketing effort.

Emphasis on time. In this type of situation, the company philosophy is:

> If this person isn't interested, don't waste your time. Go on to the next one who is.

Figure 8.2

Every phone should be in operation and every operator in hot pursuit of a sale.

The key to success in this case is knowing when to hang up. Generally, operators are instructed to disconnect the call and start another one if:

- the phone rings more than three times.
- the prospect has no interest in what you have to say.
- the prospect offers objections.
- you are put on hold for more than 30 seconds.
- the prospect is rude.

Callers work the yellow pages, or a Polk or zip code directory, or some other listing of names by geographic area. After sales are closed, a supervisor telephones the prospect to verify the information, and a "runner" or driver is sent out to collect the money and get a signed contract.

Telemarketing efforts like this are often used to sell discount coupon books for local services (drycleaners, hair dressers, delis, video rentals, etc.), or to market entertainment businesses such as movie theaters, restaurants, or amusement centers. High-volume calling also works for the distribution of newspapers, magazines, special foods (lobster, steaks, oranges), and household supplies from light bulbs to ladders.

In most cases *operator turnover is high*. They burn out quickly. However, training costs are negligible, because there really isn't any, except "on-the-job-training," and the pay scale is correspondingly low. High-volume telemarketing firms tend not to build long-term employee relationships or loyalty. Operators are easy to find, and easy to replace. Telephone salespeople are hired primarily because they have a positive, "upbeat" personality, and seem friendly and comfortable with the telephone. They usually start out by observing other callers in action for an hour or two—maybe even a whole day, then work the first week at reduced pay, and finally go on to an above-minimum wage rate with a bonus arrangement for so many completed sales.

Closing rates are also high. Until she burns out, a good operator can make 200 or more calls a day *if she knows when to hang up*. She can also close between 25 and 40 percent of those calls. Her typical sale is a compulsive buyer, often young, female, and a frequent telephone caller herself.

As a rule, the sales interview also requires the operator to obtain demographic information about each purchaser so that the company's database and buyer profile can constantly be updated. When one geographic area is exhausted, another is opened, and the callers start on a new directory. Generally this type of operation works from one directory and from one location for an extended period of time, taking advantage of outgoing WATS lines[4] or other long-distance services for their telephone needs.

This is a fast-paced, high-volume sales technique. The time from the moment the sale is confirmed until the contract is delivered is often less than an hour. This type of telemarketing is often used in conjunction with other forms of direct marketing such as direct mail.

Emphasis on sales. The more traditional, professional form of telemarketing is particularly useful in fund-raising, ticket sales, and consumer services such as family photography and health insurance, and business-to-business marketing. This type of telemarketing depends on a carefully orchestrated sales track. The sales cycle takes a longer time to complete, but profits are high, and long-term loyalty is often built between companies and their clients, and their employees.

A lot of bank card companies are now using this technique. In one thirty-day period, for instance, a well-known financial institution offered a plan to supplement medical insurance with payments directly to the card holder in the event of a claim, a discount home-shopping service, and special auto insurance rates, all of which could be billed directly to the card-holder's account merely by answering "Yes" to the telemarketer's call.

Unlike high-volume telemarketing, telephone operators are usually much better trained and much better paid. They are usually well versed in telephone techniques and can skillfully turn objections into benefit statements. They are prepared to call back as many times as necessary to close a sale. Sales tracks, although "canned," are so well learned that it never sounds as if the caller is "reading" a prepared presentation.

With this type of presentation, the company's philosophy is that a sale is always possible unless the customer flatly rejects it and hangs up. Although never rude or argumentative, as long as there is even a spark of interest from the prospect, the operator will pursue it.

Long-term relationships and repeat business are the rule rather than the exception. Service after the sale is as important as the sale itself, and the company and its operators will bend over backwards to insure a satisfied customer.

Seldom does a driver or runner rush out to get the money while the prospect is hot. Instead, billing is usually handled over the phone, by credit card. Sometimes goods are shipped C.O.D. or paid for when the customer comes in to use the service, as in family photography. Experience has shown that it is better to book the sale to a credit card if possible, although some companies will also send out a preposted return envelope for the customer to use for sending in a personal check.

Developing Sales Skills

Telemarketing is an audible appeal rather than a visual one. Most people, however, tend to be visual, so it takes some special skills to sell over the phone.

Word pictures.   The technique of painting "word pictures," or helping the customer to "see" what you are selling offers some unique selling opportunities to the telemarketer. Since space is not a factor (as it is in copywriting), you have an opportunity to explain your product in greater detail. By using strong action verbs, and colorful, expressive nouns and adjectives, you can easily describe how your products taste, look, and feel. Look at the sets of statements in Figure 8.3. In each pair, notice how the second one says so much more than the first. In each case, the caller, by using highly descriptive words, can help the prospect to visualize what she is selling.

Power words.   Certain special words will help you close sales. Look at the list of words in Figure 8.4. These are words that have a strong

Figure 8.3
Painting Word Pictures

1. It comes in red or blue. Which would you prefer?

   You can order it in a vivid, Christmas red, or we also have it in blue — sort of the color of the sky on a clear summer day. Would you like to order the red one, or does the blue sound better to you?

2. Wouldn't you like to have a nice framed color picture of your family?

   Your family's picture will be printed in full glowing color, on the finest quality paper. We will frame it in a beautiful gold frame, suitable for hanging on your living room wall, or placing on your mantle. We also have a lovely, burnished silver frame, if you would prefer that. This will make a thoughtful gift for grandparents or other family members, don't you think?

3. Our exercycle will help you lose weight.

   This exercycle is guaranteed to make you look slimmer and more attractive after only one week, and you won't even feel sore after using it, if you follow the simple directions.

4. This course will help you plan your investments.

   People who have taken this course say they feel smarter right away. They even start reading the financial pages every day, and a lot of them say they can predict the market after just a few of our lessons!

5. We have eight shows this season, and all of them are very good. I'm sure you will enjoy them.

   All eight plays are exciting. Three of them are done by our Shakespeare company, who, as you know, enjoy a national reputation as one of the finest Shakespeare companies in the United States. Two more are lively new off-Broadway comedies destined to go on to Broadway. A local playwright wrote and directed "Summer's Eve" which has had excellent reviews. And the last play is our major production for the season. The sets and music are outstanding — colorful, contemporary, and truly a treat. I know you will find all eight plays a rewarding experience.

In each set of statements, the second one "paints a word picture," which makes it much easier to "see" what the operator is selling.

Figure 8.4
POWER WORDS

ADMIRE	NEEDED
BEAUTIFUL	POPULAR
COURAGEOUS	POWERFUL
COURTEOUS	PROGRESS
DURABLE	REPUTATION
EXCELLENT	SAFE
FREE	STATUS
GENUINE	SUCCESSFUL
GUARANTEE	THOUGHTFUL
HELPFUL	TIMELY
INDEPENDENT	VALUABLE

emotional appeal, and draw the prospect into the sale on a personal level. (Review the sections in Chapter 2 that deal with psychographics, and the things that motivate people to buy.) Power words are "hot buttons" which stress benefits such as *value, reputation,* and *independence.* Look at the statements again in Figure 8.3. See if you can spot the power word in each second statement.

   Listen. What your prospect does *not* say is often as important as what he or she *does* say. Learn to listen for hidden meanings and objections. This is not as easy as it sounds. How often have you been right in the middle of a thought or a word when somebody interrupted you as if you hadn't been speaking at all? When someone else is talking, do you really listen, or are you, as most of us are, thinking about what you are going to say next? Think back over the last time you were busy, really busy, and someone asked you a question. Did you have to ask "What?" once or twice before the speaker's question sunk in? Did you hear the question at all?

Ask probing questions. The answers to these questions will give you a pocketful of clues that you can use to make a sale. Suppose you were selling the series of eight plays described in the final set of statements in Figure 8.3. You opened the conversation with your name, and the fact that you were selling subscriptions for the winter season. You then asked, "Would you like to purchase a subscription for the series?"

The prospect promptly replied, "I'm not interested."

If your company philosophy was time dependent, you would hang up at this point and try another number. In this case, however, because you are working a qualified list that says this prospect has a fairly high propensity to buy theater tickets (maybe he supports the opera, or an art foundation, or belongs to a civic theater group), you have a reasonable expectation of selling him a season ticket. So, you might respond by asking, "Are you interested in the theater, Mr. Jones? What was the last play you saw?"

In the example above, the first question is a **closed question**. That is, it can be answered only by a *yes* or a *no*. Asked alone, it leaves no opening to continue on to another objection or to obtain any further information from the prospect. The second question, however, which asks what play Mr. Jones last saw, is an **open question**. It presents him with an opportunity to tell you something about himself, something which will be helpful in understanding why he said he was not interested. By probing gently with several open questions in a row, you can find out a great deal about Mr. Jones, and each bit of information will help you sell him a season ticket, if there is any interest there at all.

Each time Mr. Jones answers one of your questions, his response indicates a growing interest in your proposition. With each answer he gives, you are closer and closer to making a sale. Lead him gently to the close by asking a few closed questions. Keep the mood positive, however; make sure your questions will elicit a "yes" from Mr. Jones.

"Do you belong to the community theater, Mr. Jones?" (You know he does, because you got his name from the community theater list.) He answers, "Yes."

"Have you had season tickets to the Broadway before?" you ask, knowing the answer to that one too, because his name is on the list of previous season ticket holders. "Then, wouldn't you like them again this year?" you probe hopefully.

Mr. Jones says, "Yes, I would. But we had some financial problems this year, and I really don't think we can afford it."

Aha. Now you know the *real* objection. It isn't lack of interest, as he first told you, but a price problem. Very seldom is the first answer the real objection. Unless you establish some rapport with the prospect, however, you will probably never know what the true objection is. Now, you can use your skill as a salesperson, and your knowledge of the company and its policies, to create a solution (a discount series) that will let him see some of the plays, which he obviously wants to do, and yet not strap him financially. By proposing the discounted series, you not only have made a sale, you also made a friend. Next year when it's time to sell season subscriptions again, Mr. Jones will be at the top of your list. And he will buy.

Identifying Your Customer

Most people can be loosely classified as one of four major *personality types*. Various schemes have been devised to name and categorize them, but for the most part, you can identify them as:

Analytical	Directive
Accommodating	Persuasive

Although most people are a combination of all of these qualities, one is usually dominant. An analytical engineer might drive you crazy trying to view something from every possible angle before reaching a decision about it. Or an accommodating person may agree with whatever you say, because that person doesn't want to hurt your feelings. Your neighbor down the street may be a company manager who carries his executive habits home with him, and directs every neighborhood project, from doghouse-building to the Fourth of July street parade. And of course, we all know the persuasive guy, the one who talked you into a used car you didn't want, or got you to hire twice as many kids for the summer youth project as you had planned to do.

Figure 8.5

Most people can be loosely classified as one of four major personality types.

A few probing questions should help you discover which type of personality you are dealing with. Usually. Most people are a conglomerate of all four types, however, and it is hard to pigeonhole them. If you can identify a few personality traits which indicate that your prospect leans toward one corner or another, it can be helpful. You can alter your style a little to accommodate hers, make her more comfortable, and close the sale with far less effort—on both of your parts.

Knowing what kind of person you are dealing with will also help you avoid a few major traps. As a rule, there are several things you should avoid in telephone sales. When you speak to your customers, don't:

- argue.
- badger.
- bully.
- use the word *but*.
- insult their intelligence.
- talk down to them.
- overwhelm them with technical terms.
- treat them rudely.

Flexibility.   Do take your prospect's attitudes and personality into consideration. If you are dealing with a directive type, don't waste time but get to the point quickly; let her think she is *controlling* the interview and leading you to a close. It will be surprisingly easy to sell her. If you are speaking with an accommodating woman, ask her how she feels, draw her out, try to get her to *suggest* what it is that she wants. And then supply it. Analytical people need to be presented with several viewpoints, and because they, like accommodators, have trouble reaching a decision, reach it for them. Give them a limited amount of time to fuss, then go for a direct close. Persuasive people, like most salespeople, are the easiest of all to sell. All you have to do is let them buy.

Technical talk.   Although it is not usually a good idea to use technical talk, there are exceptions. If your product, for example, is one aimed at engineers, and if you are talking to one, there is no reason why you can't talk to him in his own terms. If your product is pharmaceutical supplies, however, and you are talking to a drugstore manager, rather than to the pharmacist, technical jargon could be out of place. Unless you use terms your buyer can easily understand, he won't buy.

Don't argue.   Badgering or arguing with the customer is never productive. You will almost certainly make an enemy. If someone truly doesn't want what you have to offer and is fair enough to say so, then accept it gracefully and go on to the next person.

And never, never treat a customer rudely, no matter how rude that individual has been to you. If the speaker on the other end of the line is rude or obnoxious, it is that person's problem, not yours. Don't take it as a personal reflection on you. Ignore it, hang up, and call someone else who is more fun to talk with.

THE SALES CYCLE

If your marketing plan and company philosophy call for a long-term telemarketing approach, you and your operators will need to develop a sales track to follow. Although all types of telemarketing involve an opening and a close, the time-dependent form doesn't bother with handling objections or answering a great many questions. Instead, that method just moves on to the next name on the list. The longer form, however, works carefully through objections, viewing each one as a chance to cement the sale. Time is not a problem, and the operator uses as much of it as necessary to reach a mutually satisfactory conclusion to the phone call.

The Opening

Many telemarketing workshops suggest opening a sales call with a remark like one of the following:

> "Hi, Mr. Marks. How are you today?"

> "Mr. Marks, this is Tracy at Ajax Cleaners. Isn't this terrible weather we are having?"

> "How about those Padres? Wasn't that some game?"

These are all great ways to start a call, if you are talking to a friend, but since you have only about 15 seconds to get someone's attention in a telemarketing call, it seems a silly waste of time to open up with trite remarks like these. It's much better to get down to business, especially if your call is to a business person. Many people resent the intrusion of a phone call, particularly if they are busy. Until you know what type of personality you are dealing with, it is best to be friendly, but get straight to the point of the call.

> "Mr. Marks, this is Tracy at Ajax Cleaners, and we would like to offer you the chance to have your entire office cleaned at a 50 percent savings. It will take only a brief moment for me to explain the program to you."

If Mr. Marks says, "Not right now, I'm busy," find out when would be a better time to talk, and book it. Then call back at the agreed-upon time. Failing to follow through as promised is death to any telemarketing effort! This technique will help you get through the "secretarial screen" later. When you call back, you can say to the secretary, "I'm calling Bill back at his request."

If you can, try to make the opening personal as well as businesslike. Establish mutual interest right from the start by relating your remarks to the prospect, his business, or something else that is personal. In most cases, because you have a qualified prospect list in front of you, you already know something about the prospect which will help you put the call on a personal level.

"Mr. Jones, I understand you have been a season ticket subscriber with us before. I am calling to see if you would like the same number of tickets again this year."

"Mrs. Nantucket, since our project is similar to the music fund, the Coordinated Arts Council was hoping that you would be able to help us this year. May we count on you for a similar donation?"

If your product or service will offer your prospect a savings in time or money, or help him expand his market, you might try opening the conversation by telling him so. Appeal to his business judgment, which should also flatter him. Flattery, if used carefully, is a good technique. Just remember the "don't" list, and if you decide to use flattery, do it subtly. You don't want to come across as talking down to the prospect. Trying to sound like an expert when you are not can cause problems, too.

"What do *you* know about my industry?" he may reply. No matter how you respond, you will sound defensive and argumentative.

Benefit Selling

Unless you get very lucky (and telemarketing doesn't owe much to luck; it's more a matter of skill), your prospect will probably not jump through the phone to take you up on your offer. Instead, you will have an opportunity to list all the selling features and benefits of whatever it is that you have to sell.

Selling-features talk about the product. They describe it, tell what it is, what it does, how it works. If you are selling color photos, for instance, they may be cheaper, glossier, larger, crisper, or whatever.

When confronted with all of this information, the customer is likely to respond, "So what?"

In Chapter 2, you learned that the first question a prospect asks is "What's in it for me?" Telling her that your photo service will give her a nice, clear, clean, crisp picture doesn't do a whole lot for her. Telling her that your crisp photos are finished so that they will last for years, staying clear and bright even when locked up in a photo album or dresser drawer without any light, so that she and her family may continue to enjoy them for a long time, is telling her something that will offer a *benefit*.

Benefit statements answer the question, "What's in it for me?" They take a selling feature and explain how it affects the customer. By asking the prospect a few questions, you will be able to point out benefits that appeal specifically to the person.

The best time to make a list of benefit statements is *not* while you are on the phone talking to the customer. The time to figure out what benefits your product offers is *before* you pick up the phone. Refer to the statements in Example 3 in Figure 8.3 on page 167. We are selling an exercycle, and we know that it offers the following features:

- lightweight
- built-in chronometer
- adjustable seat
- folds up
- digital read-out
- aluminum
- toe straps
- adjustable handlebars
- electronic speed-set
- complete instructions

Each of these points is a selling feature, and most of them won't mean much to your customer unless you can translate these cold facts into benefits.

"The seat is adjustable, so you can use the exercycle for a longer period of time without any discomfort. Adjustable handlebars make it more comfortable, too. This bike is aluminum, so it won't rust if you have to store it outside part of the time. Because it is lightweight, and folds up, it hardly takes up any space at all, and is easy to store, no matter where you decide to keep it. Electronic speed-setting and digital read-outs take the guesswork out of using it. Just preset it to the prescribed distance and terrain—hilly or flat, for example (complete instructions are enclosed with it), and you are on your way to losing weight easily and quickly. Because it is so easy to move, you can even set it up in front of the TV and pedal while you watch your favorite show!"

Suppose you are selling computer supplies and your company offers paper that has invisible perforations. How does this benefit the customer? (Smooth, unragged edges make paper look like stationery instead of torn-off sheets from continuous-form printout.) You also sell snap-in, preinked printer ribbons. (Easy to install. Keeps hands clean.)

If your employees are new to the company, or if you are using an outside telemarketing firm to do your telemarketing for you, make sure you *supply the operators with a complete list of selling points and benefits.* Take time to look at your product from the customer's point of view. Look for things that will meet the motivators shown in Figure 2.7 in Chapter 2.

Sometimes the benefits will be obscure, such as the fact that the exercycle can be pulled in front of the TV. But if your probing questions discover that this woman likes to watch TV and that she doesn't want to go out to exercise at a gym because she feels she is "too fat," then offering her a chance to work out at home, in private, in front of her TV is a nice benefit.

Objections

Much has been said about objections. They are the major cause of fear and frustration in most salespeople, and they don't need to be. Objections are really questions, and as such, *they indicate an interest in what you are selling.* If the prospect wasn't interested, he or she wouldn't take the time to offer an objection!

Of course, you need to spot the difference between outright refusal and a qualified objection. Refusal sounds like, "No. I do not want to buy your product. Thank you anyway. Goodbye." followed by a click as the prospect hangs up the telephone.

Objections sound like, "I don't really want one," followed by a pause, while the prospect waits for you to continue the conversation. There are several kinds of objections, and several ways to handle them. Most objections are one of four main types.

1. Price.
2. Postponement.
3. Product.
4. Personal.

The first two objections are the easiest to handle. If you can justify the price because of superior benefits, you have a sale. The second is not too bad, either. Usually the individual wants to discuss the offer with a spouse, or partner, or another employee. You may have to remake the sale, from another personality point-of-view, but since you already have the first person on your side (he told the other person about it didn't he?) you have an ally. Your job is much easier.

With the third type, the customer is balking because of something about the product or service itself. "Thank you, Marie," Mr. Biddle says, "but I'm really not interested in a prepaid legal plan. Our own legal department handles that sort of thing." If you can find a loophole — does his legal department handle auto injury cases, for example — you may still have a sale. This may also be a legitimate no sale, and if you see you really cannot provide a real benefit, don't waste his time or yours. Thank him for his time, and hang up. (Many telemarketers might use this opportunity to

Figure 8.6

If she thinks she's too fat to exercise in public, offering her a chance to work out at home, in private, might be a nice benefit.

ask if Mr. Biddle knows anybody who *would* be interested. After all, if he was polite enough to listen, he might have an idea of somebody else who might need the service. It's worth a try.)

The fourth type of objection is a tough one. For some reason the prospect doesn't care for your company. The problem could be past reputation, or something someone else has said about your policies or products. If is *very important to find out why* the prospect feels this way. Obviously there has been a misunderstanding of some sort, and it has to be cleared up before you can continue with the sale. Try to establish communication (after all, the gripe isn't with you personally, it's with the company). Ask questions and try to find out what caused the problem. At this point, the problem may have to be referred to another department, but if the problem can be resolved to the mutual satisfaction of the company and the prospect, you can get back on the sales track again.

No matter which type of objection you hear first, the first one usually isn't the real one. It's a red herring. The prospect, after all, doesn't know you and has no reason to trust you, so why should he confide in you? (This is especially true if your offer is something he wants, but thinks he cannot afford.)

By probing with open and closed questions, you can find out what the problem really is, verify that you understand what it is, answer the objection, and then point out a benefit of your product that will meet that need. The path looks like this:

OBJECTION ▷

        ◁ Listen carefully to the problem.
        ◁ Verify that you understand it.
        ◁ Answer the objection.
        ◁ Show a corresponding benefit.
        ◁ Ask for agreement.

OBJECTION ▷

Let's take a look again at Mr. Jones and the theater ticket problem. Here's how the salesperson might handle that sale:

PROSPECT	SALESPERSON
We really can't afford to go out much this year. We're on a pretty tight budget. ▷	I can sympathize with that. You've really enjoyed the theater in the past, though, haven't you? ◁
Yes, we have. It's too bad we can't do it again this year. ▷	If I can show you a way that it would be possible, would you be interested? ◁
Sure. I guess so. ▷	If you buy season subscription tickets, you will have several preplanned, prepaid evenings to look forward to, without putting an unexpected strain on your budget. We can set it up so that, although you won't get the entire series this year, you will still be able to see several really good plays, *and* you will keep the excellent seats you have had for several years. Would that work for you? ◁
How much would it cost? ▷	

Right here, you've got a sale. You will still have to answer a price objection, but Mr. Jones wants those tickets. Once you've justified the price, you will have a satisfied customer.

This sales example takes advantage of an objection technique known as the "feel, felt, found" method. In it, the salesperson responds to an objection with statements that sound like,

> I know how you *feel*.
> I've *felt* that way too.
> But we've *found* that . . . .

The problem with using this technique is that it has been done so often, many people are put off when they hear it. Try to avoid using the actual terms, *feel, felt*, and *found*; instead, substitute other phrases that accomplish the same purpose, without offending the prospect. Look again at the preceding example and see how the salesperson handled it.

As soon as you answer an objection, get right back on the sales track. Your presentation should lead straight to the close. Before you proceed, however, make sure that you really have solved the problem raised by the objection. Get some agreement, then go on.

Close

If you've done your job right, closing is just a formality. Surprisingly, a lot of salespeople have trouble at this point. They are uncomfortable asking for the money. Or, worse yet, they don't know when to shut up. By now, you should have answered all of the customer's objections. The only thing left to do is write up the sale and log the customer into the customer list.

Don't oversell. If, at some point, your customer says, "That sounds fine—what do you need from me?" then stop right there and take the order. If she indicates she is in a hurry and says something like, "I have an appointment in ten minutes; do you have all the information you need?" go for it. The sale is closed.

Implied close. In this case, you assume the sale is going to proceed with no further objections, and begin to write it up. You would close by saying something like this:

> "Do you want to take advantage of the discount and order all three now, or shall we ship just one and call you back about the other two?"

"Normally we send this out by parcel post. Will that be OK?"

"Which will work better for you, Monday morning or Thursday afternoon?"

"How many do you want?"

In each of these cases, you have asked an open-ended question which has only a limited number of answers, and none of them are "No."

Order close.   This is another version of the implied close. Instead of asking for an answer, you begin taking the order, using the information from your calling list together with the things the customer has told you.

"Are you still at 1234 Fourth Avenue, Mr. Jones?"

"Let's see, your seats are row 6, seats 12 and 14, is that right?"

"Will this go on your Visa card again, or do you want us to put it on another card?"

In these examples, you never really asked for confirmation of the order. Instead, you began filling it in as soon as Mr. Jones sounded like he was ready. The danger with either of these assumptive closes is that if you move too soon, you will make the customer angry, and you will have to backtrack a long way before you can work back up to this point.

Direct close.   On this one, you ask a closed-end question, one that can be answered only with a yes or a no. If you are fairly sure the sale is going to happen, this works well. But asking for the sale and getting a "No" means starting all over again, that is, if the prospect will let you. Most times the prospect won't.

Whichever closing method you choose, try not to hang up before the customer hangs up. The click can be annoying, and after you have worked so hard to achieve a positive atmosphere, it is hardly good business to leave the customer with the feeling that you have already forgotten about her in the rush to get on with the next call!

AFTER THE SALE

The sale does not end with the click of the receiver—no matter who hung up first. Two things should take place immediately, before you make another call. The order should be checked for accuracy and forwarded to the right people for filling. Often this means no more than sticking the order blank in the proper slot or pile on your desk. And the database you are updating should be marked—which could simply mean putting a red check beside a name in the phone book.

Filling the Order

In a high-volume, quick sales telemarketing operation, the supervisor's follow-up call should take place right away. Many time-dependent telemarketing firms conclude a sales call by saying, "My supervisor will call in a few minutes to verify the correct address and other delivery information. And our delivery driver will be there within the hour. Will you be home?"

The long-term philosophy, however, allows time for checking credit and ensuring that the shipping department has the correct information to fill the order. With this more traditional telemarketing style, a definite program should be established to track the sale from the moment the operator hangs up until the merchandise is delivered and the payment banked. If telemarketing is being used in conjunction with another system, such as direct mail, the two efforts should be coordinated. And, in all cases, it is important to make sure that lists are not duplicated and that satisfied customers who have already been contacted are not contacted again (by the same or by some other salesperson) with the same offer.

Accountability

The rules of direct marketing dictate that: 1) a sales effort must be part of an interactive system and, 2) the response to that system must be measurable. The telephone interchange between buyer and seller that either does or does not result in a sale is certainly an interactive exchange. To follow through on the second rule, you must record and measure the responses to your sales efforts.

Let's say, for example, that you are a time-dependent telemarketer and that your company distributes magazines. During the course of one day, 10 operators, each working six hours, make an average of 150 calls each. That's 1,500 calls a day. If each operator closes 30 calls, and the two best people each make 200 calls and close 55 apiece, the overall average closing ratio is 21 percent. For those two top callers, the ratio is 27.5 percent. When your company moves into a new territory, assuming the buyer profile and list source is the same, or if you decide to use the same type of list again for a similar marketing effort, you can reasonably expect similar results.

Perhaps you are a traditional telemarketing firm, a business-to-business supplier of office products. Your calling list is about 70 percent previous buyers, a good solid base; 15 percent rented, to supply fresh, new names; and 15 percent response names, people who responded to a print ad which included both an 800 toll-free number and a mail-back coupon. As you complete each call, you will update your customer base, noting a reorder on the part of the names on the house list and adding new names to it from the rented names and outside responses that you got. This procedure will enable you to track the effectiveness of the rented list against your house list and to compare the response of both lists to those of the print ad. (Review Chapter 3 for more about testing lists, and Chapter 11 to find out more about testing and comparing results of advertising methods.)

SUMMARY

Telemarketing offers the direct marketer some unique opportunities. Like direct selling, it allows the seller to interact with each prospect on a personal level. Objections can be countered on the spot, and benefit statements can be designed to meet each customer's own special needs. It is fast, there is no travel involved, and the entire process is controlled from start to finish. The seller initiates the call and follows a preplanned path. If the prospect turns out to be a poor one, the seller can hang up and call another person who is more likely to buy. Cost of reach is comparatively low, and because callers are working from a target market list — either a house list or an external one — measuring response can be very precise.

ENDNOTES

1. A Spectrum Book. Published in 1984 by Prentice-Hall in Englewood Cliffs, NJ.
2. To find out about a telephone sales workshop in your own area, contact the local telephone company. Additional information can be obtained also through the American Telemarketing Association in Glenview, Illinois, telephone (312) 724-7700, or see the lists in the Appendices at the end of this book.

3. Check the local library, or contact the Direct Marketing Association in New York for information about their own publications on telemarketing.

4. WATS is an acronym for Wide Area Telephone Service. Once a rather simple concept whereby you purchased blocks of time at a discount rather than pay for the calls individually, it is now an extremely complicated concept. To find the best rates for long distance service, you must contact AT&T and the other competitive services as well as your local telephone service representative. As of this writing, you will find that:

1. Calls within your service area are billed through your local telephone service.

2. Calls originating from or terminating within your service area but coming from or going to an area outside it, can be billed through the local telephone company if AT&T is used. Calls within your state would be handled much the same way.

3. Calls outside your state, incoming or outgoing, can be handled by AT&T or a competitive service. Since one company may be more competitive in one area than in another (even when those areas are adjacent), you may want to research each area where you plan to make calls.

4. No one individual, from one service, will give you a straight answer, because, although many are friendly and helpful, not one of them has access to enough information to put a long-distance calling plan together for you.

(You may want to hire a full-time individual, just to research how to save money on long-distance service. It's probably the simplest solution!)

9

RADIO

"Words, sounds, music, even silence are woven together by the [radio] writer to produce a moving tapestry of thought, image, and persuasion. Connection with the listener is direct, personal, emotional, primal."

—Bob Stone

Radio offers some unique possibilities. It already has a built-in demographic profile, so you know what kind of buyer will be listening. If your buyer profile matches the station's, you are halfway home. Also, it has been proven through various educational studies that people tend to remember things better if they *hear* them than if they see or read them.

LOYAL LISTENERS

Radio listeners are loyal. They tune in, and stay tuned in, to a particular station, even when some commercials are irritating, or one particular dee jay is not necessarily a favorite. Radio listeners don't switch channels like television viewers do, frequently changing from one program to another.

Many listeners set their alarms to wake them up with their favorite radio station. Radio goes where you go. It follows you into your car, the elevator, your office. It even follows you home and to bed. A radio is portable; it goes to the beach, the mall, or on a morning run strapped to your head and hip. Radio programs bring news, tell you what kind of day to expect, warn you when to take an umbrella or roll back over and sleep through a snowstorm, and entertain you with your favorite music all day long. When schools are closed, when a riptide is running which prevents surfing, or there is a speed trap on the street you always take to work, how do you find out in time? You tune into your favorite radio station, of course.

Because of the number of station-sponsored contests, and other promotions that involve them, listeners often stay with their radios all day long. Proof of their loyalty is in the number of calls each station gets during the day. Requests, promotions, call-ins, and popular opinion polls are all devices that entice listeners to interact with specific stations and programs. Even in your

Figure 9.1

Radio listeners are loyal. Most of them have a favorite station and a favorite dee jay.

car, you are not immune. Traveling along a busy freeway, or, perhaps, a quiet side street, you might be approached by a boldly lettered van festooned with antennae, advertising, and a giant loudspeaker announcing, "If you are driving a red Toyota with the license plate E12345, call XYZ in the next fifteen minutes and you will win $100!"

"What's your favorite radio station?" the dee jays ask. And the listeners jam the telephone lines to tell them.

Radio is community supportive. Local stations sponsor little league games, kid's soccer teams, park projects, summer work for teenagers, and charitable drives for the city, or special people within it. Dee jays show up at school dances, or talk about neighborhood projects on the air.

DEFINABLE DEMOGRAPHICS

Because it is so personal, you must take care that your spots, or commercials, are personal, too. Each station has a specific type of audience, and a corresponding segment of the radio audience. Your decision to advertise

Figure 9.2

If your license plate number is E12345, call XYZ in the next fifteen minutes to win $100!

on a particular station should be based on common demographics. You wouldn't want to advertise an acne medication on a classical music station, for example, and you wouldn't want to try to generate leads for a hospital medical plan on the rock station.

In San Diego, KIFM,[1] a local station whose programming includes jazz and soft rock, appeals to an upscale audience in the 25 to 54 age bracket. Restaurants, better clothing stores, jewelry stores, and dealers of luxury automobiles, in particular, enjoy success in their radio advertising on that station, as do banks and travel services. The station does not, however, do much advertising for surf boards or rock concerts. For a San Diego direct marketer, offering package trips to Hawaii, for example, this station would be an excellent choice, because its defined audience likes to travel, has the income to do it, and purchases that kind of package on a consistent basis.

Ratings

Media buyers select radio times based on ratings, just as they do for television. Both the advertisers and the stations themselves depend on a rating service to help them match product profiles to station demographics. Arbitron Ratings Company[2] in New York is used by most stations to supply radio listener profiles, and market share during various times of the day for every metropolitan (or rural) area across the country. (See their sample Radio Prototype in Figure 9.3.)

Advertising representatives of local radio stations will be happy to provide you with the demographics of their station upon request. You will find that even though the *overall* demographic is what you are looking for, certain times of the day will prove more responsive than others.

Prime time in radio is often referred to as "drive time" — the time in the morning and evening when commuters are in their cars, traveling to and from work. In the past, this had been a poor time for direct response advertising, for obvious reasons. The listener had to scramble around to write down a phone number and information about the product or service she wanted to order. Once near a phone, she had to interrupt her regular schedule (checking in at work, dashing off to the office, or arriving home to a houseful of hungry, screaming kids) to process the order. Not many orders happened in the time period immediately preceding or following drive time. And, like all forms of direct response media, the more time that elapses between seeing and buying, the less chance there is for a sale.

Car Telephones

Now there is a new wrinkle in the program. The car telephone, or cellular telephone, is fast becoming a standard item in many cars and trucks. Once reserved for emergency use or for the few who could afford them, car phones are now easily within reach of most commuters and salespeople. In many parts of the country, most notably the East and West Coasts, not only are car phones a status symbol, but they have progressed to the point where they are a necessity. For stations like KIFM in San Diego, this could be an important consideration, as a large (but as yet undetermined) percentage of their audience probably have car phones and use them.

Car phones make a great response device. Your audience is completely captive. If your prospect is sitting in a traffic jam on the freeway or speeding along the highway toward a morning sales call, and hears something interesting advertised on the radio, he has merely to push a single button to call the station (car phones can be preprogrammed to dial commonly used numbers), and place an order.

Car phones also break one of the major caveats of direct marketing. The customer often calls back! If the station's studio line is busy, the number can be redialed automatically, again, by pushing a button. Since the driver doesn't have much else to do but drive, and is stuck in the car anyway, he will often keep trying until he gets through.

Figure 9.3

Target Audience
_____ Persons 18 - 34 _____

	MONDAY - FRIDAY 6AM - 10AM				MONDAY - FRIDAY 10AM - 3PM				MONDAY - FRIDAY 3PM - 7PM				MONDAY - FRIDAY 7PM - MID				WEEKEND 10AM - 7PM			
	AQH (00)	CUME (00)	AQH RTG	AQH SHR	AQH (00)	CUME (00)	AQH RTG	AQH SHR	AQH (00)	CUME (00)	AQH RTG	AQH SHR	AQH (00)	CUME (00)	AQH RTG	AQH SHR	AQH (00)	CUME (00)	AQH RTG	AQH SHR
WAAA METRO / TSA	80 / 88	600 / 638	1.1	4.0	90 / 107	589 / 666	1.2	4.3	86 / 95	693 / 731	1.1	4.6	45 / 45	419 / 419	.6	4.8	44 / 45	564 / 603	.6	3.5
WBBB METRO / TSA	211 / 245	1023 / 1269	2.8	10.4	200 / 223	1005 / 1124	2.7	9.5	167 / 206	1008 / 1185	2.2	8.9	55 / 63	577 / 702	.7	5.8	81 / 99	987 / 1144	1.1	6.4
+ WCCC METRO / TSA	60 / 64	305 / 319	.8	3.0	104 / 114	262 / 276	1.4	4.9	60 / 68	275 / 289	.8	3.2	7 / 7	113 / 113	.1	.7	20 / 23	220 / 272	.3	1.6
WDDD METRO / TSA	40 / 40	141 / 141	.5	2.0	28 / 28	262 / 262	.4	1.3	48 / 48	410 / 410	.6	2.5	23 / 23	222 / 222	.3	2.4	40 / 40	421 / 421	.5	3.1
WEEE METRO / TSA																				
WFFF METRO / TSA																				
WGGG METRO / TSA																				
WHHH METRO / TSA																				
WSVB METRO / TSA																				
WJJJ METRO / TSA																				
WKKK METRO / TSA																				
WLLL METRO / TSA																				
WMMM METRO / TSA																				
WNNN METRO / TSA																				
WOOO METRO / TSA																				
WPB																				

ARBITRON RATINGS
RADIO • TELEVISION • CABLE

Press Information

1350 Avenue of the Americas
New York, New York 10019
(212) 887-1300

CONTACT: Alison J. Conte
212-887-1318

RADIO: A CONSTANT COMPANION

Since radio is a portable medium, the proport in of listening that is at-home, in-car, or some other place varies by the time of day. According to Arbitron Ratings, the country's largest radio research company, 96% of us listen to radio each week, on an average of 25 hours per week. 83% of all full-time working women listen to radio regularly. The most people tune in when they're getting up for work — between 7 a.m. and 10 a.m. — and when they're home relaxing on Saturday between 10 a.m. and 3 p.m.

It's early morning. The sky lightens and, if your inner alar... down, what finnally brings you to full wakefulnes... Back, rock, or the local traffic report o...

Consider what por...
station ...

1987 Market Survey Schedule *(continued)*

Rank		Markets	Spring 1987	Summer 1987	Fall 1987	Winter 1988
C	187	Lake Charles, LA	•			
S	113	Lakeland-Winter Haven, FL	•			
S	107	Lancaster, PA	•	•	•	•
CM	98	Lansing-East Lansing, MI	•	•	•	•
CM	74	Las Vegas, NV	•	•	•	•
C	193	Laurel-Hattiesburg, MS	•			
C	232	Lawton, OK	•			
S	128	Lexington-Fayette, KY	•	•	•	•
S	168	Lincoln, NE	•			
S	84	Little Rock, AR	•	•	•	•
C	188	Longview-Marshall, TX	•			
CM	2	Los Angeles, CA	•	•	•	•
CM	45	Louisville, KY	•	•	•	•
S	161	Lubbock, TX	•			
C	222	Lufkin-Nacogdoches, TX	•			
S	140	Macon, GA	•	•	•	•
S	122	Madison, WI	•	•	•	•
S	182	Manchester, NH	•			
		McAllen-Brownsville, TX				

1987 Market Survey Schedule *(continued)*

Rank		Markets	Spring 1987	Summer 1987	Fall 1987	Winter 1988
C	216	Naples-Marco Island, FL	•			
CM	48	Nashville, TN	•	•	•	•
CM	12	Nassau-Suffolk (Long Island), NY	•	•	•	•
C	83	New Bedford-Fall River, MA	•			
S	81	New Haven-Meriden, CT	•	•	•	•
CM	31	New Orleans, LA	•	•	•	•
CM	1	New York, NY	•	•	•	•
CM	33	Norfolk-Virginia Beach-Newport News, VA	•	•	•	•
C	225	Northwest Michigan, MI (Traverse City-Petoskey-Charlevoix)	•			
C	148	Odessa-Midland, TX	•	•	•	•
CM	43	Oklahoma City, OK	•	•	•	•
CM	69	Omaha-Council Bluffs, NE-IA	•	•	•	•
CM	51	Orlando, FL	•	•	•	•
C	248	Owensboro, KY	•			
S	108	Oxnard-Ventura, CA	•	•	•	•
C	192	Palm Springs, CA	•			
C	229	Panama City, FL	•			
C	196	Parkersburg-...WV-OH	•			

Sample radio prototypes.

Source: Arbitron Ratings Company

Ask your favorite radio station how many winners of recent call-in contests did it from car phones!

Auto redial and delayed impulse reaction.   The automatic redial feature is not limited to car phones. Most office phones and many home phones have it, too. Thus, if your commercial is aired frequently — so that the customer becomes familiar with the idea, she is apt, after hearing it advertised one or two times, to try to contact the station more than once, *even when she is busy doing something else.* This occurs in part because of the common habit of calling in to a station for news, weather, or other information. It occurs also because of the continual use of interactive contest or polling devices by the station itself. Since the station needs constantly to update its demographic profile (to share with prospective advertisers as proof of its audience), they actually condition the viewers to respond to a call for action.

BUYING RADIO TIME

Radio is probably the best bargain of all direct marketing methods. It has by far the lowest cost per thousand (about $2, as compared to $300 or more for direct mail!). Stations are usually as creative as the advertiser in putting together mutually agreeable deals. Time can be purchased in any number of different ways, for an unlimited amount of time slots. If your pockets are deep and there is not much at the bottom of them, many stations (especially the most innovative ones), will even let you "barter" for time. Col. Saunders Kentucky Fried Chicken got started that way. The Colonel (really R. David Thomas, founder of Wendy's hamburger chain) was short on cash and long on chicken, when he made a deal with a local radio station.

Spot Buys

Radio time is usually bought by the "spot" (a segment of time normally computed in 30 second intervals). Most direct sale spots are one to two minutes long, enough time to get the message across without belaboring the point. (The single purpose of the direct sale spot is to generate a sale.)

Shorter spots can be used to generate leads. Also known as **direct lead** or two-step, these spots are used to encourage the buyer to call in (or write in) for additional information. Direct lead spots are usually run by companies whose products are too difficult or complicated to run in the limited amount of time in a direct-sale radio commercial.

Support spots are short—usually only 30 seconds—and are run simply to create an awareness for some other type of direct marketing media or to give instructions regarding it:

"Watch your mail for Woody's Car Service Coupons."

"Within the next week, your prize packet will be mailed directly to your home. Please fill out the enclosed order blank and return it immediately in the specially marked envelope to qualify for the million dollar prize!"

Payment

It is possible to buy spot time for a specific time frame. It is possible, but it is also expensive. Since prime time drive time is usually not the best time for direct response advertising, buying discount time can save money and will probably produce higher responses. Commercial spots bought with discount time, however, are subject to instant replacement the moment a full-paying advertiser comes along.

Pre-emptive is the EDM term for this "bumping" of commercials from the air. Because your commercial could be bumped for any number of reasons, you will need to buy more time (a *lot* more time at some stations) than you think will be needed to reach your customers. Still, the discount is usually substantial enough that direct marketers have no problem with this kind of arrangement.

Run-of-station, or ROS, means that the station will air your spot when it can. This could be during any "day part" of the station's choosing. (Day part is the EDM term for a specified block of time during the day as determined by the station's ratings. "Drive time" is a day part.) Since both your audience and the station's audience are much the same, ROS commercials should work well, no matter when the station runs them.

Per-inquiry, or PI, is a frequent favorite with new direct response advertisers. Payment takes place *only when a response takes place*—a sale, in the case of one-step or direct-sale spots, or a lead, in two-step, or direct lead spots. Since this initially means that the station is providing free air time, before they will give you a PI contract, you will have to prove to them that your product is likely to sell. Without a prior track record (the problem with new advertisers or new products), you will have to buy time with real money — almost always upfront — first!

Conversely, if your spot does exceptionally well, this arrangement could get expensive. Since the station gets a cut on each and every response generated, if the product really takes off, you will spend far more in advertising costs than you would have if you had paid straight rates.

Negotiate. The best way to buy time is to negotiate. Each station has a different need, just as each advertiser does. One may need cash and want to be paid up front. Another may have too much inventory and will be willing to work almost any deal to fill up air time. Before you plan or cost-out your spots, check first with the radio stations you want to use to see what kind of arrangements you can make. Generally, the bigger the "buckets" of time you are willing to buy, the better deal you can negotiate. And, of course, it goes without saying, the better your track record with the station (and your product), the better deal you can put together.

CREATING A RADIO SPOT

Radio follows the AIDA concept, just as all other direct response advertising does.

- Attention.
- Interest.
- Desire.
- Action.

Getting the prospect's attention can be as simple as having the announcer casually lead into the commercial or jump into it with a resounding clash of symbols and a drum roll. Radio is imaginative. You can create atmosphere just by background sounds, like falling rain, or a running brook, or the happy laughter of children playing outside on a summer evening. Once started, you can use your imagination to stimulate interest, increasing sound, using testimonials, building desire as you outline key selling points and features.

Short But Sweet

Just as the copywriter often gets caught in the trap of overwriting, so too, does the radio writer get caught in the trap of overexplaining. Time is

Figure 9.4

The announcer may jump into a spot with a resounding clash of symbols and a drum roll.

limited. You want to build desire, but not confuse the issue. Your commercial should clearly follow a path, with one point supporting the next, to the call to action. Obviously you want to stimulate desire, but don't give so many benefits and features that the listener loses interest. You won't have much time, so make the most of them.

Ad-Libbing

Especially effective if the announcer is a popular one, ad-libbing is an unwritten commercial, done on the spot by the announcer. Having a well-liked dee jay talking about your product on the air is tantamount to a personal endorsement or testimonial. Ad-lib commercials are also effective because the announcer can lead into them so gradually the listener hardly realizes that a commercial announcement is in progress.

What's more, if the dee jay likes you, or your product, that enthusiasm will show. Frequently the commercial will run over the alloted time space (and that extra time is free time to you!)

The drawback of course, is that you will get a poor announcer, or one who doesn't know or like your product and cannot explain it well. Worse yet, he may forget to announce the necessary details the listener needs in order to buy it.

Prewritten Scripts

Read live by the announcer, pre-written scripts can solve the problem. Because there is a script to follow, no details will be left out. The announcer can succinctly point out everything the customer needs to know, including benefits, features, and instructions for placing an order. On the positive side, then, your entire message is sure to be heard on the air. If the announcer is a poor one, however, or is having a bad day, the message may sound unexciting and dull, which makes your product sound dull too.

Canned Scripts

Pre-recorded or taped presentations offer another solution. Problems can be ironed out on tape, so that the final version is letter perfect. Although the message may be clear and distinct, if it is delivered by someone other than the dee jay currently working the show, the intrusion of the new voice may be jarring. Loyal listeners usually know who is on at what time, and when they recognize a new voice, they know a commercial is coming and mentally tune it out. If the announcer is from another station, the listener may pay more attention to figuring out who the announcer is than he will to your message.

Still, studio-produced tapes may offer the best alternative. They allow a great deal of creativity and interest-getting devices — background sounds, music, dual voices.

One word of caution about studio tapes: **use professionals**. Recently the announcer on a San Diego radio station was heard to make this comment after a locally produced commercial was run: "Isn't that the worst commercial you ever heard?"

His listeners must have agreed. The commercial stopped airing a few days later.

The right voice at the right time can go a long way toward success-fully promoting your product. Wolfman Jack, a well-known radio an-nouncer, whose unique sales skills are legendary, managed to sell thou-sands of live baby chicks over the air from a remote station in the Southwest.

You never know what will happen until you try.

TESTING

Testing is probably one of the best features of radio response advertising. Because scripts can be changed, *even while they are being aired*, changes can be made immediately and inexpensively. Since the audience is so well defined and can be selected because of definable demographics, radio is an excellent and inexpensive way to test offers before running them in a more expensive media such as print.

Radio spots are also easily convertible. Scripts translate easily into copy for print media or direct mail. With the addition of visuals, they can be transformed smoothly into television spots. The flexibility and creativ-ity of the medium is endless. And the cost is so low, that for most beginning direct marketers, radio is often the best way to go.

ENDNOTES

1. KIFM Radio 98.1 FM. 5125 Convoy, Suite 304, San Diego, CA 92111. Information used by permission.
2. Arbitron Ratings Company, Metropolitan Tower, 142 W. 57th Street, New York, NY 10019. For the office nearest you, call their headquarters at (212) 887-1300.

TELEVISION

"Television direct marketing is the purest form of advertising there is. You know right away if it's going to work or not."

— Jay Kholos, President
World Communications, Inc.
Carlsbad, California

Television is the newest member of the direct response advertising family. It is also the fastest growing, and because it is so young, the most unpredictable. Together with other forms of EDM, or Electronic Data Marketing (notably, radio and telemarketing), television accounted for $15 billion in marketing revenues last year. It is growing at a phenomenal rate (educated guesses range from 7 to 15 percent a year), and by the time you read this, that number may be old news.

Interestingly enough, nobody knows exactly why.

They do know, however, that television EDM works. There are a number of schools of thought, of course. While one entrepreneur in the field quotes statistical probabilities, another swears his success is based strictly on "gut instinct." Both, apparently, are right, but until the medium has settled down (which it has no appearance of doing right now), most successful efforts will be based on a potpourri of luck, skill, past history, and the creative use of new technology.

ONIONS AND EVANGELISTS

Like direct mail, television got a rural start. Television evangelists were probably one of the first groups to realize its potential. Televised appeals for money to support churches and ministries brought in a flurry of envelopes containing donations of one dollar, five dollars, and even ten dollars. All this happened at a time when even a dollar meant a big sacrifice to most folks. Quick to recognize a good thing when they had it, television preachers never stopped to ask why the money poured in; they hustled the donations straight to the bank, and went right back on the air to ask for more.

While television evangelists were saving souls, another group of saviors were saving housewives' time in the kitchen with a handy little gadget that could slice up an onion in 100 different ways and turn it into everything from onion rings to onion soup. This gadget was demonstrated by a fast-talking huckster who always seemed on the verge of cutting off a few fingers but never actually did. The television audience who watched him may well have been fascinated with how he managed to keep his fingers out of the flying onion bits. Fascinated or not, they bought the gadget, and a lot of other products as well when the announcer told them, "Call in right now, right this minute, to order your miracle onion slicing machine!!!"

Taking a page from the evangelists' notebook, these early television advertisers tried using "testimonials" to "prove" the viability of their products. In a fevered pitch of happy acceptance, a member of the TV audience would rise to her feet and proclaim, "I *love* this product," much in the same way that she might shout, "I've been saved." This format was particularly popular in Florida and other parts of the South.

As acceptance grew, the audience grew too, and programs went cable to increase viewing audience. New formats were developed, some of them a

Figure 10.1

Fast-talking hucksters were always on the verge of chopping off a few fingers.

direct copy of the TV "Talk Shows" made popular in the sixties and seventies. Audiences loved it. They got a chance to be a star temporarily when they were given the opportunity to testify about the products they had bought.

Impulse buyers were the driving force behind the evangelistic approach to early televised direct marketing. "When you see it, buy it!" was their motto. Television made it ridiculously easy.

Positive Response

The world of televised direct response advertising chugged along for awhile, with big-toothed salesmen assisted by scantily clad girls barely out of their teens, creating a carnival-like atmosphere that sold thousands of gadgets and cars, and overstuffed furniture with fake zebra-skin covers. Most of the ads were shown on sit-com reruns or on late night TV. Announcers made outrageous claims, and created a climate of urgency that kept buyers coming back and back again.

Then one day somebody looked up and wondered about the slick presentations on network TV placed by the general advertising media. They looked great. But did they sell?

The key to direct response advertising is accountability. One thing that the "hucksters" had over the general media people was positive response. They could point a finger and say, "See? Look at these results! One 30-second spot got 100 calls within 10 minutes of the time it aired. What did you get for *your* $15,000 display ad? How many times did *your* telephone ring?"

AT THE HEAD OF THE PACK?

The question was a valid one. Of all forms of direct marketing, televised EDM is probably the most cost effective and the most cost accountable. One single presentation reaches more people at one time than any other direct marketing method. (With satellite communications, every individual on the entire planet who has access to a television set could be watching your commercial.) When TV direct marketing is used concurrently with incoming telephone lines, the response is immediate (less than fifteen minutes in most cases). The advertiser knows almost instantly if the ad is going to work or not. If it doesn't, the advertiser can try something else.

TV IS NOT FOR THE INEXPERIENCED

Television meets all the other tests, too. It is visual. It is verbal. It is personal. It is certainly interactive, and it most definitely is measurable. Best of all, the break-even point is relatively low (in many cases, about three dollars per thousand).

Viewed from those perspectives, television marketing certainly has the *potential* to ride at the head of the direct marketing parade. But right now, because technology has outstripped technique (at least for the time being), it can't rightfully claim the position. Televised direct response advertising *can* claim, however, to have progressed from infancy to adolescence. Media people are no longer skeptics. They may not like television very much—as Jay Kholos of World Communications puts it, "Television is the most honest form of advertising there is. Feedback is immediate. You know what the real world is all about." For the business person though, this is a dream come true. You really *do* know whether your product is selling or not. And you know right away.

While television may be great, it is *not* a medium which the average business person can jump right into. TV advertising can be complicated, expensive beyond comprehension to the uninitiated, and difficult to understand. (Even many of the self-professed pros aren't exactly sure why it works. There are, however, many highly qualified professionals in this

Figure 10.2

Feedback is immediate.

area. See Appendices.) Because it is new, many old-line agencies and media people are unfamiliar with the nuances of the media, and the newer, "creative" producers often fly right over the heads of solidly grounded business managers and owners.

In many aspects, television EDM still holds that "rural flavor" with down-home testimonials and product "interviews" reminiscent of television 20 years ago for the home shopping channels. At the same time, high-speed, high-tech catalogue shopping based purely on telecommunications is developing faster than the developers can put it on the screen. Most television advertising, however, is based on item and price. Some of the biggest sellers are record albums and tapes. Televised direct response made country singer Slim Whitman a household word, and brought yodeling into every American home, whether they wanted to hear it or not.

A Communication Gap

It is no surprise, then, that there is still a lack of communication between the business community and the advertising community. The average business person never had a course in this kind of marketing. If he or she came up through the ranks the hard way, electronic direct marketing was out of reach of most businesses; there was little opportunity to experiment with the media and learn how to use it.

Get professional help. Today, the field is wide open; however, unless you are well-versed in the language of television direct-response advertising, you should proceed slowly. (This is *not* the same thing as general or "image" advertising where the purpose of the spot is to increase product awareness rather than initiate an immediate sale.) There are a number of competent direct marketing producers who provide services to television advertisers, from creative through the actual production. (See the lists in the Appendices .)[1] You will also need telemarketing support, and the firm *must* be equipped to handle the expected crush of calls resulting from a successful promotion. If the viewer gets a busy signal on the first try, the chances of another attempt diminish as the seconds tick by.

The costs for production and telephone support vary as widely as the producer's experience in this medium. The old caveat "you get what you pay for" applies, so if you decide to use professional help (and you should, unless you are very, very good), make sure you get someone who knows what they are doing.

Overcoming Objections

Television EDM is still suffering from the same malady that plagued direct mail. Shoddy products, poor service, and haphazard fulfillment gave it a bad name that will take time and effort to overcome. Many viewers still associate this form of advertising with evangelism and potato peelers and feel uncomfortable purchasing through this media. As more and more knowledgeable users and producers come on board, this image will undoubtedly improve.

Learning the Ropes

Meanwhile, some advertisers, like Academic Guidance Services in New Jersey, have mastered the medium, and can produce effective commercials of varying lengths and formats. Dr. Mark Cohen, President of AGS, has even taken his program to a national audience, airing it on the national cable weather station with excellent results. Most advertisers, however, are still struggling through the trial stages of television EDM. As Don Pesce, Advertising Director of SMI in Waco, Texas, says, "The potential is clearly there. But, it's hard to break into this media. And harder still, to know where to find quality creative for a reasonable price."

Some companies, such as World Communications in Carlsbad, California, have built a successful business based solely on television marketing. This company does the entire promotion in house, and farms out only the telemarketing and fulfillment portion of the business. Thus, although it does not actually manufacture a product, it qualifies as both a user and a producer, of direct marketing — much like National Pen, also in the San Diego area, which does produce its own product.

BROADCAST AND CABLE

Using television for direct marketing offers several possibilities. Like World Communications, television marketing can be a business in itself. For AGS, it is a primary marketing tool. For retailers or groups that promote sweepstakes, television EDM can be a support vehicle, designed to prepare prospects for a promotion using another direct marketing method. In many cases, EDM is used to generate leads, which are then followed up by some other means.

It is not the purpose of this book to provide you with a technical guide for developing your own productions.[2] Accordingly, various methods of television EDM, how they might be used, and how to purchase air time will be discussed; but it is strongly suggested that should you decide to use television, you contact knowledgeable, experienced people to help you design the actual production.[3] Only after you have successfully mastered the medium should you strike out on your own.

Programming

Broadcast TV sends network programming from coast to coast, and country to country (when satellite is used), to reach huge audiences. In America alone, there are almost 90 million households that own a television set. Consider that most of those households contain two or three people. Add in the number of viewers in other countries, and the potential audience begins to defy imagination!

Cable TV is a utility which delivers an enhanced broadcast signal via a cable utility hookup. In contrast, broadcast programming is beamed to your television whether you have the hookup or not. To watch it, you have only to turn on the set, assuming you have the proper reception to receive it. And therein lies the problem. Most localities receive only a few stations. The rest are blocked out by natural barriers like mountains, or send out a signal too weak to cover a large geographical area. *Cable hookup provides the viewer with increased reception.*

Even with a cable hookup, viewers still cannot receive all the available channels unless they pay an additional fee for the programming that is sent out on a scrambled transmission (like the Playboy channel, Disney channel, or popular movie channels such as Home Box Office, Showtime, and Cinemax.) If you want to watch one of these channels, you have to pay extra for the privilege.

Cable viewers have the opportunity to be more selective than general broadcast viewers. Whether they are or not is open to question, as the rating systems for cable television are not as thorough as those for broadcast. Nielson and Arbitron, both of which provide ratings for network programming, do not track cable as closely as they do general broadcast. New technology is changing that situation very quickly, however, with the addition of "people meters" such as ScanAmerica℠.[4] (See the section on buyer graphics in Chapter 2.)

Within the cable stable, the scrambled channels (such as Disney and HBO) probably offer better demographic profiles. The viewers fit a specific buyer profile, and subscribe to these channels or cables because they like the programming. We can *infer* who they are and what they like because they have purchased the channel hookup, but it is still inference only, because there are no solid data to substantiate it.

Restricted advertising.   Not all cable companies will accept advertising on all channels. One of the great things about certain cable channels is that they have little or no advertising. For the viewer who finds commercials intrusive (and most all of us do), this type of cable offers a welcome change from the constant bombardment of products and services.

Cable classifications.   Cable comes in roughly three different classes: local, national, and super-cable. National cable, carrying financial news, R-rated movies and shows, or weather, offers a broader base for its advertisers than local stations do. Super-cable receives broadcast signals via satellite and airs them on unused channels. As an advertiser (for an additional cost, of course), you can take advantage of the increased audience without resorting to purchasing time on regular broadcast TV. WTBS, broadcasting out of Atlanta, for example, is a super-station. Running an advertisement on that station should assure you of a national, even an international, audience. Of course, although there are more than 80 million sets in the U.S. alone, there are also 13 VHF channels on each of them; and for those who have UHF or cable, the number goes up to 70 or more. What are the real chances that somebody is watching your commercial?

Time and Charges

Of all the elements that count most in television EDM, time counts the most. It is the key factor in deciding between broadcast or cable.

The cost of television advertising varies widely, but generally spots on network or network affiliate stations are more expensive than those on local or independent stations. The Super Bowl, for instance, which is probably the most expensive program time there is, cost about $20,000 for 30 seconds of time on local San Diego stations in 1986. That same 30-second spot cost $275,000 via network for the same game. Network, remember, gives you a much wider audience than a local spot.

For all channels, advertising costs during "prime time" TV watching are generally more expensive than fringe or off-hours. Ratings create demand, which in turn, creates higher costs. To give you an idea of the low end, a preemptable, non-prime-time spot on late-night TV costs about

$50. You get what you pay for, of course. Obviously if you need to reach as many people (in your targeted audience) as possible, it is highly unlikely that a $50 spot will do a whole lot for you.

Commercial "spots" (or blocks of time) in broadcast network, or network affiliate stations, are shorter (10 to 30 seconds on the average) than nonnetwork or local spots. Time is less available — especially on the big network affiliates. (You are competing with the larger, "image" buyers who want to gain product recognition over a wide service area.) If you buy "discount" time (at cheaper rates), and most direct marketers usually do, you could easily get "bumped" if a major buyer wants your slot. (See the sections on ROS and preemptive time on pages 207 and 208.)

Network affiliates are paid to carry certain advertising and programming. They can preempt, up to a point, for local advertising or programming, but there may be limits. Local or totally independent stations, on the other hand, can pretty much do what they want. There is less demand for their time, so there is more time available.

The choices between network and nonnetwork, and between local or general broadcast, really depend on the audience you want to reach, and the programming the audience members like to watch. Products that appeal to older people, for example, might do well on channels that run old movies. These are often local stations, or cable stations. Advertisements for sports-related items, including certain foods and beverages, generally belong on national broadcast network television, since they have a wide appeal. A local distributor of sporting goods equipment, however, might find far more success on the local channels. And, of course, if delivery was not possible outside the immediate area, advertising on national televsion would make no sense at all. Children's products, such as toys, cereals, and clothing, do very well on Saturday morning cartoon shows, no matter how or where they are broadcast. For products distributed nationally, for example, broadcast or "super cable" might be the best choice.

When Is the Best Time to Run a Spot?

There are two distinct schools of thought on this subject.

The inverse proportion theory. Many direct marketing books, especially those written before 1987, suggest that programs with less-engrossed viewers attract more buyers. The theory is that if a viewer is engrossed in the news, for example, or a favorite show, he will be less inclined to run to the phone to order something. And he will be even less interested in deserting the screen altogether to hunt for a pencil and pen to write down the toll-free number that flashes (all too quickly) on the screen. The theory goes on to say that if the viewer is uninterested in the program on the screen, the interruption is almost a welcome one, and the viewer will take the necessary steps to place an order. For this reason, many direct marketers who use television choose to air their commercials on late-night TV, or in conjunction with reruns of older programs.

The proactive viewer theory. Recent studies seem to indicate that the viewer who is alert and involved in a program, such as a newscast, is *more* likely to buy. Proponents of this theory say that commercials aired during highly rated programs or prime-time viewing will be more effective because the viewer is more involved in the foreground programming.

And the "couch potato" who dozes away on the sofa, munching snacks and paying only minimal attention to the program will probably not make the effort to get up to order anything, much less write it all down to order later.

HOW TO BUY AIR TIME

Inventory

Supply and demand is a major factor in determining the cost of air-time. If a station has a large "inventory" of unused air time, an offer to purchase time will be welcomed with open arms. Inventory, however, is often based upon popularity. The higher the station's ratings, the less available inventory they will have. Everybody wants to buy into success!

Unpredictable inventory makes accurate planning difficult to achieve. If you are a small business and dependent on television response advertising to generate business, this situation could pose a serious cash flow problem! To avoid being faced with the news that the station is "sold out" of inventory when they want to run a spot, most advertisers plan and contract for advertising two or three weeks in advance.

Ratings

The cost of broadcast programming is usually based on GRPs (gross rating points). The higher the ratings, the higher the cost of the spot. Simply put, one point equals 1 percent of the viewers at any one time. Thus, if a program has a rating of 30, one-third of the households with televisions are supposedly watching the show. (You know better, of course. Frequently the TV is left on when no one is in the room or even in the house.) Prime time ratings generally run 30 to 32 percent. Local news, on the other hand, might be around 15 to 17 percent. A 30 to 40 percent share (number of actual households watching within that rating) is about average.

Spots

Time can be purchased directly from the station (or network) or through "Rep" firms. Rep firms can be, and usually are, independent, but some of them are O&O (owned and operated by the network). Most direct marketers, especially local firms, prefer to negotiate the best deal directly with the station, if possible. Rep firms, however, can be very helpful, especially to larger companies interested in regional or national buys which allow them to be *selective* about which geographic regions will carry their products.

When a short "spot" is aired, a toll-free "800 number" is usually flashed on the screen. Average spots last from 30 to 60 seconds. Independent stations may have a high enough inventory (amount of empty or unused time to air commercials) available, making the purchase of 120 seconds (two minutes) of time possible. Network affiliates usually have a large percentage of their air time scheduled by the network to which they owe their allegiance. Not only is it more expensive to buy air time, it is also more difficult. With less "inventory" available, advertisers are usually relegated to 30-second spots. (Recently that number has dropped to allow some 15-second spots.)

Since it is expensive to produce spots of varying lengths to be shown on different stations, most advertisers produce one 30-second tape which can air on broadcast or cable, local or network, whenever or wherever it is appropriate.

Cable stations with a large block of unsold inventory sometimes allow advertisers to buy a half hour (or more) of "programming" time. This method is especially popular with financial services. The "program" is advertised in the cable or television guide as "advertising," but it gets a listing as well as extended, fairly inexpensive air time. ("Programmed" advertising is rarely found on network or network affiliates. Time is too short and costs too high to make this effective for the station or the advertiser.)

Run-Of-Station (ROS)

Allowing the station to select your air time based upon their overall schedule (i.e., when there is an excess of dead air time), can be economical. If the station is overstocked with unsold inventory, it will be happy to discount time to you. Of course, if an advertiser comes in who can afford to pay regular rates, your commercial will be "bumped" (just like what happens when you fly standby; if the regular ticket holder shows up, you get "bumped" off the flight to make room for the person who paid full fare).

Preemptive

Spots which can be "bumped" or preempted by another advertiser are fairly inexpensive. For a slight charge, most stations will even permit you to specify when you want your spot aired. Unless you pick prime-time programming, your commercial has a fair chance of being shown when you want it aired.

Most seasoned direct marketers buy "buckets" of preemptive spots based on certain types of programming which they feel is demographically homogeneous with their own buyer profile. The theory is that because of overall reach and frequency, responses will be high enough to make the promotion worthwhile.

The problem with this for the *inexperienced* buyer is that you may very well negotiate a deal where nobody ever sees your spot because it never runs!

Per Inquiry (PI)

This is popular with direct response advertisers, especially new ones who are operating on a tight budget. *PI* means "Per Inquiry." The station does not charge for the air time, but it takes a percentage of the response when there is an inquiry. In other words, you pay only when somebody buys. It's a good way to get started, but not a very accurate way to run a direct marketing campaign. Because you have no control over the media, you can never be sure if or when someone is likely to buy. One of the major problems with this method is fulfillment. Unless you stock a large inventory, you could be caught shorthanded after a particularly successful commercial. (The law requires that you be able to deliver what you offer. See FTC regulations in Chapter 12.)

Bonus-To-Pay-Out

This is similar to PI, except an arrangement is worked out with the station that guarantees a minimum response. Everybody wins on that one, because everybody gets paid within a set period of time.

The real key to buying TV time is negotiation. Because the needs of individual businesses and the policies of each station vary greatly, every deal needs to be negotiated separately.

CREATIVE AND PRODUCTION

Air time is not a part of the cost of producing a television commercial. Production is entirely separate. As with print advertising, your direct response piece (or, in this case, commercial spot) must be laid out, designed, and produced. And, like print, the producers may include printers, typesetters, graphic artists, and many other people who design for the print media. But because this is a visual as well as a verbal medium, the creative process is a little different, and the array of professional people you need will be much more diversified.

If you have a background in EDM, there should be no problem; but if you don't, you will need qualified help.[5] You will also need skilled people to present your ad in addition to those who design it.[6] (There is nothing sillier than Joe, the businessman boss, pitching his discount furniture store on television. He may be a retailer, but chances are he is a terrible television announcer!)

Production

Generally, television advertising is designed using a device called the "story board." This "picture story" sets up a columnar layout showing pictures and copy running side by side down the board. The video portion is then filmed, and the sound track overlaid. Since production is rarely live (almost all productions are taped), production problems are ironed out before the viewer ever sees the commercial.

Production costs vary widely, as does the expertise of the producer. Be prepared to spend in the neighborhood of $25,000 to $50,000 or more to prepare a solid promotion and then to test it using a national agency and "heavy" talent (big names) to promote your product. Most stations can produce their own spots for advertisers, however, at a far more reasonable cost. According to Jeff Anderson of KFMB-TV, Channel 8 in San Diego, "the average cost to produce a spot ranges between $1,000 to $2,500."

Figure 10.3

Story boards are used to design advertising promotions.

Videotape Versus Film

One other consideration is the choice between videotape and film. Videotape produces a sharper, cleaner picture, which often enhances the feeling of urgency. It also gives a very clear representation of your product. With videotape there is no processing involved; it is ready immediately. (It's like shooting some footage of little Johnny at the zoo with a home-movie camera, then plugging the cassette into the VCR at home and watching little Johnny at the zoo all over again.) Because tape is immediate, you can look at it right away and decide whether you have produced the right commercial or not. If not, there will be plenty of time to correct any mistakes. (New technology makes videotape almost as versatile as film for cutting, editing, and splicing.)

Film produces a soft, expensive feeling. It romanticizes the product. (Image advertising and large national promotions are done on film.) Pictures are smooth, sensuous, often lush, with the edges softly blurred.

The final choice may not be yours to make at all. Some agencies and stations are far better equipped to use videotape. Others, most notably network and high-end agencies, are more comfortable with film. The choice should really be left up to the creative directors. You are paying for their expertise. Let them do what they do best.

Testing

As with all other forms of direct marketing, you should build in a budget for testing. Fortunately, although it may be initially expensive (the overall cost is actually lower than most other forms of direct marketing), television direct response advertising is quick. If your program spots ran as planned (that is, no preempts and long time delays until the station does or does not run your piece), you should be able to determine right away whether or not your campaign is going to work. With most other media, you must complete the run (or insertion) before you know if the design was a good one. Television lets you make fast changes and quick substitutions — with the station's blessing, usually. Just don't try to pull the ad off the air if you don't like it, and then ask for a refund. When you come back six months later to renegotiate another contract, the station won't be very interested in talking with you.

It is also a good idea to run a comparative test with another media, such as radio or print, to see which works best for you in terms of costs to response. Split-run testing (two almost identical commercials with a slight change as to price or offer), or multimedia testing can be very helpful. For more about testing, see Chapter 11.

ONE-STEP, TWO-STEP, AND SUPPORT

Television makes it possible to hit all the hot buttons, the motivators discussed in Chapter 2. In the hurry to get the message across, urgency is conveyed. Your presentation can be made so appealing that the viewer is consumed with desire to have whatever it is. And it is that overwhelming desire — which lasts only a few seconds, or minutes at the most — that will draw a positive response. When your spot runs, you have approximately five seconds to grab the viewer's attention, and fifteen minutes to get a response once it is off the air. That is a very fast turnaround time. But it works only if you did everything right, and with television EDM, there are a lot of variables — many of which you cannot control.

Direct Sale

Also known as one-step EDM, the purpose of this type of spot is to force the viewer to take action immediately. The spot, be it 30 seconds or 30 minutes, is designed to draw the viewer in, build selling momentum, and climax it with a strong appeal for urgent action. Usually an 800 number is flashed on the screen, and often an address is given as well.

Everything that the viewer needs to know in order to buy must be covered during that spot. Color, size, weight, special ordering information, cost: whatever it is, all information about that item must be conveyed clearly and accurately. You must do everything you can to make it easy for the viewer to buy.

Two-Step, or Direct Lead Sale

Here the purpose of the spot is not to force the viewer to buy immediately but to generate leads which can be followed up through another direct marketing method such as personal sales or telemarketing. The two-step is often used by insurance companies, financial institutions, and companies whose products are complicated enough to require a more complete explanation than the brief one possible during air time. Usually a toll-free number flashes on the screen, and the viewer is invited to call in for more information. Because less material needs to be covered in a direct lead spot, it can be of a much shorter duration. Most advertisers have found one or more 30-second spots, followed by a fast 10-second reminder with the toll free number, have proven to be the most effective combination.

Support

Support advertising follows a similar format to direct lead sales, but with this method, the purpose for airing the commercial is to warn or apprise the customer of an impending action. One of the best known examples is Publisher's Clearing House, which twice yearly sends out a sweepstakes offer. Just before the offer is mailed, media advertising announces it is coming, and suggests that the viewers watch their mailboxes for a sweepstakes packet. This technique has proven so successful that it can raise response rates by as much as 50 percent.

TWO-WAY TV

From the interactive marketing that developed in the seventies, television EDM followed two distinctly different paths. Broadcast and cable spots, as discussed above, were designed to give a quick pitch, make a strong appeal, and present the viewer with an easy way to order—by calling or writing in.

The other form of televised EDM, which is still really in its infancy, is a spin-off of the fast-paced, fast-talking onion slicers. In this system, a host describes (even demonstrates) the products, one at a time, on the screen. When the viewer sees something he wants, he can call in and order it on the spot. This marketing method became so popular (and profitable) in places like the bay area in Florida and in New Orleans, it was produced on 24-hour cable channels. Before long, it had gone national, and then onto the satellite. HSM, the first satellite, became a full-fledged network.

Home Shopping

The latest technology provides the home shopper with a service that lets her shop without ever leaving her chair. (Most home-shopping buyers right now are women, and about 60 percent of what they buy is jewelry.) The viewer is equipped with a touch-tone phone and a booklet of instructions. When she sees what she wants, she punches in the item number on her telephone.

Today, the big advertisers are getting into home shopping. A new network, backed by J.C. Penny, is testing in Chicago (as of this writing). Another one, America's Value network, has started a channel aimed at home dish owners (individuals who have their own satellite dishes).

Full Service Sales

Impulse buying—which is what this really is—has triggered a revival in interactive service. Teleaction in Chicago, for example, offers a wide variety of items, including pizza, for home delivery. McDonald's is handing out direct mail pieces for HSC, showing the familiar "testimonial" from viewer/buyers.

Today you can buy just about anything from a television shopping service—airline reservations, financial services, tickets to sporting events, and microwavable food that is delivered to your door, ready to heat and eat.

Figure 10.4

Equipped with a touch-tone phone and a booklet of instructions, the television shopper never needs to leave her chair.

Delayed Ordering

The new trend is toward services that permit the buyer to order something *after* it leaves the screen as long as he remembers the item number. If he forgot it, he can call in and ask. Telephone operators are standing by, ready and willing to help.

Customer Service

Twenty-four hours a day, seven days a week, the smart shopping services are offering full customer service, helping customers who forget item numbers or those who want to return merchandise, no questions asked.

Undoubtedly, experienced print catalogers will be on the bandwagon before long. The opportunity is just too good to miss!

WHAT'S NEXT?

It took barely 10 years for home catalogue services to develop from an onion grater. It took only one or two more years to develop a full range of products from just a few. On the drawing board now are home banking services, complete travel services, pharmaceutical supplies, and network credit cards. Already one network has established an Easy Pay Plan (Cablevision is experimenting with it now), which will permit customers to pay for larger purchases by budgeting their payments (much as they do now with department stores). One network already has an automatic phone response system called TOOTIE which permits total electronic ordering.

Technologies are changing too. The way we transmit information to our buyers is constantly undergoing revision and improvement.

Teletext

Using the "vertical blanking" intervals of broadcast, Teletext allows homes to get up to 100 pages of a catalogue, "on line" or available at one time.

PC Pickup

A number of services now use personal computers rather than television screens to deliver information to the customers. Using cable lines, a continuous stream of data is transmitted to home computers. One of them, Financial News Network, sends information (much like stock market quote equipment in your broker's office) on a short delay basis.

Express Information Services also delivers a data stream to computer owners, but this one offers a wider selection and takes it a step further. Including general information, news, and sports, the network is designed for the entire family to access. Although it is not on the vertical blanking system like Teletext, it is completely interactive. Viewers, with the aid of an instruction book, can press various keys to make their selections.

The future looks bright for this kind of hookup. Most systems work on any IBM compatible, Apple, or Commodore. And in most cases, they operate on standard modems (hookups from the computer to the telephone line), such as the ones manufactured by Hayes.

Video Disks

Video disks operate with an interactive "disk" on a special cable channel. The viewer sees a "visual" or picture of what he wants and uses a touch tone to interact. He can also page forwards or backwards through the "disk" to find the information he needs. Most information is pictured via "slides," much as you would see on a home movie projector. For example, the code for J.C. Penny might be "10." He would punch in that number, and then continue punching in choices, much like a multiple choice test, until he zeros in on the item he wants. All of the visuals are stored on the disk, which can be updated frequently, much like a box of slides, or an accounts payable file on your office computer.

An interesting variation of this is TCI's Video Jukebox Network out of Miami. The network operates by request. The viewer touches her phone, orders a video, and sees it in minutes. Sort of like demand MTV.

Although video disks do not currently have a wide audience, the potential is clear. GTE, in conjunction with Apollo Cablevision in Cerritos, California, is experimenting with a video on demand system. The viewer tunes into a special channel, touches a button on the telephone, and instantly sees a "menu" of choices, much like a card catalogue at the library. From the menu, she can select a show or event she wants to watch, *in the future*, program it in, and watch it when she wishes.. The system is like having the resources of your own public library, stored on disk, in your own home. The possibilities are limitless.

Video catalogues are one variation on this theme. The viewer might punch in a request to page through Bloomingdales, or Sharper Image, for example, and browse through an entire catalogue of products.

If you are a retailer, this is one chance you really don't want to miss!

ENDNOTES

1. Contact your local direct marketing club or association for names of agencies or producers in your area who are familiar with this type of advertising. The Direct Marketing Association in New York City can also help you. A partial list of their resources follows in Appendices A and B of this book.

   The most important thing to remember about television EDM is that not all agencies understand the technique or are equipped to handle it . If you decide to use professional help (and newcomers to the medium definitely should), make sure you choose someone who knows EDM.

   Another point: Using television as a one-step advertising program is very different from using it as a support medium. Many conventional agencies can design highly effective *support* campaigns in this media, but if your aim is to broadcast and sell, all in one commercial,then find a producer who has experience in producing that particular kind of advertising.

2. To date, few technical references have been written about television EDM. Bob Stone discusses it briefly in his most recent edition of *Successful Marketing Methods*. One of the more comprehensive short treatments was written by G. Scott Osborne (*Electronic Direct Marketing*, Prentice Hall, 1984). Check your local library's reference system, under the heading "electronic direct marketing" or "television, marketing" for current writings.

   Other than that, your best bet is to contact the Direct Marketing Association.

3. The Direct Marketing Association in New York has an excellent reference guide and can put you in touch with a number of associations or services that can help you. Please see the listings in the Appendices for additional information.

4. ScanAmerica is a Service Mark of Arbitron Ratings Company, New York.

5. Most direct response agencies that are knowledgeable in this field are in Chicago or on the East Coast. There are also a few on the West Coast. Check the listings in the Appendices, and check also the *Standard Directory of Advertising Agencies* which should be available in the local library.

6. Your ad agency should be able to help, but if it cannot, check the talent agencies in your area who *book* talent (not just manage it), and have a stable of people experienced in television commercial work. Qualified agencies are usually members of AFTA and Actor's Equity.

THE TOTAL MARKETING PLAN

11

"In today's Baskin-Robbins society, everything comes in at least 31 different flavors." —
—John Naisbitt, in Megatrends

What does all this mean to you, the business person? If you plan to be a part of the marketing picture in the nineties, you had better have a grasp on direct marketing. It's no longer a back-room operation; direct marketing is both a full-scale discipline and an art, that produces big profits for everybody.

- Direct mail has been refined into a scientific profit-producing machine which by the year 2000 will be so prolific that its output should equal or even top first-class mail production.
- Telemarketing can be inbound, outbound, or both-way bound as businesses talk to each other and to their customers, speeding orders and credit processing with the marvels of telecommunications.
- Catalogue shopping has jumped from the printed page to the television set in your home, office, or even in your automobile. As technology improves, and two-way television EDM is refined, there will literally be a rush of retailers and manufacturers to sign up for interactive marketing spots.
- Electronic data marketing has turned "direct" marketing into "immediate" marketing. Whether it is a chance to air your own commercial, or a chance to be a "page" in an electronic catalogue, the businesses that survive into the next century will be the ones that know how to use EDM.
- *And, because marketing methods are becoming increasingly interdependent, the successful marketer will also have to understand the dynamics of mutually dependent advertising and marketing media.*

We are in the grip of another social revolution. Today, most adults work and have less time to shop. And most households have both a television and a telephone. (See the section on the market in motion in

Chapter 2.) Americans, whether they like it or not, have been catapulted into the age of information. It's an advertiser's dream, if he or she knows how to take advantage of it.

YOU NEED A MARKETING PLAN

You might get lucky and be inundated with orders after sending out your first mailing. You might, but you probably won't. For your initial tele-marketing effort, you might find a man or a woman with the sexiest telephone voice ever heard—and bring in bundles of business. There are always exceptions to every rule.

The success or failure of any business ultimately depends on its sales. Without sales, there *is* no business. To orchestrate a successful sales path requires designing, developing, and *following* a successful sales path. Direct marketing gives us a proven path to follow, and provides us with methods and techniques to use which are *guaranteed* to improve profitability. The trick is to follow the rules and master the art of "mixing" marketing media to get the most out of your marketing dollars.

Figure 11.1

You might get lucky and be inundated with orders.

Building a marketing plan is fun. It's exciting. (And, it's almost always very profitable.) Because direct response advertising is based upon previously proven results, and because it follows an established, predefined goal path with built-in milestones, the job of the market planner is not only fun, it is also easy!

Even more exciting, because direct marketing uses a "database" approach to marketing (see Chapters 2 and 3), it is a highly accurate method of successfully matching product and buyer. Computer processing makes it easy to compile and store information relative to prior sales. Credit cards make it easy to buy more, and to buy more often. And the zip code allows us to target our market precisely, yet cut costs while reaching it.

Through the use of constantly updated databases, an amazing array of information is at the disposal of the direct marketing planner. Product research defines, locates, catalogues, and analyzes products or services to be sold and the firms or individuals who can supply them. Results of prior or similar advertising efforts suggest the most profitable marketing methods. Surveys, tests, and consumer preferences of previous and prospective buyers detail who wants what, and when and why they will buy it. Market testing and segmentation further categorize buyers into endless arrays of "common groups," thanks to modern market research techniques (Chapter 2) and the miracle of mailing lists (Chapter 3). With so much information available to the seller, it would seem impossible to build a market plan that could not succeed.

FACTORS TO CONSIDER

"Nothing," said Murphy, "is as easy as it looks." In fact, if direct marketing is such a snap, why isn't everybody doing it? Probably, as we noted before, because most folks don't know what direct marketing is or how to use it. Maybe they tried it once, and it didn't work. So they gave up, without giving it a fair chance.

Most sellers either have the right tools or can find someone else who does, once they know what they are looking for, or whom to ask for help.

AIDA

Anybody who has ever been involved in selling has heard this term. AIDA stands for Attention/Interest/Desire/Action. These are the four key points in any sales or marketing plan, but in direct marketing, the first and the last "A" make or break your sale. You only have a few seconds to grab your prospect's attention:[1]

> 2 seconds — print advertising
> 5 seconds — radio, television
> 15 seconds — telemarketing
> 30 seconds (or more) with direct mail.

Faced with such a limited time span to gain the prospects' attention, you must do an exemplary job of headlining your ad, no matter how you choose to present it.

The other problem is *action*. Your piece or spot might be wonderful — intriguing, appealing, enticing. But if you don't ask the reader, listener, or watcher to *do something*, your advertising dollars have been wasted.

The call to action has to give all of the information needed for the customer to buy. Cost, shipping instructions, telphone number to order, whatever he or she needs to know, tell them now. You won't get another chance!

Flexibility

When a process you've attempted doesn't work, don't junk it; rethink it, and try doing it a little differently. A direct marketing technique which proved highly successful in the past should work well in a similar situation, given common characteristics of both sales campaigns. Just because a method worked well once, however, doesn't mean you are married to it. There is no reason why you can't experiment with other media or test new markets and products.

Direct marketing, remember, is interactive. To be successful, it depends on an appropriate response from the buyer. Sellers must always be aware of sudden changes in the marketplace. Sometimes it takes only the merest whim of a group, say a bunch of teenagers on the West Coast who decide denim is "out" and sackcloth is "in," to cancel the effectiveness of an entire marketing strategy in just a few days.

Not all buyers' whims are negative, however. What was "in" last month could become such a roaring success that the seller finds business doubled, even tripled, in a very short time. Look what happened with MTV (music television). The sudden explosive interest in video music started an entire new industry — video taped music — and opened up an advertising media that became an overnight success!

Figure 11.2

The sudden explosive interest in video music started an entire new industry.

The need for flexible market planning has never been more apparent than it is today. Direct response advertising is undergoing a technical revolution. The age of electronic direct marketing has opened up possibilities that were unheard of only a few years ago.

The Customer's Viewpoint

Even the best laid plans don't always work. Suppose you've tested and tested, and are so flexible you feel like spaghetti, but still can't get a bite on the product line. Direct marketing, don't forget, is interactive; it takes two—the buyer and the seller—acting in concert to complete a successful sale.

If your best efforts fail, the problem may very well be your choice of marketing method, or the point of view it expresses. Like the dead pet Milk Bone example, the technique you have chosen may be the wrong one for the market you have targeted.

Knowing how to excite and entice prospective buyers is every bit as important as knowing where to find them. Some people pore over catalogues, and in the interests of time or convenience buy repeatedly from them. Other people consider catalogues garbage and toss them unopened into the trash. Telemarketing encounters similar ups and downs. While one individual may enjoy telephone contact and will converse easily with a telemarketer, someone else may find the experience annoying.

Contrasting attitudes exist for every method of direct marketing. Even more confusing, a buyer may gradually turn from a dependable customer to one who shuns your advertising efforts. Individuals who open and read *all* their mail, even printed circulars, will probably clip and save coupons. If they are inundated with too much bulk-rate mail, however (or perhaps an avalanche of unwanted pornographic material), that same person may junk the lot of it. Time can also be an enemy to the direct marketer. When a mail shopper suddenly finds she has too little free time to peruse a growing stack of third class mail, she will select only the pieces that she really wants to see and pitch the rest. This "quick screen" is particularly common with business-to-business direct mail in which the screener is often a receptionist or secretary and the intended "target" prospect never even gets a chance to see the piece.

"Turned-on/turned-off" attitudes go way beyond the printed word. In many cases, you don't have much control over the final outcome. If your buyer, for example, is a late-night TV addict and responds well to advertising she sees there, she may suddenly "turn off" if she loses interest in her favorite program. She'll fall from your positive response list, and you'll never know why. Similar problems occur with radio advertisers who are dependant on station philosophy and programming. If one or the other is changed, the audience disappears before you can track it down. Should you decide to use either of these electronic medias to present your offer to a buying public, be sure that your goals meet with the producer whose attitudes and airwaves you are sharing by default.

Cost

Once you have decided upon the method or methods most likely to attract your buyers' attention, take time to assess the costs before implementing it. For example, if you cannot afford mass advertising at a national level, network television may not be suitable for you. At the other extreme, if your product is intended for the sight-impaired, using print media (other than Braille) isn't going to work, either. To meet with success, the method you choose must be compatible with your budget as well as with the characteristics of the market itself.

Product Appeal

Another consideration in the selection of a marketing method is the *product* or *service* you are selling. Often, the product itself will dictate the best method for selling it. Products with high visual appeal such as clothing and accessories, or equipment for sports and hobbies, should be marketed visually. Catalogues, television, and large color print-ads might be wise choices. Services that appeal to personal feelings such as corporate motivational seminars, and financial products such as insurance, stocks, and mortgages, often sell better with a direct mail piece that thoroughly explains what it is that you are selling and what benefits it has to offer to the buyer. These services also profit by long-spot television advertising, with a half hour more of "programmed advertising."

Products which have demonstrable qualities, such as onion slicers and automobiles, do well on television. Other demonstrable merchandise, such as cleaning products, might be best marketed through direct selling (face-to-face contact). Often a verbal appeal such as one for educational material, sports events, or rock concerts will stir interest in auditory products (even when the quality is distorted).

Familiarity

Successful advertising often is based on nothing more than the use of a familiar (and comfortable) marketing approach. A large percentage of direct marketing depends on past history. "If I did it before, I will do it again," is frequently the reaction of a buyer who is approached a second or third time for the same type of offer. Family photographs, cleaning products, and certainly campaigns for dollar donations to various causes, are heavily dependent on this factor.

Sales-Type Goals

Not all sales goals are the same. The complexity of your product often determines how you want to sell it. The choice of media is one consideration, of course. The other is what kind of action it should elicit.

One-step direct sale.   Geared to immediate action, this format gives the reader all the pertinent facts, including benefits and selling features, and then asks them to buy and to buy *now*.

Various premiums and discounts are frequently offered to move the customer to immediate action. If the product can be sold without a detailed explanation or if it is something which can easily be perceived as desirable, then radio, television, print ads, and catalogue sales work very well. For something requiring more explanation or a longer list of features and benefits to build desire, then direct mail or telemarketing would be a better choice. Clothing, records, books, tapes, jewelry, and cosmetics are frequent direct sale products.

Two-step direct lead.   Sellers whose products are more complicated, such as insurance, financial services, or learning materials, may need to give prospects a lot more information than can be contained in a short ad or 60-second spot. In that case, radio, television, and print ads are often used to spark the prospects' interest, and tell them where to get the rest of the information. The purpose of this type of ad (like the SMI ad illustrated in Chapter 7) is to elicit leads which can later be followed up by telemarketers or sales people.

This method is commonly used by auto insurance companies, for example, who mail out a letter enclosing a "quote sheet." The prospect fills out the sheet and returns it. The company then works up a quote, contacts the prospect (usually by telephone), and attempts to close the sale.

Support. The purpose of support advertising is not to sell directly, or even to generate leads (although this sometimes happens), but to support another media. Sweepstakes offers by companies such as Publisher's Clearing House are heralded by television support advertising. The latest cable shopping services to air are using direct mail to tell people to watch for their arrival in the local area. Support services are usually big-budget, and often national in scope. Small businesses can use them effectively, however, with a combination of radio and direct mail, for instance, or local TV to back up telemarketing.

MARKET MIX

As the use of two-step or support selling clearly shows, direct marketing methods are not isolated. Frequently, it takes a combination of two or more methods to cover the market thoroughly. As long as it requires a response that can be measured, and is interactive between buyer and seller, your marketing mix will ultimately be determined by both buyer preferences and your own budget. Target marketing is not shotgun marketing. It depends on several media, often one supporting another, or acting with it in a symbiotic relationship to build a bigger, better client base.

Many marketing methods are often almost interchangeable — radio and print advertising, for example. In many cases, they are also interdependent. Telemarketing is frequently used in conjunction with direct mail, print advertising, radio, and television. It can be a support mechanism, in the case of call-in telephone numbers published in a response coupon, or flashed on a television screen. It can also be an independent marketing device, or used as a backup to another campaign.

A Package Approach

The name of the game in direct marketing is, "Make it easy to buy!" Certain media combinations will help make that happen.

For example, telemarketing and direct mail work well together when the offer is first presented by one method and followed up later with the second. Almost any product or service, from moon rocks to paper socks can be sold with a strong telemarketing campaign preceded by a coupon mailer, and followed with a self-mailer order form. Reversing the order may work even better: direct mail first; telemarketing follow-up. Catalogue sales often use both a direct mail order blank and a toll-free number as response devices.

Telemarketing, direct mail, and radio or television make a profitable combination, too. Sweepstakes preannounced by television or radio spots do 50 percent better than those mailed to the same list without any fanfare. Catalogue shopping services mail out announcements of new services, put them on the air, and use telecommunications to process the order.

Radio, too, communicates with its audience via telephone. Radio listeners will call in, but as studio lines are not always as efficient as independent telemarketing operators are, they will also mail in a response. A lot depends on listeners' loyalty to the station and their affinity to the announcer, who can determine the outcome of a commercial with one quick comment. "Hey, that's a good commercial," he might say, "and they make a really good onion grater!" Listeners will buy.

Sweepstakes offers with a big enough budget often use support television advertising (and radio too), to inform prospects of an impending offer. This method also allows them to use the "testimonial" approach to verify their credibility ahead of time. Televised catalogue or shopping services are starting to use this technique, too. Several of them have reversed the sweepstakes approach and now send out a direct mail piece to inform prospects that televised shopping is on the way to their hometown TV channels.

Past History

What appeals to one demographic segment may not work as well with another. Again, results of previous direct marketing campaigns will suggest the best methods to use to reach prospective buyers. And with the new technologies introduced every day, old methods can be improved, and new ones added to increase response.

MANAGING YOUR MARKETING CAMPAIGN

How well you mix marketing media will certainly have a strong impact on the ultimate success of your marketing efforts. The more you know about each media, the better equipped you are to use it, and to call for professional help when you need it.

Outside Consultants

Unless your company is a large one, staffing a group of expensive marketing executives seldom makes good management sense. There are so many competent consultants available who can be hired, by the job, when you need them. Using outside talent removes the need for additional office space or for employee overhead. When certain specialties are required, you call for them, thus eliminating the added expense of in-house training, or worse yet—sending someone out for training. (The latter costs you double—the loss of the employee while she's away learning the new technique, and the loss of revenue from profits you could have been making if you had initiated the program earlier.)

The range and talent level of consultants vary widely. For help with a specific media, refer to your local direct marketing organization, or see the Appendices of this book. For help in designing a marketing campaign, many excellent consultants are available from full-service marketing firms to individual marketing consultants.

Budgeting

As an example, the cost to design an overall marketing plan for a firm employing ten people and anticipating $1 million in first year annual sales, with an expected growth rate of 10 percent, could cost somewhere between $5,000 and $50,000 for a marketing consultant. Production costs (such as printing, EDM advertising, even logo design) would be additional. Brochures could cost $8,000, for example, and a database marketing program another $10,000.[2]

Marketing Director

You *will* need a marketing director, someone who can work up a budget and coordinate the program. This individual should have both the training and expertise to put together a working plan and locate experts to carry it out. In a small firm, this hat is usually worn by one individual acting as the operations director, the general manager, and the chief salesperson. In other words, the boss wears all the hats, including that of marketing director. This, of course, saves money, but what is saved in dollars is usually lost in expertise. As an alternative, an outside consultant can often do the job better, and in the end, for far less money. The business owner is then free to do what *he* does best — run his business or develop his product. (If you use outside talent to draw up a budget, ask your accountant to review it — in comparison to other, similar efforts.)

Larger, more diversified firms are not faced with a cost crunch, and can support an in-house marketing director, and possibly even supportive, administrative staff. Here again, the temptation for many start-up companies (or shoe-string ventures) is to pad the payroll with "cheap" help in the name of cost efficiency. Don't let temptation overcome better judgment, however. A marketing office is not a training ground for minimum wage employees!

TESTING

How do you know what works? What if you blow the budget on a big direct mail campaign and it flops? Most advertisers solve this problem by testing — a perk of direct response advertising that is directly attributable to the miracles of computer processing. Here, again, the expertise of trained marketing people will be invaluable in selecting appropriate tests and in analyzing the results.

Not only is direct marketing interactive and flexible, it is also dependent upon a *measured response* to gauge its effectiveness. One of the best ways to measure response is to test it. Even better, test by running several advertising campaigns simultaneously, and then comparing the response of one method against that of the other.

Radio is often a favorite test medium (see Chapter 9). It is inexpensive, quick, and very flexible. Since it relies on what is essentially written copy, radio formats are also easily transformed into other forms of direct marketing.

Tests are usually based on small, representative samples or groups of prospects limited to a specific geographic location, or groups of individuals who meet certain demographic or psychographic criteria.

Be testing techniques and trying out new products on small segments before embarking on an all-out advertising campaign, corrections can be made early-on, and large-scale, costly mistakes avoided.

To market the sporting equipment discussed in Chapter 2, for example, the direct marketer might try a cooperative campaign with a single cable television company over a six-month period. The marketing device might be a pamphlet, brochure, or insert, with an appropriate response vehicle included, stuffed into the cable company's monthly statement. Customers of the cable company would serve as the **sample** (typical prospective buyers as defined in the sports buyer profile). During the test marketing phase, results would be carefully tabulated as orders for sports equipment were placed and filled. Following that, if advertising lived up to expectations (with profits and costs falling into an acceptable ratio), the marketing sample might be widened to include the customers of several other cable companies. The advertiser could continue to test the market until he was satisfied that his program would work.

At the same time, the seller might test the effectiveness of advertising his weight-training and sports equipment in catalogues. On a limited basis, he would place an ad in one or two selected catalogues (whose audience was compatible with his own buyer profile). Again, responses and costs would be measured carefully, and if cable statement stuffers were still being used, the response figures from the catalogue sales would be compared against those from the inserts.

Market Sample

Test marketing allows the direct marketer to target a specific segment of the market, usually a particular location, to get a "feel" for the product's appeal before dipping too far into the advertising budget. Many times the product will need to be revised or the campaign redesigned before the final version of either is ready for mass marketing.

For the small to medium size business, a test market sample could be a single neighborhood, or a cluster of cities or towns with common characteristics. Ads placed in local papers or magazines might be coupled with a flurry of door-to-door fliers and a barrage of direct mail. Like the Nielsen ratings, *the response of a test should be indicative of how the product will do when introduced to a larger market, provided the sample* is accurate.

Split-run advertising. Split-run advertising is a special kind of testing used to compare one or more variations of the same offer in the same media at the same time, i.e., run Ad A on Monday, Wednesday, and Friday in the local paper, and run Ad B on Tuesday, Thursday, and Saturday.

In their new book *Maxi Marketing*,[3] Stan Rapp and Tom Collins suggest **split-run advertising**[4] as an excellent technique for market testing. As with all other market research methods, split-run testing provides the advertiser with a highly accurate barometer for measuring results directly against sales. In this technique, a product is marketed using several different offers — promise, price point, even product name — simultaneously. Response to the offer (which is usually a booklet, savings coupon, or promise buried in the text of an ad) can be via an 800 number, a reply coupon, or other direct response vehicle. Whatever advertising method is chosen, it must be one that allows accurate, equal splitting of the advertising run (Type A versus Type B, Type B versus Type C, and so on). Direct mail works very well, as does newspaper or television advertising. (To qualify as split-run, the same media must be used with different offers. Thus, the example above, comparing the results of one offer advertised in two different media — cable statement stuffers and radio commercials, does not qualify as true split-run testing.)

The test Collins and Rapp used to illustrate this technique is a famous one in advertising circles. Two ads for Milk Bone® dog biscuits offered a free package of Milk Bone Snacks. The essence of both ads was the same: feeding table scraps to your dog during the summer is dangerous. It could make the poor pet sick, maybe even kill him. Much better to feed him something healthy, like Milk Bone Snacks. One ad used a negative appeal; the other a positive one. Said Ad A, "Don't Poison Your Dog!" Ad B suggested, "Keep Your Dog Safe This Summer!"

When the results were tabulated, Ad A pulled 58 percent more requests than Ad B. In other words, because a dead dog was not nearly as acceptable to a pet owner as a live one, the appeal based upon a positive viewpoint was twice as successful.

Market Tests

Used to determine the acceptance of a new product, market testing allows the advertiser to *peek* at the market before attempting a full-scale penetration of it. For instance, before a soft drink bottler comes out with a new version of the drink, the product might first be tested in a specific geographic area to test the validity of the offer (the soda itself), packaging (the can it comes in), and price. Should that test prove positive, another, larger sample may be tested before the product is released to the general public.

Spectrum Tests

Used to identify the market, spectrum tests are also particularly useful in determining expansion plans or widening market share. Three lists are tested simultaneously. The primary list contains the buyer profile you feel most correctly targets your market. The second list represents people who,

Figure 11.3

Don't use a negative viewpoint.

for various reasons, are considered good prospects even though they don't fit the primary buyer profile. A third test is also made, with still another list. Like the second one, this list also contains good prospects—but this group is chosen for an entirely different, although compatible, buyer profile.

Results of spectrum tests should each be considered separately, and should not be averaged together.

Cluster Behavior

Certain geo-demographic areas exhibit specific patterns or buying behavior. Utilizing census data and new techniques in market analysis, PRIZM (Potential Rating Index by Zip Markets) combines two independent databases to refine zip code marketing. Using clever names such as "Shotguns" and "Urban Gold Coast," this system, and others like it, help the direct marketer to predict consumer behavior within certain geographic areas and to target the most positive prospects by:[5]

- Removing the low-end of a list through negative screening.
- Pulling out the top 25 percent by PRIZM select coding (using current census data).
- Ranking a mailing by zip code.
- Building regressive analysis models (for adjusting creative approaches in long-term campaigns).
- Scoring and selecting names by multivariate, behavioral data (used in cross-selling and credit screening).

SUMMARY

Direct marketing is a delightfully dependable, highly accurate way of forecasting and following up on sales—at the same time that you are making them. Because it uses proven methods and tested, identifiable markets, one would have to work at it to miss the market! The rules are so simple:

1. Your offer must include a response device (return mail coupon, toll-free number, etc.) which is directly related to that specific offer.
2. Results must be measurable, which means that for every offer made, the response must be tabulated, even if that response is no response. (If you print 1,000 advertisements or make 1,000 telephone calls, how many people said yes? How many said no? How many did not answer at all?)

To help business people succeed, some very talented people are waiting, ready, and willing to lend expertise, and to help more and more of us learn to use a technique that can immeasurably improve our profitability.

We live in a tremendously exciting, changing world. As business people, and as advertisers, the challenge is clear: master the art of direct marketing, or fade away with the twentieth century.

Never before have we been so well equipped to locate a market and build a profitable marketing campaign to penetrate it. A wealth of information about the buying public awaits us; we have only to tap into it.

ENDNOTES

1. As a rule of thumb with most verbal (i.e., radio, TV) direct marketing, you have about three seconds to catch your prospects' attention. Written forms of communication (i.e., print, direct mail) give you more time — usually 30 seconds or so — to capture their interest.
2. The cost of consulting and outside advertising services will vary widely. Cheaper is seldom better, but the reverse is *not* true. Expensive is seldom better. Get quotes, compare them, and review work done for other clients to find a happy medium.
3. See *Maxi-Marketing*, by Stan Rapp and Tom Collins, McGraw-Hill Book Co., 1987. Says David Ogilvy, a competitor of Rapp and Collins, "Everyone who works in advertising *must* read it."
4. Split-run testing is also known as the Caples method because it was developed by John Caples, a recognized expert in the field of direct marketing.

    "The essence of [this method] of scientifically comparing two advertisements is to vary the advertisements — a different promise, different price, a different method of presentation, even a different product name — but make an effort that remains identical in presentation in both types of advertisements." (From an article by Stan Rapp and Tom Collins in *Advertising Age*, December 1, 1987.)
5. For more about psychographic overlays of geo-demographic segments, see "Psyching Out List Overlays," by Jim Mammarella, Associate Editor, *Direct Marketing* Magazine. February 1986.

HELP FOR THE DIRECT MARKETER

"Direct marketing depends on product presentation, the right marketing list, and follow up."
— Timothy H. Von Feldt
Manager, Mail Classification
U.S. Postal Service, San Diego

A number of organizations stand ready to help the direct marketer, not the least of which is the U.S. Postal Service. The Federal Trade Commission also provides helpful booklets and information about their rules concerning direct mail. The following pages share that information, and provide both a list of resources for every major metropolitan area in the United States, listed by location, and information catagorized by service classification, such as direct mail or telemarketing.

THE U.S. POSTAL SERVICE

There was a time when express mail meant a mud-caked rider spurring his horse through severe weather, sagebrush, and hostile territory. Today, Express Mail, neatly zipped up in a red, white, and blue packet, is delivered to your door by a driver in a freshly pressed blue uniform.

If delivery service has changed over the years, so has the mailer. Today's mailer is often a business, dependent on swift service to communicate a message to clients and suppliers. It stands to reason that the faster and more expert we get at communicating, the more successful we will be as marketers.

Direct mailers are really dependent upon the cooperation of the post office. A creative approach and a "teamwork" attitude can go a long way towards expediting mailings and saving problems down the line. By working closely with the local postmaster, you can improve mail flow, preplan unusually large mailings, and even anticipate and reduce mail flow problems. If you qualify, you may be eligible for on-site pickup and distribution, which avoids any processing at all through the local post office; this is helpful to you in speeding up your mailings, and helpful to the post office by not choking up their system.

Memo To Mailers

Post office regulations change frequently. Before initiating any direct mail project, consult your local postmaster. Certain restrictions apply to mailing materials, such as firearms[1] and sexual material.[2] To help you stay abreast of the latest developments in mailing services, the U.S. Postal Service publishes a free booklet which covers the latest trends and techniques in the direct mail world. Sent to interested subscribers, this publication covers topics such as the new Zip-Plus-Four conversion program and Express Mail. To get on the mailing list, contact the mail classification department of your post office.

Zip-Plus-Four Coded Presort

This new service was begun by the U.S. Postal Service to help commercial accounts manage databases more effectively. If you provide them with a copy of your mailing list (minimum 300 names) on disk or other electronic media compatible with their own equipment, the post office will standardize your list and recode it with the proper zip-plus-four designation for each address on the list.

    This service is enormously helpful, because it not only corrects zip codes, but also corrects street names, replacing any errors it finds with the correct spelling or abbreviations. Once your file has been cleaned up and standardized, you can streamline your mailings and begin saving costs with zip-coded mailings (about $9 per thousand as of this writing.)[3]

Mail Classes

Classification of mail started with two types when Ben Franklin was running the post office. Now there are four, with a lot of little subclasses that change from year to year.

First class.   Business reply permit mail, personal mail, letter-size material, correspondence, bills, statements of account.

Second class.   Periodicals, tabloids, newspapers. Originally subsidized by congress, this class was created in the 1700s in order to convey information to the general public in the fastest manner. (Most subsidies are gone now.)

Third class.   Advertising or material being distributed which is identical to all addressees (except for name and address), and is being sent to two hundred or more people. Each piece must be under one pound.

Third class mail is cheaper (almost half the cost) than first class mail, thus it is the *most common class used by direct mail advertisers*. The following rules apply to all users:

1. The body of the material must be mechanically reproduced (copied, printed, computer-printed, etc.).
2. All material must go in "like terms" to qualify (i.e., each piece must be identical).
3. The signature and greeting may be handwritten.
4. Each piece must have a unique identifier.

Rules regarding third class mail are difficult to understand and change frequently. The post office publishes a manual which explains the rules, but a visit with the local post master is essential before attempting to use third class mail. Failing to follow the rules may slow up your mailing or prevent its being sent out at all. It is not uncommon to see a new direct mailer sitting on a post office floor, resorting a seven-sack mailing. It's better to get it right the first time.

Also, within third class are several subclasses dependent on the number of pieces in each presorted section of mail. You may qualify for a rate that is *less* than half of the normal mailing cost.

Fourth class.   Material that weighs over a pound, i.e., merchandise. Maximum weight per piece is 70 pounds. This class was originally devised to deliver merchandise to rural areas (such as Sears Roebuck catalogue merchandise.)

There are no restrictions upon the use of first class mail except when used for business reply. All other classes and first class business reply require permits.

Within each class there are numerous subclasses. For example, within first class, postage is reduced by presorting (by zip code). The finer the presort, the greater the postage reduction. Carrier route presort

Figure 12.1

It is not uncommon to see a new direct mailer sitting on a post office floor, resorting a seven-sack mailing.

(which bypasses most processing) is zip-plus-four and uses a letter-sorting machine which can sort 55 letters a minute using optical character readers and a bar code reader. Banks often use presorted first class.

Another subclass is priority mail. Faster than fourth class, priority mail handles parcels and heavy packages within the first class postal rates.

Business Reply Permits

Issued by the post office, these permits require compliance with the following rules:

1. Use on letter size mail (correspondence).
2. Use to return merchandise.[4]

3. Postage is first class plus a surcharge for handling.
4. Permit holders may set up a trust account (prepay postage) or pay the postman when he delivers the mail. Another alternative is to pick up reply mail at the post office and pay the postage there.
5. Return mail must have an imprint showing the permit number and clearly stating that the piece is first class mail and U.S. Postage Paid. The city and state of origin must also show.

Other Permits

These must state the permit number, city and state of issue, and U.S. Postage Paid. Several forms are permitted.

1. Metered mail.
2. Precancelled stamps.
3. Printed indicia (using a rubber stamp).
4. Preprinted indicia (printed on envelope).

Metered Mail

This requires a license which can be obtained at the post office. The user prepays a certain amount of postage which is then available on a postage meter. Letters run through the meter are imprinted with the appropriate postage. All classes of mail can use metered mail.

Itemized Postage

The mailer and the post office agree to using a permit imprint system where mail itself is of different and varying weights. The mailer builds a weight factor into a computer to precalculate weight and postage. This method is usually reserved for large direct mailers such as National Pen.

Personal Zip Code

If your company is big enough or if the number of mailings high enough, you may qualify for your own zip code, which precludes normal processing and thus speeds up mail considerably.

Address Correction Requested

To penetrate the widest market possible, some companies send out one publication addressed to "occupant" and another, similar but more complete, edition to their regular customer list, with the added notation "address correction requested." The latter insures that the catalogue will keep up with good customers when they are on the move.[5]

Do Not Mail

If you are selling sexually explicit material or certain types of firearms or alcoholic beverages, you must comply with local, state, and federal regulations. The post office maintains a list of individuals who have asked that certain types of materials not be mailed to them. Because lists are sold, rented, and interchanged frequently, it is easy to overlook a *Do Not Mail* code and send material the recipient finds offensive. To date, the burden falls on you to avoid that mistake.

(Contact your local post office to verify that your direct marketing plans are within legal limits.)

ETHICAL ADVERTISING

The question of "ethics" deserves to be mentioned here. Over the years, direct marketing developed a bad reputation as the home of "snake oil" shysters who took your money and ran, leaving you with a bottle of nothing. The snakes are still out there, not just in direct marketing, but in all types of business. It is up to you to verify that you are not one of them. Make sure your product will do what you claim it will do before you offer to sell it to someone else. If you aren't sure, test it. If it doesn't work or live up to its claimed expectations, cancel the offer and pull the ad. Your reputation can work for you or against you. Remember, the stench of bad customer service and shoddy products will follow wherever you go. Keep your promises and don't sell swampland through cereal boxes.

There are also certain laws, rules, and regulations relating to direct marketing. Most familiar are the laws against selling sexually explicit material through the mails (with certain exceptions) and the law (which changes frequently) about selling certain classifications of firearms. You must also be careful about soliciting money through the mail. Schemes such as the "chain letter" advertisements selling a "mailing list" for a dollar to the last name on the list are illegal.

Sexually Explicit Material

As of this writing, you may send such material through the mail if the recipient has requested it.[2] You may *not* send it to minors. Those who do not wish to receive such material may register with the post office and have their names placed on a special list which is available for all direct marketers. Parents or guardians of minors may also place names of those children on the list. Should you persist in mailing offensive material to someone on this list, after someone has registered an objection to it, you could be subject to heavy penalty. See your local postmaster for details. If you have further questions, consult an attorney before embarking on the sale of "sensitive" material. Incidentally, "implied consent" is usually sufficient, and if you place an ad in a women's magazine that carries a number of other offers like yours, it is assumed that the purchasers of this magazine know what to expect before opening the covers. Thus, you are not guilty of "offending" them by placing your ad in that publication.

FEDERAL REGULATIONS

Firearms

The U.S. Government has regulations against selling handguns and certain other types of firearms through the mail to unlicensed purchasers. Prospective owners of automatic weapons must first obtain a special type of license. In addition to federal laws, some states have rules of their own regarding the sale of firearms. Before selling any type of weapon or firearm, consult the postmaster in your town and other appropriate authorities.[1]

Tax Fraud

Because certain types of direct marketing lend themselves easily to fraud, you should be careful accurately and faithfully to record sales and expenses and prepare taxes and returns on time and in accordance with all local as well as federal laws.

FTC Mail Order Rule

The Federal Trade Commission/Bureau of Consumer Protection (FTC/BCP) regulates the direct marketing industry, as it relates to the delivering of mail order merchandise and services. The rule is discussed in detail in the booklet,

"A Business Guide to the Federal Trade Commission's Mail Order Rule," available from the FTC in Washington, D.C. In essence it says:

> "The Mail Order Rule was issued by the Federal Trade Commission (FTC) to correct growing problems with late or undelivered mail order merchandise. Under this rule, you have a duty to ship merchandise on time. You also must follow procedures that the Rule requires if you cannot ship ordered merchandise on time.
>
> "When there is a shipping delay, the Rule requires that you notify your customers of the delay and provide them with an option either to agree to the delay or to cancel the order and receive a prompt refund. For each additional delay, your customers must be notified that they must send you a signed consent to a further delay or a refund will be given."

The Rule expects you to know whether problems will be encountered in shipping or timely delivery and to notify the customer in time. If, for example, there is a railroad or airline strike, you should make alternative arrangements to ship, or else notify the customer of the problem. Generally, 30 days is considered the appropriate amount of time for delivery. After that, the Rule must be invoked.

The Rule dictates how and when to send notices, and what you must say. It tells you when you *must* cancel — generally if delivery will go beyond 30 days (unless you have specified differently in your literature) and you have failed to notify the customer.

"The Rule does **not** cover:

- magazine subscriptions (and similar serial deliveries), except for the first shipment;
- sales of seed and growing plants;
- orders made on a collect-on-delivery basis (COD);
- transactions covered by the FTC's Negative Option Rule (such as book and record clubs);
- mail order photo-finishing, or
- orders made by telephone and charged to a credit card account."

The Rule also states that "only two kinds of unordered merchandise can be sent legally through the U.S. mail without a consumer's prior consent:

- free samples that are clearly and conspicuously marked as such; and
- merchandise mailed by a charitable organization asking for contributions."

Please remember that, absent the two exceptions listed above, *if you send something through the mail that was not ordered, the customer does* **not** *have to pay for it.*

ENDNOTES

1. Firearms classified as concealed handguns are not permitted through the mail unless it is between dealers, police officers, or licensed manufacturers.

    Guidelines for selling and shipping long-barreled guns, shotguns, and rifles are provided by the ATF (Alcohol, Tobacco, and Firearms) Department of the Federal Government. Also contact local and state police for appropriate permits.

    The post office prefers *not* to ship firearms. Most gun dealers use common carriers. Selling weapons over state lines is administered by the ICC (Interstate Commerce Commission) as well as the AFT.

    While it is perfectly legal to advertise war materials through the mail, delivery may pose a problem.

    The above information was furnished by the U. S. Postal Service as of July 1986. Any or all of it may have changed. Before selling or delivering any firearms through the mail, contact your local post office to verify the latest rulings.

2. Sexual or pornographic material is unacceptable by mail unless it is clearly marked with the endorsement: "Sexually Oriented Advertising."

    U.S. Title Code 18 of the Federal Law makes violators criminally prosecutable for distributing lewd or sexually oriented material (movies, devices, other paraphernalia). However, there is considerable leeway as to the definition of "paraphernalia" because the definition depends, in part, upon the user's perception and intention.

    Sending sexually explicit material to children comes under the Pandering Order. Sending such material to children whose parents have filed a Form 2150 with the post office (prohibiting receipt of such material) will result in criminal prosecution. Responsibility lies with the advertiser to know who is on that list, which is available through the local post office.

The postal laws may have changed. Any or all of this material may no longer apply. Contact your local post office for information before advertising or delivering sexually explicit material through the mails.

3. There is no charge for this service. For more information, contact your local post office. Mailing lists prepared on most standard personal or business computers (PC, XT, or AT) can be converted with no problem.

4. The post office also offers a Merchandise Return Service which might prove a better alternative to a Return Mail Permit.

5. Check with your local branch of the post office for current rates before using this technique. The added cost may be prohibitive, and certainly is warranted only in the case of proven prospects.

APPENDICES

Appendix A: Listing of Trade Associations

1. Advertising Research Foundation
   3 East 54th Street
   New York, NY 10022
   (212) 751-5656

2. American Assn. of Fund Raising
   Counsel Inc.
   25 West 43rd Street
   New York, NY 10036
   (212) 354-5799

3. American Marketing Association
   250 South Wacker Drive, Suite 200
   Chicago, IL 60606
   (312) 648-0536

4. American Society of Association
   Executives
   1575 Eye Street NW
   Washington, DC 20005
   (202) 626-2723

5. American Telemarketing
   Association
   1800 Pickwick Avenue
   Glenview, IL 60025
   (312) 724-7700

6. Census Bureau
   Herbert C. Hoover Building
   14 Street & Constitution Avenue NW
   Washington, DC 20230
   (202) 763-4040

7. Direct Selling Association
   1776 K Street NW, Suite 600
   Washington, DC 20006
   (202) 293-5760

8. International Advertising Association
   475 Fifth Avenue
   New York, NY 10017
   (212) 684-1583

9. Magazine Publishers Association
   575 Lexington Avenue
   New York, NY 10022
   (212) 752-0055

10. National Mail Order Association
    5818 Venice Boulevard
    Los Angeles, CA 90019
    (213) 934-7986

11. National Retail Merchants
    Association
    100 West 31st Street
    New York, NY 10001
    (212) 244-2780

12. Newsletter Association
    1341 G Street NW, Suite 700
    Washington, DC 20005
    (202) 347-5520

13. Newspaper Ad Bureau
    1180 Avenue of the Americas
    New York, NY 10036
    (212) 921-5080

14. Printing Industry Association
    1730 North Lynn Street
    Arlington, VA 22209
    (703) 841-8100

15. Promotion Marketing Association of
    America
    322 8th Avenue, Suite 1201
    New York, NY 10001
    (212) 206-1100

16. Standard Rate & Data Service
    3004 Glenview Road
    Wilmette, IL 60091
    (312) 256-6067

17. Third Class Mailers Association
    1341 G Street NW, Suite 3103
    Washington, DC 20005-3103
    (202) 347-0055

18. USPS Consumer Advocate Line
    475 L'Enfant Plaza WSW
    Washington, DC 20260
    (202) 268-2000

Mail Order Statistics

1. Marketing Logistics
   (Arnold Fishman)
   175 Olde Half Day Road, Suite 145
   Lincolnshire, IL 60069
   (312) 634-4700

2. Maxwell Sroge Co., Inc.
   (Maxwell Sroge)
   The Sroge Building
   731 North Cascade Avenue
   Colorado Springs, CO 80903
   (303) 633-5556

Source: Direct Marketing Association, 6 East
43rd Street, New York, NY 10017. Reprinted
by permission.

Appendix B: Listing of U.S. Direct Marketing Clubs and Contacts by Geographic Location

ARIZONA

Phoenix

Phoenix Direct Marketing Club
Mr. Richard Moore
c/o Marketing Connections
10227 N. 53rd Avenue
Glendale, AZ 85302
(602) 264-8794

The Phoenix Direct Marketing Club
(PDMC)
P.O. Box 8756
Phoenix, AZ 85066
(602) 268-5237

CALIFORNIA

Los Angeles

Direct Marketing Club of Southern
California
Mr. Howard Oberstein
c/o The Marketing Place
8615 Tamarack Avenue
Sun Valley, CA 91352
(818) 768-8500

Orange County

Direct Marketing Association of Orange
County
Mr. Robert Zack
c/o S. K. Zack Associates
17371 Sandalwood
Irvine, CA 92715
(714) 786-3040

San Diego

San Diego Direct Marketing Club
Mr. James R. Rosenfield
c/o Buchanan/Vinson/Rosenfield Direct
1335 Hotel Circle South
San Diego, CA 92108
(619) 293-3940

San Francisco

San Francisco Advertising Club
Ms. Cathy Clifton
c/o Forms Engineering Co.
300 Broadway Street, Suite 23
San Francisco, CA 94133
(415) 391-2580

COLORADO

Denver

Rocky Mountain Direct Marketing Club
Mr. Al Stieffel
c/o M.L. Associates
1380 S. Santa Fe Drive
Denver, CO 80223
(303) 777-4280

DISTRICT OF COLUMBIA

Falls Church

Direct Marketing Association of
Washington
Ms. Catherine Lincoln
c/o The Viguerie Company
7777 Leesburg Pike
Falls Church, VA 22043
(703) 356-0440

Washington, D.C.

Women's Direct Response Group
1210 North Taft Street, Suite 711
Arlington, VA 22201
(703) 527-2772

FLORIDA

South Daytona

Florida Direct Marketing Association
Mr. Stuart Oleson
c/o Response Graphics
P.O. Box 4550
South Daytona, FL 32021
(904) 756-0060

GEORGIA

Atlanta

Southeast Direct Mail/Marketing Club
Mr. Jerry Eaves
c/o Hooper Holmes Direct Marketing
290 Interstate Parkway North
#230-235
Atlanta, GA 30339-2401
(404) 952-0220

HAWAII

Honolulu

Direct Response Advertising &
Marketing Association
Mr. David Erdman
c/o Travel Management Associates
4 South King Street
Honolulu, HI 96813
(808) 531-4336

ILLINOIS

Chicago

Chicago Association of Direct Marketing
Mr. Donald Harle
c/o Mid-America Mailers, Inc.
430 Russell Street
P.O. Box 646
Hammond, IN 46325
(219) 933-0137

CADM
221 North LaSalle Street
Chicago, IL 60601
(312) 346-1600

Women's Direct Response Group
Ms. Dorothy Rosen
c/o Gruen & Sells
645 N. Michigan Avenue
Chicago, IL 60611
(312) 943-8189

INDIANA

Indianapolis

Direct Marketing Association of
Indianapolis
Mr. Jim Lindsay
c/o American Legion
P.O. Box 1055
Indianapolis, IN 46206
(317) 635-8411

KENTUCKY

Louisville

Louisville Direct Marketing Association
Mr. Guy Miller
c/o Kentucky Easter Seal Society
233 East Broadway
Louisville, KY 40202
(502) 584-9781

MARYLAND

Baltimore

Maryland Direct Marketing Association
Mr. Douglas McCrea
c/o MacDantz Direct
120 W. Fayette Street
Baltimore, MD 21201
(310) 837-4966

MASSACHUSETTS

Boston

New England Direct Marketing
Association
Mr. George Wojtkiewicz
c/o New England Mutual Life Insurance Co.
501 Boylston Street
Boston, MA 02117
(617) 266-3700

MICHIGAN

Detroit

Direct Marketing Association of Detroit
Mr. John Hobart
c/o Consultant
41805 Rayburn
Northville, MI 48167
(313) 362-4830

MINNESOTA

St. Paul

Midwest Direct Marketing Association
Ms. Joanne Clark
c/o I.C. Systems
444 E. Highway 96
St. Paul, MN 55164
(612) 483-0585

MISSOURI

Kansas City

Kansas City Direct Marketing Association
Mr. James Thorman
c/o Professional Computer Resources
4710 E. 63rd Street, P.O. Box 17536
Kansas City, MO 64130
(816) 444-1626

St. Louis

Direct Marketing Club of St. Louis
Mr. Ralph Barber
c/o Creative Office Systems
1601 Washington Avenue
St. Louis, MO 63103
(314) 436-2800

NEBRASKA

Omaha

Mid-America Direct Marketing
Association
Mr. Ray Golden
c/o Wats Marketing of America
9706 Mockingbird Drive
Omaha, NE 68127

NEW JERSEY

Ridgefield

Women's Direct Response Group
Ms. Meryl Boggs
c/o Rubin Response
712 Bergen Boulevard, Suite 10
Ridgefield, NJ 07657
(201) 945-6416

New Brunswick

Fulfillment Management Association
Mr. Jack Beardsley
c/o Beardsley & Associates
1265 Omaha Road
New Brunswick, NJ 08902
(201) 828-7337

NEW YORK

Hudson Valley

Hudson Valley Direct Marketing Club
Mr. Robert Foehl
c/o Direct Media, Inc.
220 Grace Church St.
P.O. Box 1151
Port Chester, NY 10573
(914) 937-5600

Long Island

Long Island Direct Marketing Association
Ms. Cathy Greiger
c/o Beautiful Visions
810 S. Broadway
Hicksville, NY 11802
(516) 822-3760

Direct Marketing Club of New York
Mr. Mal Dunn
c/o Mal Dunn Associates, Inc.
Hardscrabble Road
Croton Falls, NY 10519
(914) 277-5558

New York City

Direct Marketing Creative Guild
Ms. Emily Soell
c/o Rapp & Collins, Inc.
475 Park Avenue South
New York, NY 10016
(212) 725-8100

Direct Marketing Idea Exchange
Ms. Florence Peloquin
c/o Woman's Day
1515 Broadway
New York, NY 10036
(212) 719-6000

Direct Marketing Minority Opportunities
Ms. Barbara Lewis
c/o Thomas Publishing Company
One Penn Plaza
New York, NY 10119
(212) 290-7224

Women's Direct Response Group
Ms. Shirley Stevens
c/o Furgiuele, Stevens & Associates
37 West 26th Street
New York, NY 10010
(212) 481-0250

OHIO

Cincinnati

Ohio Valley Direct Marketing Club
Ms. Ruth Van Gordon
c/o Merten Co
1515 Central Parkway
Cincinnati, OH 45214
(513) 721-5167

Cleveland

Ohio Direct Marketing Association
Mr. Robert Silverman
c/o Robert Silverman, Inc.
1375 Euclid Avenue
Cleveland, OH 44115
(216) 771-6332

OKLAHOMA

Tulsa

Direct Marketing Association of Tulsa
Mr. Mike Goldberg
c/o Kraftbilt
P.O. Box 800
Tulsa, OK 74101
(800) 331-7290

OREGON

Portland

Portland Direct Marketing Group
Mr. Richard Rosen
c/o PSW Direct
517 Southwest 4th Avenue
Portland, OR 97204
(503) 228-4000

PENNSYLVANIA

King of Prussia

PDMA
198 Allendale Road
King of Prussia, PA 19406
(215) 337-0117

Philadelphia

Philadelphia Direct Marketing
Association
Mr. Doug Allen
c/o Archibald Allen & Associations
Union Hill/Industrial Park
30 Clipper Road
West Conshohocken, PA 19428
(215) 825-2570

TEXAS

Dallas/Ft. Worth

Direct Marketing Association of North
Texas
Mr. Jim Rosenthal
c/o Texas Refinery Corp.
1 Refinery Place
Ft. Worth, TX 76101
(817) 332-1161

Houston

Houston Direct Marketing Club
Ms. Alice Thomas
c/o Grizzard Advertising, Inc.
1002 Texas Parkway
Stafford, TX 77477
(713) 499-4547

WASHINGTON

Seattle

Seattle Direct Marketing Association
Mr. Lin Applequist
c/o Herring-Newman Direct Response
605 First Avenue
Seattle, WA 98104
(206) 343-9654

WISCONSIN

Brookfield

Wisconsin Direct Marketing Club
Mr. Timothy J. Keane
c/o Communique, Inc.
250 N. Sunnyslope Road
Brookfield, WI 53005
(414) 785-0400

Source: Direct Marketing Association, 6 East
43rd Street, New York, NY 10017. Reprinted
by permission.

Appendix C: Listing of Magazines and Trade Journals for Direct Marketing

Ad Age Focus
Crain Communications
1400 Woodbridge Avenue
Detroit, MI 48207
(313) 446-6012
Monthly

Adweek
ASM Communications
49 East 21 Street
New York, NY 10010
(212) 661-8080
Weekly

Advertising Age
Crain Communications
740 N. Rush Street
Chicago, IL 60611
(312) 649-5200
Weekly

American Demographics
American Demographics, Inc.
P.O. Box 68
Ithaca, NY 14851
(607) 273-6343
Monthly

ARF Transcript Proceedings
American Research Foundation (ARF)
3 E. 54 Street
New York, NY 10022
(212) 751-5656
ARF con. time

Association and Society Manager
Brentwood Publishing Corporation
1640 Fifth Street
Santa Monica, CA 90401
(213) 395-0234
Bimonthly

Association Management
American Society of Association
    Executives
1575 I Street NW
Washington, DC 20005
(202) 626-2722
Monthly

Broadcasting
Broadcasting Publishing, Inc.
1735 DeSales St. NW
Washington, DC 20036
(202) 638-1022
Weekly

Business Marketing
Crain Communications
740 N. Rush Street
Chicago, IL 60611
(312) 649-5260
Monthly

Business-to-Business Catalog Marketer
Maxwell Sroge Publishing, Inc.
731 Cascade Avenue
Colorado Springs, CO 80903-3205
(303) 633-5556
Biweekly

Business-to-Business Council
    Newsletter
Direct Marketing Association
6 E. 43rd Street
New York, NY 10017
(212) 689-4977
Quarterly

Business Week
McGraw-Hill, Inc.
1221 Avenue of the Americas
New York, NY 10020
(212) 512-1221
Weekly

Cable Marketing
Associated Cable Enterprises, Inc.
352 Park Avenue South
New York, NY 10010
(212) 685-4848
Monthly

Cablevision
International Thomas Communications
600 Grant Street
Denver, CO 80203
(303) 860-0111
Biweekly

Catalog Age
Catalog Age Publishing Co.
Box 4949
6 River Bend
Stamford, CT 06907-0949
(203) 358-9900
Bimonthly

Catalog Council Newsletter
Direct Marketing Association
6 E. 43rd Street
New York, NY 10017
(212) 689-4977
Quarterly

Catalog Marketer
Maxwell Sroge Publishing, Inc.
731 Cascade Avenue
Colorado Springs, CO 80903-3205
(303) 633-5556
Biweekly

Circulation Council Newsletter
Direct Marketing Association
6 E. 43rd Street
New York, NY 10017
(212) 689-4977
Quarterly

Communications Briefings
Encoders, Inc.
806 Westminster Blvd.
Blackwood, NJ 08012
(609) 589-3503
Monthly

Crain's NY Business
Crain Communications Inc.
220 E. 42 Street
New York, NY 10017
(212) 210-0100
Weekly

The Delay Letter
Crain Communications
220 E. 42 Street
New York, NY 10017
(212) 210-0100
Biweekly

Direct Line
Direct Marketing Association
6 E. 43rd Street
New York, NY 10017
(212) 689-4977
Monthly

Direct Marketing Magazine
Hoke Communications, Inc.
224 Seventh Street
Garden City, NY 11530
(516) 746-6700
Monthly

Direct Response Magazine
Macro Publishing Limited
Conbar House, Mead Lane
Hertford, Herts
SG137AS, United Kingdom
(4992) 54233
Monthly

Direct Response Newsletter
Creative Direct Marketing Group
25550 Hawthorne Blvd., Suite 114
Torrance, CA 90505-6828
(213) 373-9408
Monthly

DM Directions
Direct Marketing Association
6 E. 43rd Street
New York, NY 10017
(212) 689-4977
Biweekly

DM News
Mill Hollow Corporation
19 W. 21st Street
New York, NY 10010
(212) 741-2095
Biweekly

DMA Matters
Direct Marketing Association
6 E. 43rd Street
New York, NY 10017
(212) 689-4977
Quarterly

DMCA Input
Direct Marketing Computer Association
315 W. 58th St., 25th Floor
New York, NY 10019
(212) 245-0167
Bimonthly

Family Computing
Scholastic, Inc.
730 Broadway
New York, NY 10003
(212) 505-3580
Monthly

Federal Register
Office of the Federal Register
National Archives and Records
    Administration
Washington, DC 20408
Daily

Financial Services Council Newsletter
Direct Marketing Association
6 E. 43rd Street
New York, NY 10017
(212) 689-4977
Quarterly

Financial World
Financial World Partners
1450 Broadway
New York, NY 10018
(212) 869-1616
Biweekly

Folio
Folio Publishing Corp.
Box 4949
6 River Bend
Stamford, CT 06907-0949
(203) 358-9900
Monthly

Forbes
Forbes, Inc.
60 Fifth Avenue
New York, NY 10011
(212) 620-2200
Biweekly

Fortune
Time, Inc.
1271 Avenue of the Americas
New York, NY 10020
(212) 586-1212
Biweekly

Fraud and Theft Newsletter
Fraud and Theft Information Bureau
217 N. Seacrest Blvd., Box 400
Boynton Beach, FL 33425
(305) 737-7500
Monthly

Friday Report
Hoke Communications
224 Seventh Street
Garden City, NY 11530
(516) 746-6700
Weekly

Harvard Business Review
Harvard Graduate School of Business
    Administration
Soldiers Field Road
Boston, MA 02163
(617) 495-6800
Bimonthly

Inc. Magazine
Inc. Publishing Co.
One Penn Plaza, 250 W. 34 Street
New York, NY 10001
(212) 290-7336
Monthly

Incentive Marketing
Bill Communications, Inc.
633 Third Avenue
New York, NY 10017
(212) 986-4800
Monthly

Info World
Popular Computing, Inc.
1060 March Road, Suite C-200
Menlo Park, CA 94025
(415) 328-4602
Weekly

Information Marketing
Mark Nolan Advertising
7837 Greenback Lane, Suite 234
Citrus Heights, CA 95610
(916) 723-3070
Monthly

Inside Direct Marketing
Marketing Confidential, Inc.
Business Office, Suite 116
440 Main St.
Ridgefield, CT 06877
(704) 298-5705
Monthly

Insurance Council Newsletter
Direct Marketing Association
6 E. 43rd Street
New York, NY 10017
(212) 689-4977
Quarterly

International Advertiser
Directories International
150 Fifth Avenue
New York, NY 10011
(212) 807-4301
Bimonthly

International Management
McGraw-Hill Publications Overseas Corp.
14 Ave. d'Ouchy, CH-1006
Lausanne, Switzerland
021-274411
Monthly

International Videotex/Teletext
Arlen Communications, Inc.
7315 Wisconsin Avenue, Suite 600E
Bethesda, MD 20814-3202
(301) 656-7940
Monthly

Journal of Advertising Research
Advertising Research Foundation
3 E. 54th Atreet
New York, NY 10022-3180
(212) 751-5656
Bimonthly

Journal of Business/Industrial Mktg.
Grayson Associates
108 Loma Media Rd
Santa Barbara, CA 93103
(805) 564-1313
Quarterly

Journal of Consumer Research
Lancaster Press, Inc.
Prince and Lemon Streets
Lancaster, PA 17603
(717) 394-7241
Quarterly

Journal of Data Collections
Marketing Research Association
111 East Wacker Drive
Chicago, IL 60601
(312) 644-6610
Annually

Journal of Direct Marketing
Medill School of Journalism (DMEF)
6 E. 43rd Street
New York, NY 10017
(212) 689-4977
Quarterly

Journal of Marketing
American Marketing Association
250 S. Bracker Drive
Chicago, IL 60606
(312) 648-0536
Quarterly

Journal of Marketing Research
American Marketing Association
College of Business, University of Texas
Austin, TX 78712
(512) 471-6002
Quarterly

Journal of Retailing
New York University
202 Tisch Hall, Washington Sq.
New York, NY 10003
(212) 988-4153
Quarterly

Lead Letter
Market-Direct Publishing
2674 E. Main Street, Suite C-170
Ventura, CA 93003-2899
(805) 658-7000
Monthly

List Council Newsletter
Direct Marketing Association
6 E. 43rd Street
New York, NY 10017
(212) 689-4977
Quarterly

Lotus Magazine
Lotus Publishing Corp.
55 Cambridge Parkway
Cambridge, MA 02142
(617) 494-1192
Monthly

Madison Avenue
Madison Avenue Magazine
369 Lexington Avenue
New York, NY 10017
(212) 972-0600
Monthly

Marketing Communications
Media Horizons
50 W. 23rd Street
New York, NY 10010
(212) 645-1000
Monthly

Marketing Council Newsletter
Direct Marketing Association
6 E. 43rd Street
New York, NY 10017
(212) 689-4977
Quarterly

Marketing and Media Decision
Decisions Publications, Inc.
1140 Avenue of the Americas
New York, NY 10036
(212) 391-2155
Monthly

Marketing News
American Marketing Associations
250 S. Wacker Drive, Suite 200
Chicago, IL 60606
(312) 648-0536
Biweekly

Marketing Review
American Marketing Association
420 Lexington Avenue
New York, NY 10170
(212) 962-1991
10 times/yr.

Marketing Week
ASM Communications
49 E. 21 Street
New York, NY 10010
(212) 661-8080
Weekly

Research Alert
Min Publishing, Inc.
18 E. 53rd Street
New York, NY 10022
(212) 751-2670
Biweekly

National Underwriter
The National Underwriter Co.
420 E. 4th Street
Cincinnati, OH 45202-3396
Weekly

News Week
Newsweek, Inc.
444 Madison Avenue
New York, NY 10022
(212) 350-4000
Weekly

New York Magazine
News America Publishing Co.
755 Second Avenue
New York, NY 10017
(212) 880-0700
50 issues/yr.

New York Times
The New York Times Co.
229 W. 43rd Street
New York, NY 10036
(212) 556-1234
Weekly

Non-Profit Marketing Insider
Wordsworth Communications, Inc.
P.O. Box 5311
Evanston, IL 60204
(312) 475-5855
Biweekly

Non-Store Marketing Report
Maxwell Stroge Publishing, Inc.
731 N. Cascade Avenue
Colorado Springs, CO 80903-3205
(303) 633-5556
Biweekly

On-Line
On-Line Access Publishing Group
53 W. Jackson Boulevard
Chicago, IL 60604
(312) 922-9292
Bimonthly

Personal Computing
Hayden Publishing Co., Inc.
10 Mulholland Drive
Hasbrouck Heights, NJ 07604
(201) 393-6165
Monthly

Pryor Report
Fred Pryor Seminars
2000 Johnson Drive
Shawnee Mission, KS 66205
(913) 722-3990
Monthly

Psychology and Marketing
John Wiley and Sons, Inc.
605 Third Avenue
New York, NY 10158
(212) 692-6026
Quarterly

Research Council Newsletter
Direct Marketing Association
6 E. 43rd Street
New York, NY 10017
(212) 689-4977
Quarterly

Sales & Marketing Management
Bill Communications Inc.
633 Third Avenue
New York, NY 10017
(212) 986-4800
16 issues/yr.

Target Marketing
North American Publishing Co.
322 Eighth Avenue
New York, NY 10001
238-5300
Monthly

TCMA Newsletter
Third Class Mail Association
1341 G Street, Suite 500
Washington, DC 20005-3103
(202) 347-0055
Weekly

TMC Council Newsletter
Direct Marketing Association
6 E. 43rd Street
New York, NY 10017
(212) 689-4977
Quarterly

Telemarketer
Phone Marketing America
521 Fifth Avenue
New York, NY 10175
(212) 674-2540
Bimonthly

Telemarketing Magazine
Technology Marketing Corp.
One Technology Plaza
Norwalk, CT 06854
(203) 852-6800
(800) 243-6002
Monthly

Telephone Selling Report
TeleMarketing Design, Inc.
15427 Summerwood Drive
Omaha, NE 68137
Monthly

Teleservices Report
Arlen Communications, Inc.
7314 Wisconsin Avenue, Suite 600E
Bethesda, MD 20814
(301) 656-7940
Monthly

The Gallagher Report
The Gallagher Report, Inc.
230 Park Ave.
New York, NY 10017
(212) 661-5000
Weekly

Time
Time, Inc.
1221 Avenue of the Americas
New York, NY 10020
(212) 586-1212
Weekly

Video Print
International Resource Developers, Inc.
6 Prowitt Street
Norwalk, CT 06855
(203) 866-7800
Bimonthly

Wall Street Journal
Dow Jones and Co.
420 Lexington Avenue
New York, NY 10170
(609) 520-4000
Daily

Washington Report
Direct Marketing Association
1101 17th Street
Washington, DC 20036
(202) 347-1222
Monthly

What's Working in DM-Fulfillment
JPL Publications
4550 Montgomery Avenue, Suite 700N
Bethesda, MD 20814
(301) 656-6666
Biweekly

Who's Mailing What
Denison Watch
Box 8180
Stamford, CT 06905
(203) 329-1996
Monthly

World Direct Trader
Direct Marketing Association
    (Int'l Dept.)
6 E. 43rd Street
New York, NY 10017
(212) 689-4977
Quarterly

Appendix D: Suggested Reading List
Direct Marketing Association Publications

Guiding Catalog Growth: Successful
Strategies, Management and
Techniques, 1984. 299 pages.

Product Selection Criteria Used by
Catalog Merchandisers, 1983. 85 pages.

The Effectiveness of 800 Numbers in
Direct Mail Catalogues, 1983. 94 pages.

The Retail Revolution: Direct
Marketing, 1984. 366 pages.

How to Write Successful Direct Mail
Copy, by Maxwell Ross, 1976. 31 pages.

Standards for Computerized Mailing
Lists, by Arthur Blumenfield (second
edition), 1986. 16 pages.

Mailing Lists and Legal Relationships,
by Arthur Winston, 1982. 16 pages.

Sweepstakes: A Guide to Laws and
Regulations, by Arthur Winston, 1984.
50 pages.

Source: Direct Marketing Association, 6 East
43rd Street, New York, NY 10017. Reprinted
by permission.

Appendix E: Additional Reading

STRATEGIC DIRECT MARKETING

Successful Direct Marketing Methods
By Bob Stone
Crain Books

Tested Advertising Methods (4th ed.)
By John Caples
Prentice-Hall

The Direct Marketing Handbook
By Edward L. Nash
McGraw-Hill

Ogilvy on Advertising
By David Ogilvy
Crown Publishers

Direct Marketing Success
By Freeman F. Gosden, Jr.
John Wiley & Sons

Maximarketing
By Stan Rapp & Tom Collins
McGraw-Hill

Profitable Direct Marketing
By Jim Kobs
Crain Books

Direct Marketing Design: The Graphics of Direct Mail & Direct Response Mktg.
By the Direct Mktg. Creative Guild
DM Creative Guild

Winning Direct Response Advertising
By Joan Throckmorton
Prentice-Hall

Direct Marketing: Strategy, Planning, Execution
By Edward L. Nash
McGraw-Hill

MAIL ORDER

Direct Mail and Mail Order Handbook
By Richard B. Hodgson
Dartnell Corp

Building a Mail Order Business
By William A. Cohen
John Wiley & Sons

Elements of Direct Marketing
By Martin Baier
McGraw-Hill

Mail Order Know How
By Cecil B. Hoge
Business Studies

Mail Order Selling: How to Market Almost Anything by Mail
By Irving Burstiner, PhD.
Prentice-Hall

How to Start and Operate a Mail-Order Business
By Julian L. Simon
McGraw-Hill

Direct Mail Copy That Sells
By Herschell Gordon Lewis
Prentice-Hall

CATALOGS

Catalog Marketing: The Complete Guide to Profitability in the Catalog Business
By Katie Muldoon
R.R. Bowker

How to Build a Multi-Million Dollar Mail Order Business by Someone Who Did
By Lawson Traphagen Hill
Prentice-Hall

How to Create Successful Catalogs
By Maxwell Sroge Publishing
Maxwell Sroge Pub.

TELEMARKETING

Telemarketing Campaigns That Work
By Murray Roman
McGraw-Hill

Telephone Marketing: How to Build Your Business By Telephone
By Murray Roman
McGraw-Hill

Successful Telemarketing
By Bob Stone & John Wyman
National Textbook

LISTS

Mailing List Strategies
By C. Rose Harper
McGraw-Hill

TELEVISION DIRECT RESPONSE

Electronic Direct Marketing
By G. Scott Osborne
Prentice-Hall

Response Television: Combat Advertising of the 1980's
By John Witek
Crain Books

BUSINESS-TO-BUSINESS

Handbook of Business Direct Mail Advertising
By Edward N. Mayer & Roy G. Ljungren
Business Publishers Assoc. of America

LEGAL

Direct Marketers' Legal Advisor
By Robert J. Posch
McGraw-Hill

DIRECTORIES

The Direct Marketing Market Place
By Edward Stern
Hilary House Pub.

Directory of Mail Order Catalogs (New 3rd Edition)
By Richard Gottlieb
Grey House Pub.

The Great Book of Catalogs
By Steve and Betsy Pinkerton
Pinkerton Marketing

Mail Order Business Directory
B. Klein Publications

GLOSSARY

AIDA CONCEPT: A formula which postulates that to be effective, a sales offer must generate four distinct responses on the part of the prospect: Attention, Interest, Desire, and Action.

BENEFIT STATEMENTS: An important part of a sales presentation which answers the customer's basic question, "What's in it for me?"

BROADCAST TELEVISION: Network programming which broadcasts a television signal to huge audiences.

BUYER-GRAPHICS: A form of psychographics which studies the product purchasing behavior of certain groups of people.

BUYER PROFILE: The ideal buyer of a given target market, as defined by demographics (who), census-tract data (where), and psychographics (what and why the buyer will buy.)

CABLE TELEVISION: A utility which delivers an enhanced broadcast signal via a cable utility hookup.

CATALOGUE: A printed or electronically produced (televised) publication which displays a number of offers in a single presentation. Usually includes a toll-free ordering number and/or a mail-back ordering coupon.

CENSUS-TRACT: Geographic characteristics of a buying group that defines it by specific location.

CIRCULATION: Readership. The number of readers of a newspaper or magazine. (May be calculated as the number of subscription buyers or newsstand purchasers, and may also include a factor for "pass-on" or secondary readership.)

CLASSIC FORMAT: A direct mail term which refers to a mailing piece made up of an outer envelope with one or more inserts.

CLOSED QUESTION: A question which can only be answered by either a "Yes" or a "No." (Example, "Do you want to buy this product?")

CLOSING RATE: The number of sales actually made in comparison to the number of sales attempted by a salesperson or advertisement.

CLUSTER: Subgroups within each broad buyer group or segment. (See Segment.)

CONSUMER: The person who buys a product or service.

COST OF REACH: The cost to produce and deliver an advertisement to a specific, targeted audience.

CORRELATION ANALYSIS: A testing method which refers to an interdependence between mathematical values (assumed to be positive) that is used to relate the validity of one factor to another.

COPY: Verbal or written part of an advertisement that describes the product or service being offered for sale.

COST PER SALE: Computed by dividing the total cost of an advertisement by the number of sales which resulted from it.

CREATIVE: An advertising term. 1) The process of conceptualizing and creating an advertisement or an offer, or 2) the product that results from that process, as in, "this ad clearly shows the results of good, solid creative."

CUSTOMER BASE: Target market or group of regular, repeat customers.

COMPILED LIST: An external list containing individuals or businesses grouped together by a common denominator (such as zip code, sex, or income level). Often a number of psychographic or demographic factors are used in compiling such a list.

DATABASE: 1) A qualified list of individuals or businesses who have certain common demographic or psychographic factors that make them more likely to buy your product or service, or 2) a list of previous buyers.

DAY PART: The EDM term for specified block of time during the day as determined by the station's ratings. (Example: "Drive time" is a day part for radio advertising.)

DEMOGRAPHICS: Common socio-economic factors of a buying group, such as age, sex, marital status, income, or educational background, which pertain to a specific location or geographic unit such as a given zip code.

DIRECT LEAD ADVERTISEMENT: Used to encourage the buyer to call in (or write in) for additional information.

DIRECT MAIL: Distributing advertising material—by mail or any other delivery service—directly to prospective customers.

DIRECT MARKETING: An interactive system of marketing which uses one or more advertising media to effect measurable responses and/or transactions at any location.

DIRECT SALE ADVERTISING: An advertisement designed to force the viewer to take immediate action.

EDM: Electronic data marketing. Includes television, radio, telemarketing, and any other form of marketing which requires electronic communication between buyer and seller.

EXTERNAL LIST: List of potential customers, which comes from outside your own company. Usually rented from a list provider, but may also be bought, traded or borrowed from another source.

FULFILLMENT: Filling a customer's request by sending them merchandise or performing a service they have ordered and paid for.

FREQUENCY: A statistic noted in a customer list which gives the number of times a customer has placed an order (or made an inquiry) within a specified time frame.

GRPs: Gross Rating Points. Used to determine the number of television viewers at a particular time. One point equals one percent of the viewers. (Example: a GRP of 30 indicates that one-third of the households with televisions are supposedly watching a given show.) (See Ratings.)

HOME SHOPPING: An interactive form of marketing which allows a television viewer to order merchandise from a "televised" catalogue with the use of his home telephone.

HOUSE LIST: Information pertinent to customers who have bought from you before, or have answered inquiries regarding your own products and services. Also known as an "Internal List".

INVENTORY: The amount of commercial air time a radio or television station has for sale.

INTERACTIVE: Requiring actions from both a buyer and a seller.

INVOLVEMENT DEVICES: Special techniques, such as pull-off stickers, or paste-on notes, that involve the recipient of advertising material.

LIST: A group of individuals or businesses, usually related by one or more common factors, such as zip code, which can be used for direct mailing an offer to those individuals whose names appear on the list.

MAIL ORDER: See Direct Mail.

MAIL ORDER RULE: A Federal Trade Commission (FTC) rule which requires that if merchandise cannot be shipped on time, the vendor must offer the customer a prompt refund or obtain written consent for delayed shipping.

MARKET RESEARCH: The process of studying a prospective market to predict future consumer behavior based upon certain common characteristics which include demographic and psychographic factors as well as geographic location.

MARKETER: The person or company who markets a product or service.

MEASURED RESPONSE: The results obtained by tracking a given sales campaign by the number of individuals who responded to it.

MEDIA: A communication device such as radio, television, newspaper, or direct mail which allows a seller to communicate a message to potential buyers. (Also called medium.)

MERGE: Combine two or more lists (databases).

MILLINE RATE: The cost per reader for a given advertisement, calculated by multiplying the line rate (amount charged for each line of copy) by one million, and then dividing the result by the circulation.

MONETARY VALUE: Total amount of sales (dollars actually spent) recorded for a specific customer within a given time frame (usually a 12 month period).

MULTIVARIATE TEST: A method of testing a list which allows the user to locate and correlate a number of variables and determine their interdependence. These common groups are then clustered by zip code and identified as key market prospects.

NETWORK AFFILIATE: A television (or radio) station that is paid to carry network programming and advertising.

OFFER: 1) What you have to sell, or 2) the presentation of what you have to sell.

OPEN QUESTION: A question designed to elicit information rather than a straight "yes" or "no" answer. (Example, "What do you think about this product?")

PERCENT OF RETURN: Percentage of responses which resulted in a sale, calculated by adding two zeros to the number of sales and then dividing the result by the number of replies that were received.

PER-INQUIRY (PI): A frequent favorite with new direct response radio advertisers. Payment takes place only when a response takes place — a sale, in the case of one-step or direct-sale spots, or a lead, in two-step, or direct lead spots.

POSITIONING: Placing yourself in a specific market "niche" or corner of the market which will fill a need from your customers' standpoint.

POWER WORDS: Words — such as helpful, thoughtful, and valuable — that have a strong emotional appeal, and draw the prospect into the sale on a personal level.

PRE-EMPT: An EDM term referring to "bumping," or removing a commercial spot in order to make room for another one.

PRIME TIME: An EDM term which refers to the time of day when the number of listeners or viewers are at their highest.

PRO-ACTIVE VIEWER THEORY: A theory which proposes that a commercial aired during highly rated programs or prime time viewing will be more effective because the viewer is more involved in the foreground programming.

PRODUCER: A firm that supplies the actual mechanics of getting an offer to the targeted public.

PROSPECT: 1) A search for buyers for a product or service, or 2) a potential buyer or customer.

PSYCHOGRAPHICS: Common characteristics of a buying group that define their buying patterns by motivations and predictable consumer behavior.

PURGE: Remove duplicate or unwanted names from a customer list.

RFM: Recency, frequency and monetary value. The three factors by which most databases or customer lists are analyzed. (See Recency, Frequency and Monetary value.)

RATINGS: Factor normally used in radio or television advertising which determines listener profiles and market share during various times of the day for every metropolitan (or rural) area across the country. (See GRPs.)

RECENCY: The most current purchase, inquiry, or other activity recorded for an individual or company on a specific customer list.

REGRESSION ANALYSIS: A testing method which uses values established from one (or more) variables to determine the validity of another variable.

RESPONSE COST: Cost of a response to an advertisement, calculated by dividing the total cost of the ad by the number of replies sent in.

RESPONSE DEVICE: A method which allows the targeted prospect of a direct marketing offer to respond to it. Frequently the response device is a toll-free telephone number, a mail-back coupon, or a pre-addressed, pre-posted post card.

RUN-OF-STATION (ROS): An EDM term referring to the time when a station will air a commercial. ROS means that the station will air a spot (commercial) during any "day part" of the station's choosing. (See Day Part.)

SALES STIMULATOR: A device, such as an overwrap or early-order stimulator, designed to draw the prospect into a sale.

SEGMENT: A specific section of a customer base as defined by geographic location, or common characteristics such as hair color, favorite food, or any other demographic or psychographic data.

SEGMENTING: Dividing the market into segments, or like groups of individuals. (See Segment.)

SELF-MAILER: A type of direct mail piece that is totally self-contained. The offer and the envelope are all one piece.

SELLING FEATURES: Description of the product that tells what it is, what it does, how it works.

SPECTRUM TEST: Simultaneous testing of three lists. The primary list contains the target market buyer profile. The second list contains good prospects even though they don't fit the primary buyer profile. The third one contains good prospects chosen for an entirely different, although compatible, buyer profile.

SPLIT-RUN ADVERTISING: A special kind of testing to compare one or more variations of the same offer in the same media at the same time.

SPOT BUY: A television or radio term which refers to a specific block of time (usually 30 seconds) purchased for an advertisement to be aired.

STORY BOARD: Used to create television advertising. A columnar layout or "picture story" showing pictures and copy running side by side down the board. The video portion is then filmed, and the sound track overlaid.

SUPPORT SPOTS: Short advertisements (usually only 30 seconds) run simply to create an awareness for some other type of direct marketing media or to give instructions regarding an offer and how to respond to it. (Example: "Watch your local newspaper for details on how to order this product.")

TARGET MARKET: Prospective customers.

TELEMARKETING: Soliciting sales by telephone.

TEST MARKETING: Offering a product or service on a limited basis to certain geographic locations or like groups of buyers before exposing it to the market as a whole.

USER: A firm or individual who uses a direct marketing provider's services to get a product to market. (The user may also provide some of its own services, and thus also be a producer as well.)

INDEX